I0483184

A Boy Named

The artwork of René Capone

Copyright © 2014 René Capone

All rights reserved.

ISBN-13: 978-0615966076

ISBN-10: 0615966071

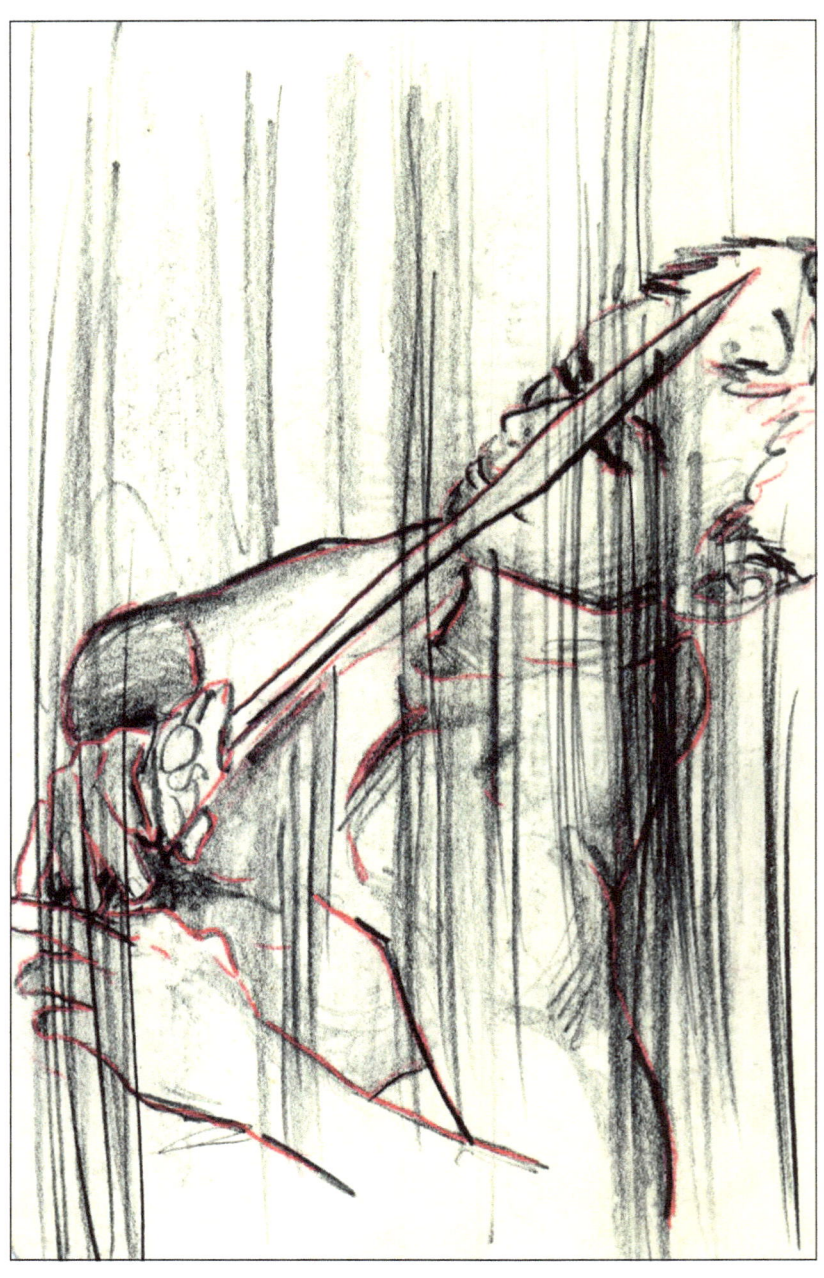

FOREWORD

When I first met René I knew it was a friendship that had already crossed space and time. We were both in our teens finding our way out of tumultuous childhoods and diving headfirst into unconventional adulthood. He the artist and I the musician, we would spend hours together ... René drawing, me playing guitar and us both making each other laugh really hard. We knew even then that our friendship was life saving for us both.

We went our separate ways for some years, after high school, René going off to NYC to attend Parsons and then on to San Francisco. I don't know if he ever realized during the years we were living our different lives how proud I was to call him my best friend. How I would brag that "my René" was off being an artist in California and doing a damn good job of it I might add.

Now it is almost 20 years later and little has changed, including the awe that he inspires in me every time he picks up a brush or a pencil ... he lives his life his way, the brave way, for his art. Never giving up his dream, never choosing the easy path, because he knows without his art that life could never be worth living.

Lian Fitz, 2014

FOREWORD

I first met René Capone my first year teaching at high-school level in the fall of 1995 in my Advanced Studio in Art class. Although he was on my roster at the beginning of the school year, it wasn't until midway through the quarter that René appeared in my art room.

René was a student whose passion for Art and self-motivation were evident within the first hour of being in his presence. Later that year, I remember with amazement René's ability to organize and secure a one-person show of his work at a nearby café. Even at the youthful age of seventeen, his artwork was an honest reflection of who he was – an openly gay teenager with a somewhat complicated life.

With that said, he was not a young man who liked to come to school. In fact, by his own admission, there were days when it took everything in his power to get himself to class. René later admitted to me that it was my interest and attention along with my genuine care about his future education plans that resonated with him and got him to school each day – albeit kicking and screaming. Ultimately I became his mentor.

René and I have continued to keep in touch throughout his years in NYC at Parsons School of Design and his eventual move to San Francisco. It has been a pleasure to watch him grow as an artist as well as an adult. To this day, he continues to make me a proud teacher.

This book – and the work included within – is a reminder of the fact that one person can make a difference in the life of another. I'm moved by the imagery and reflect upon the maturity of René both as an artist and individual, which in effect makes me reflect upon my own life as well. It is proof that somewhere along the journey the student can become the teacher – and has.

Stephen Honicki, 2014

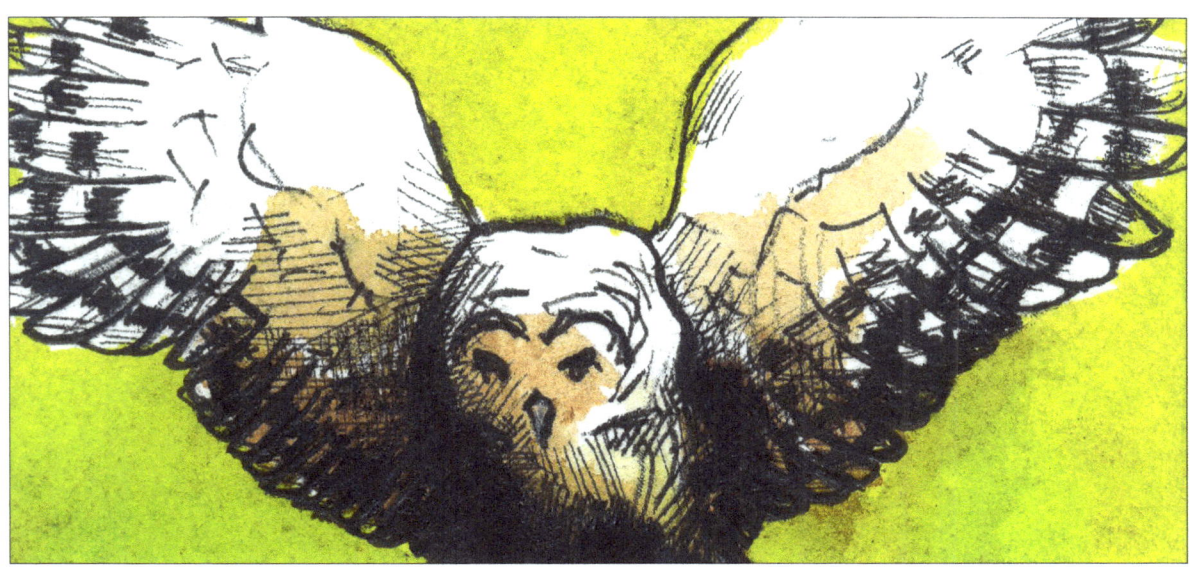

Dedicated to my grandmother, Janet Patterson

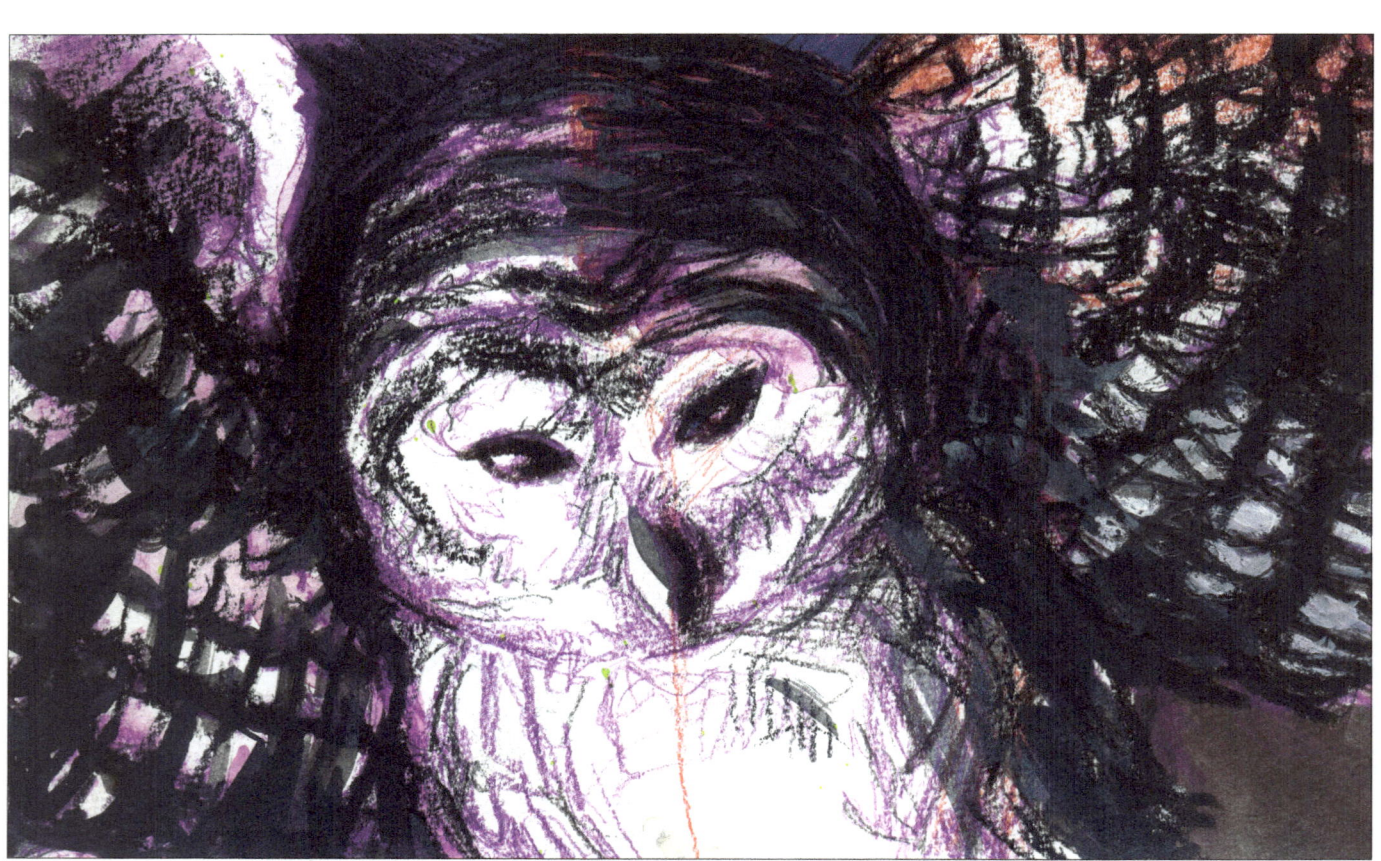

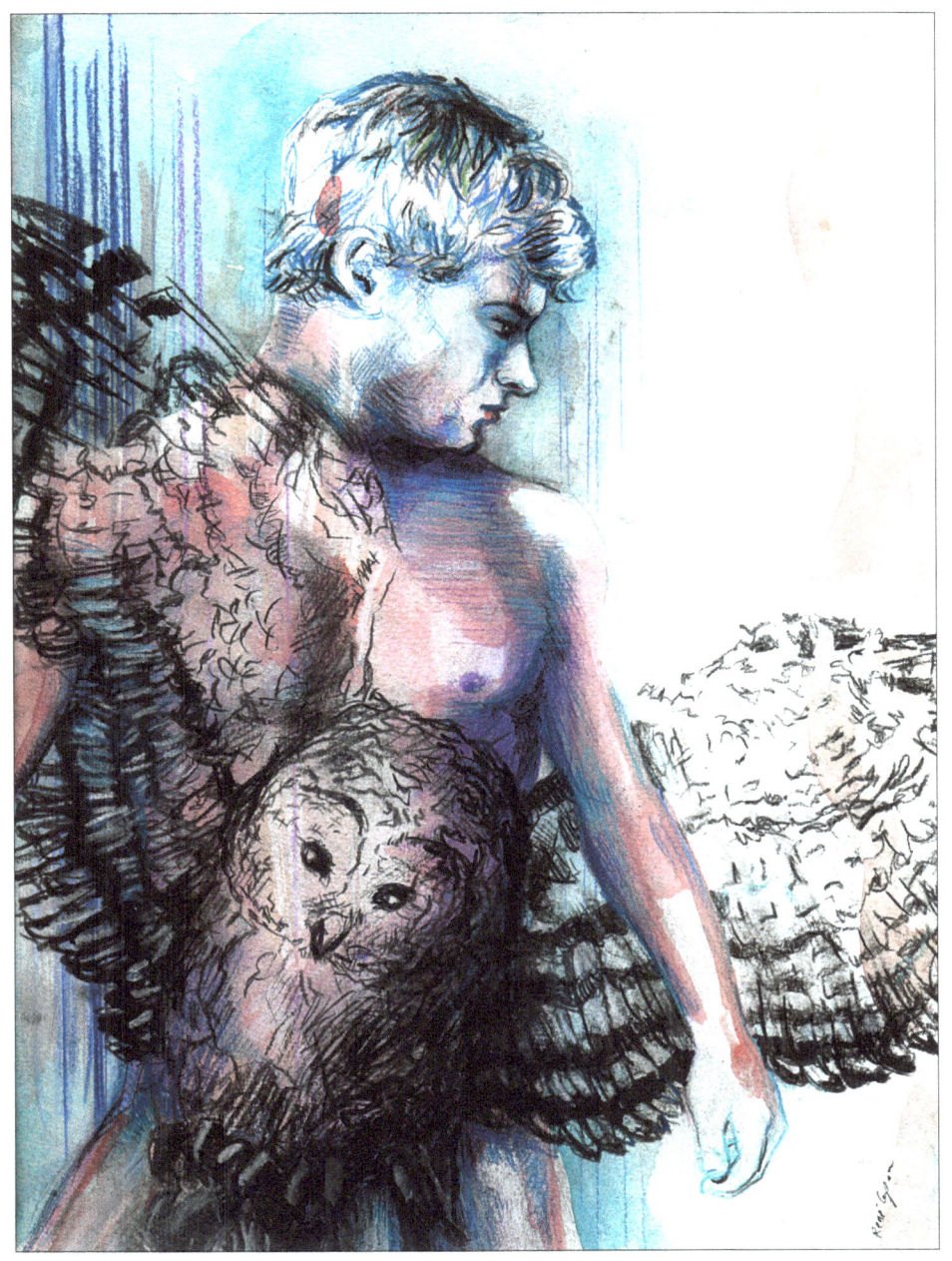

"A Boy Named Wind" watercolor & color pencil, 9"x12", 2012

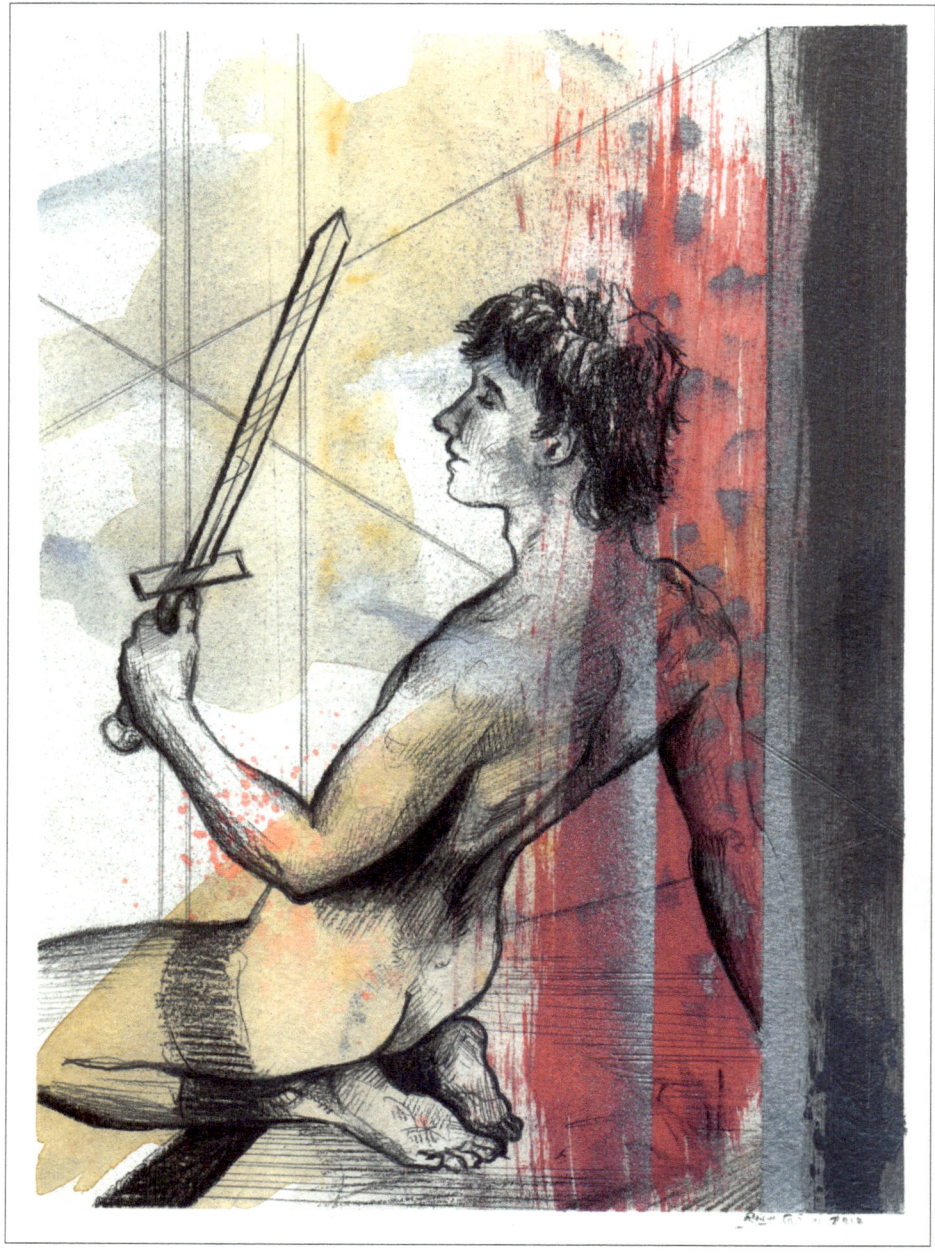

"A Boy Named Strength" watercolor & pencil, 9"x12", 2012

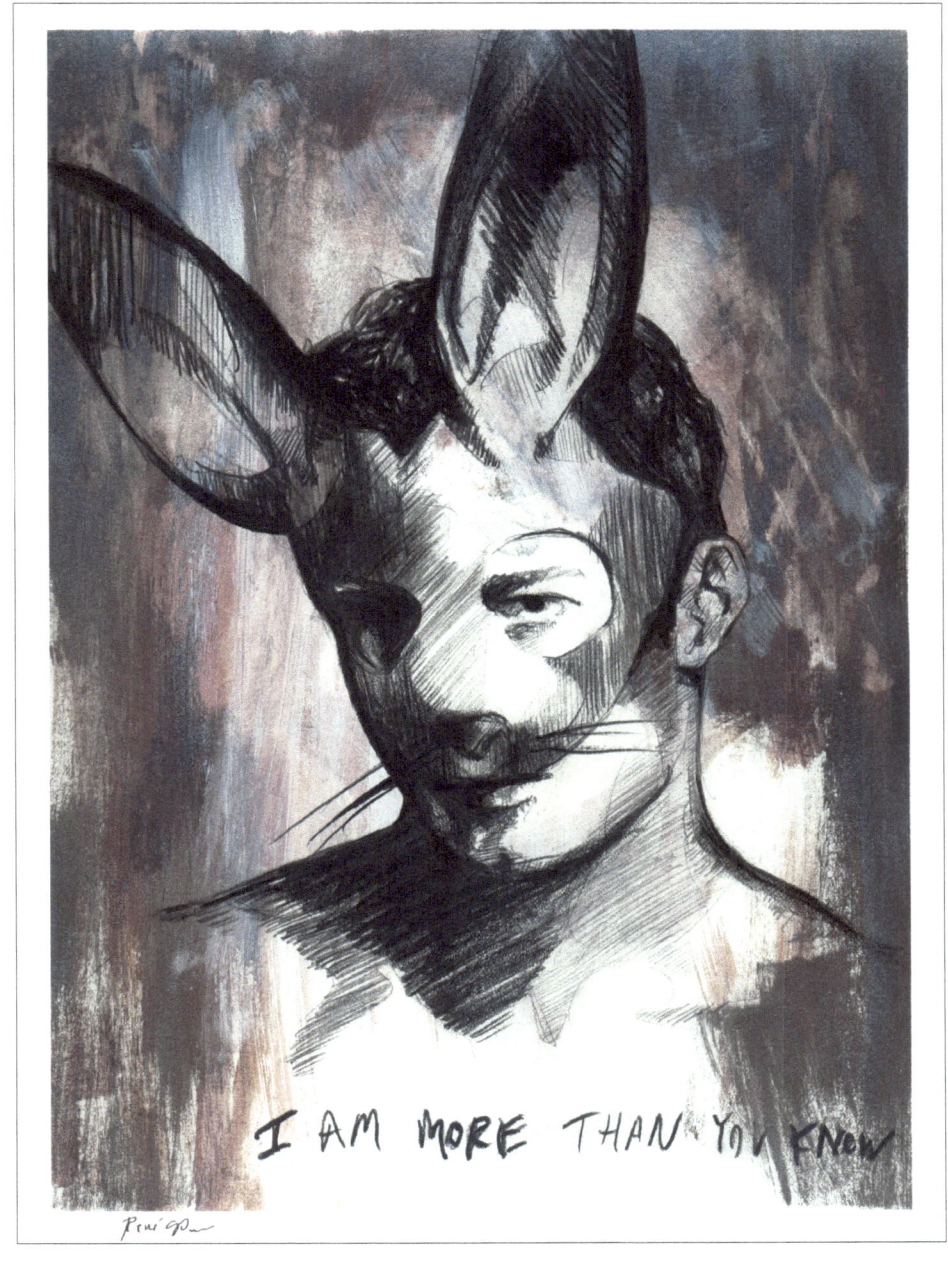

"A Boy Named Truth" watercolor and pencil, 9"x12", 2013

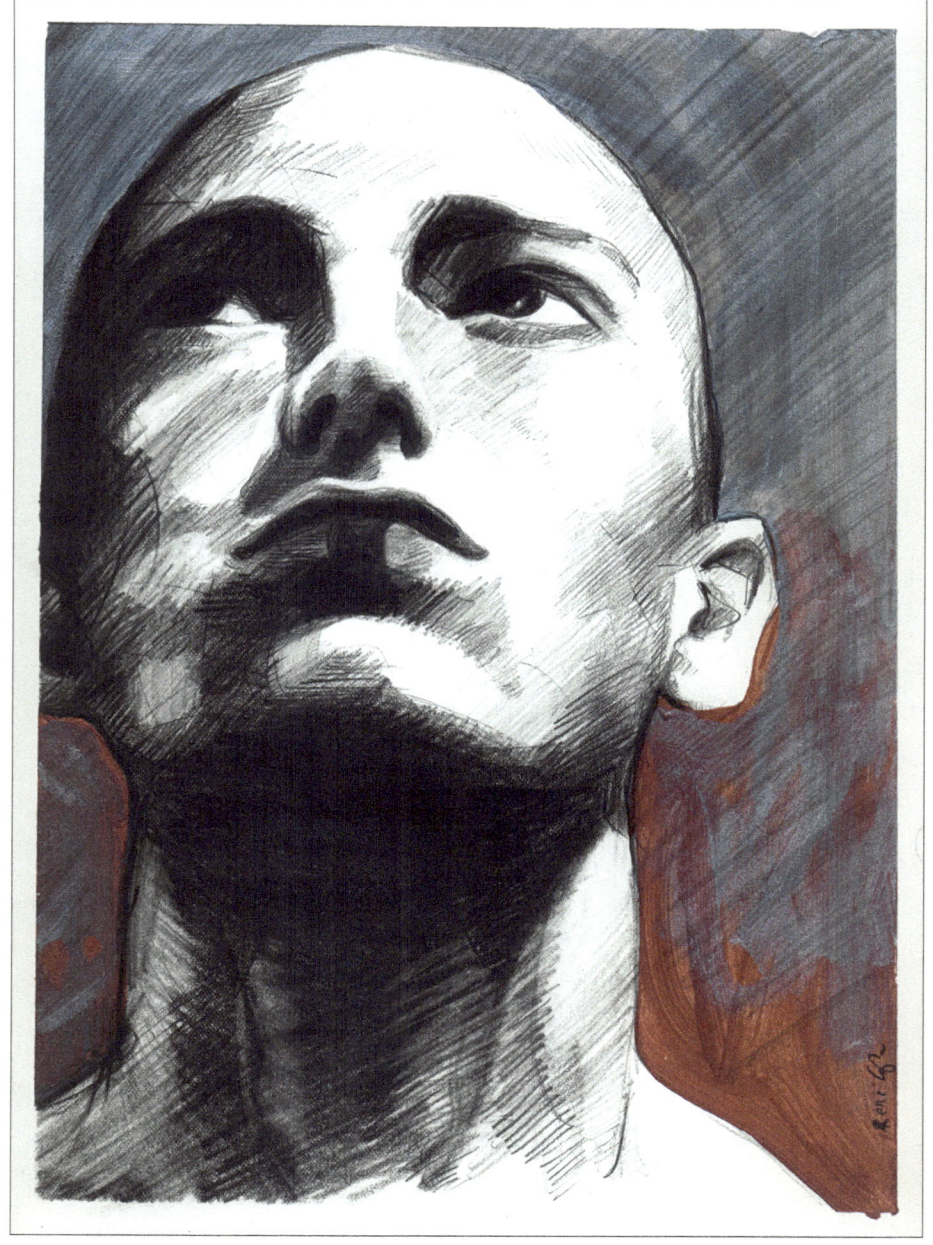

"A Boy Named Patience" watercolor and pencil, 9"x12", 2012

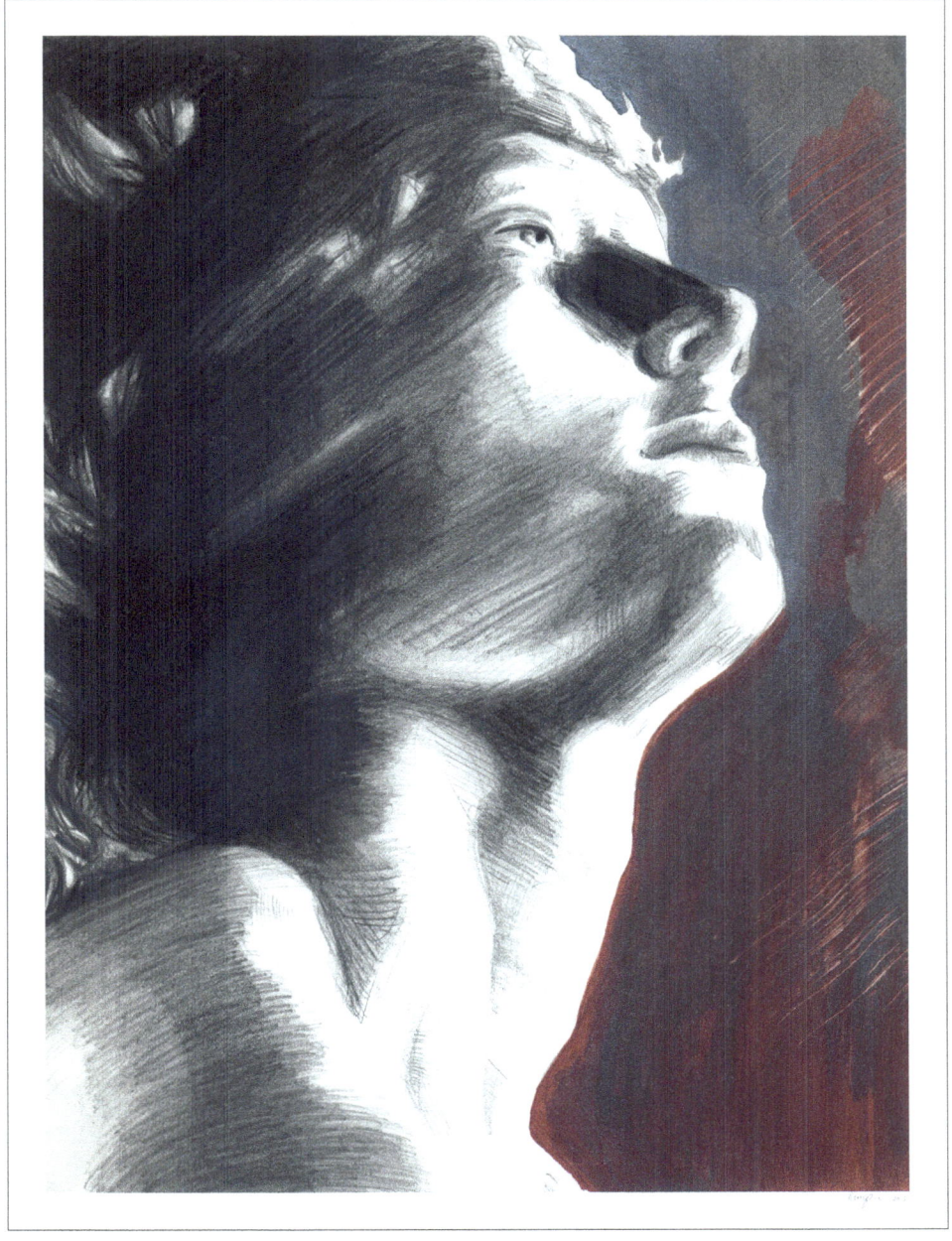

"A Boy Named Faith" watercolor and pencil, 9"x12", 2013

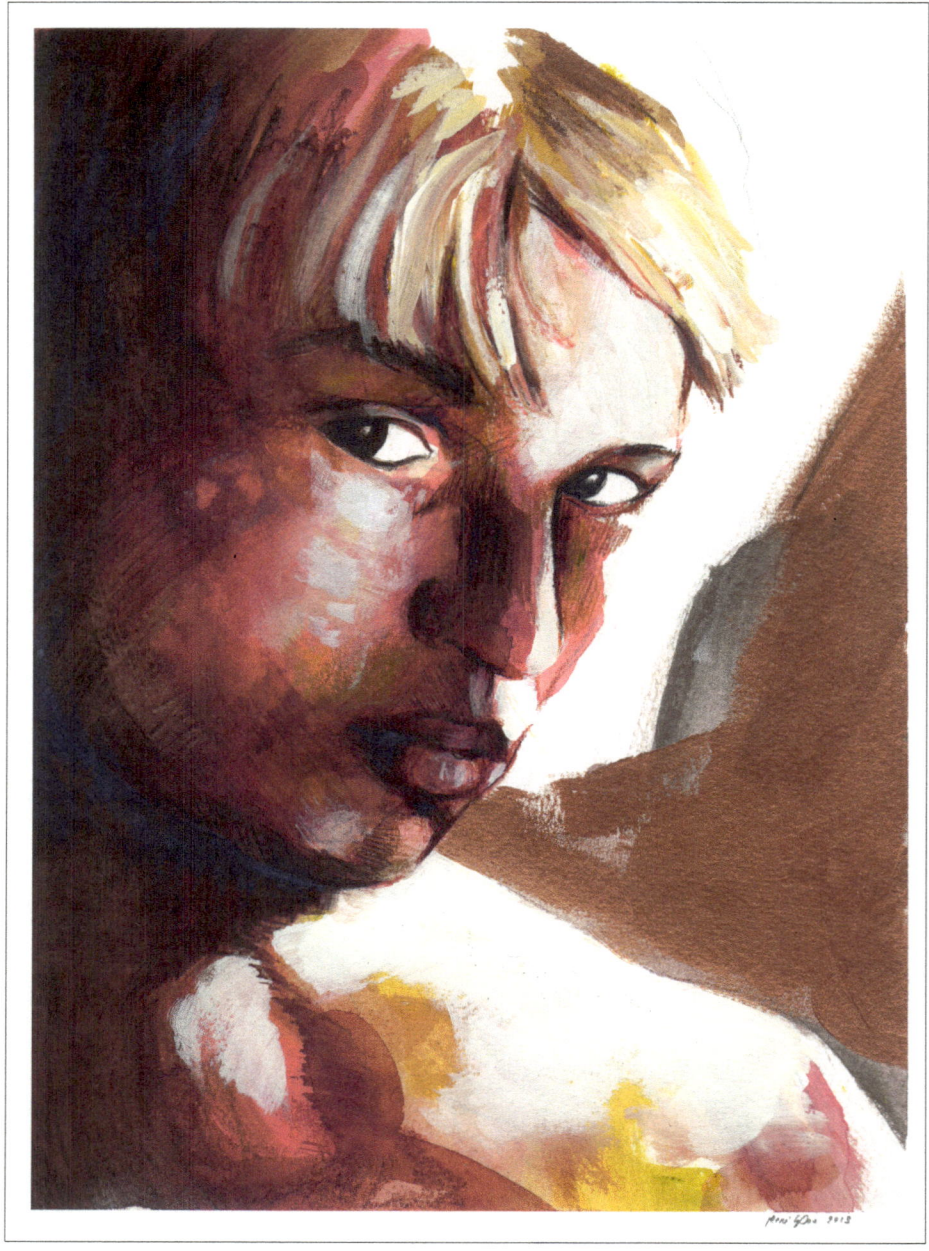

"A Boy Named Scarlet" watercolor & color pencil, 9"x12", 2013

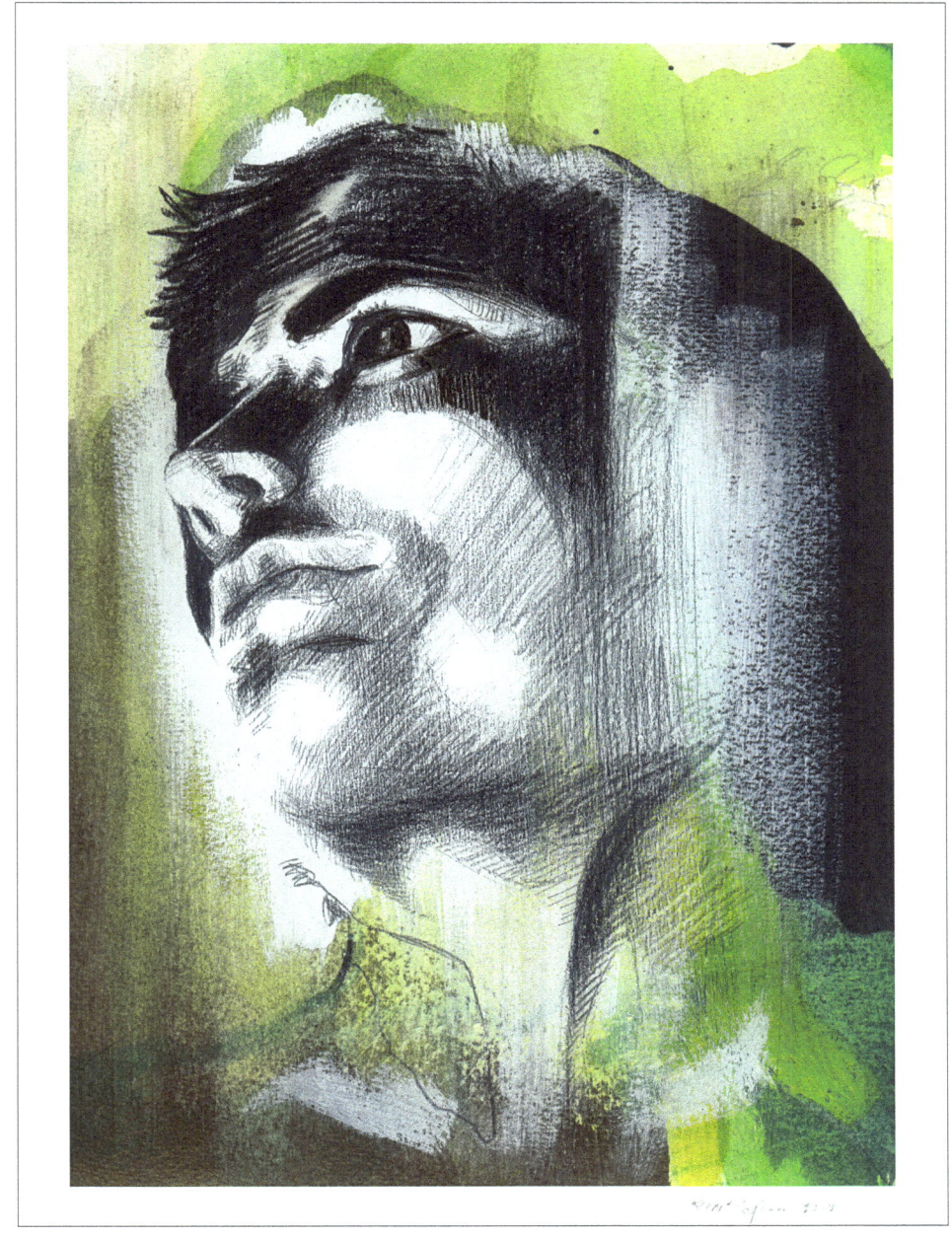

"A Boy Named Persistence " watercolor & pencil, 9"x12", 2013

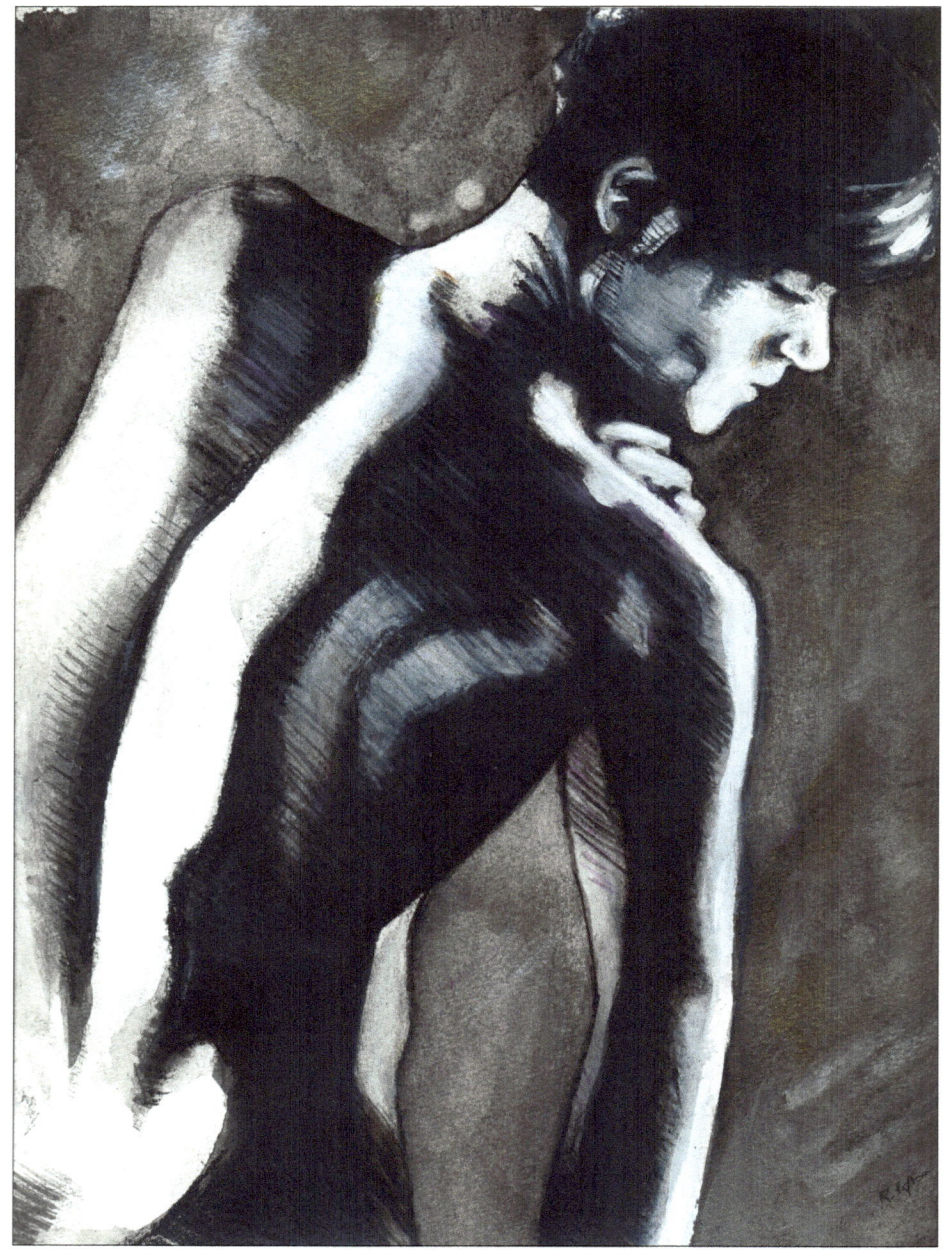

"A Boy Named Shadow " watercolor & color pencil, 9"x12", 2011

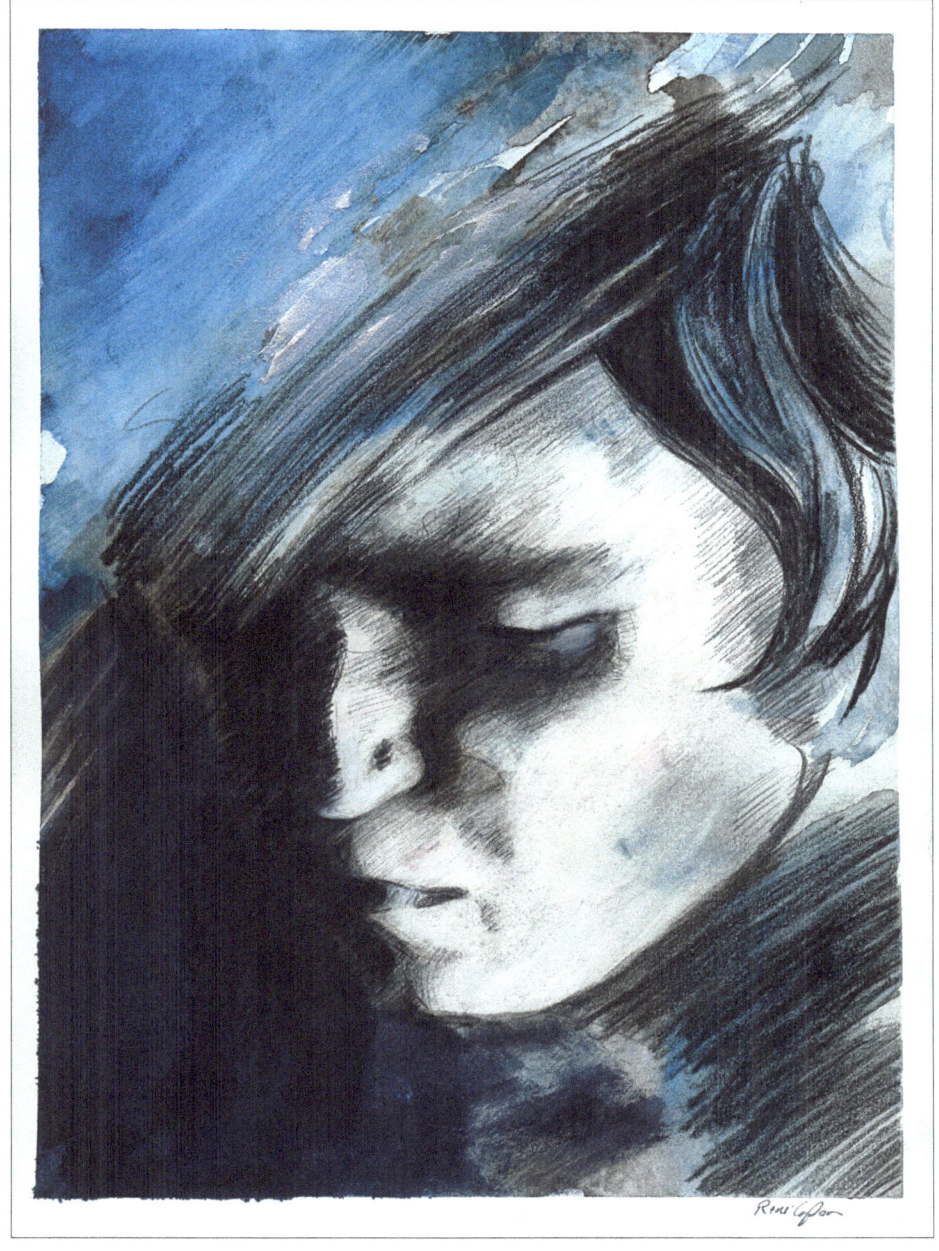

"A Boy Named Sorrow" watercolor & color pencil, 9"x12", 2012

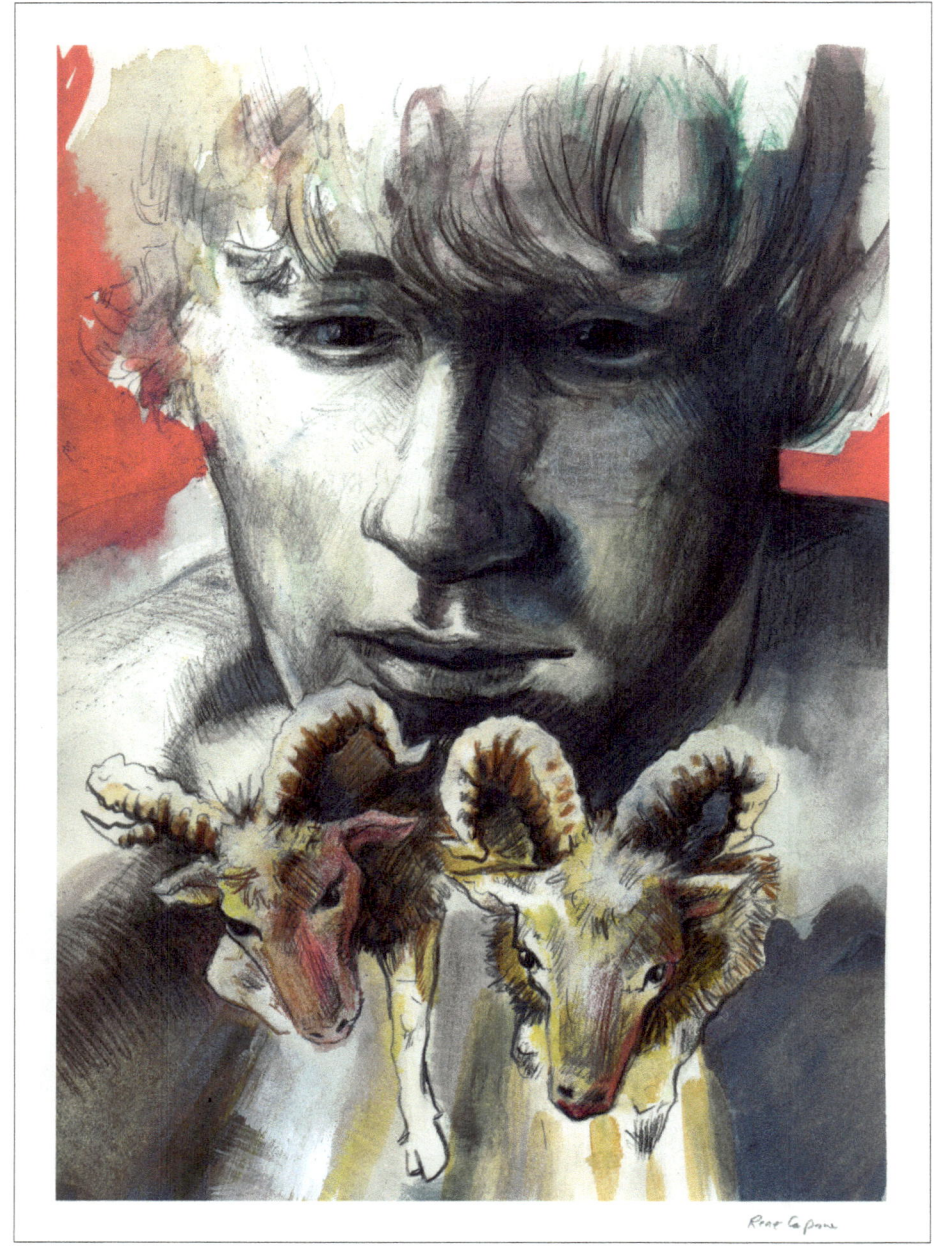

"A Boy Named Stubborn" watercolor and pencil, 12"x14", 2013

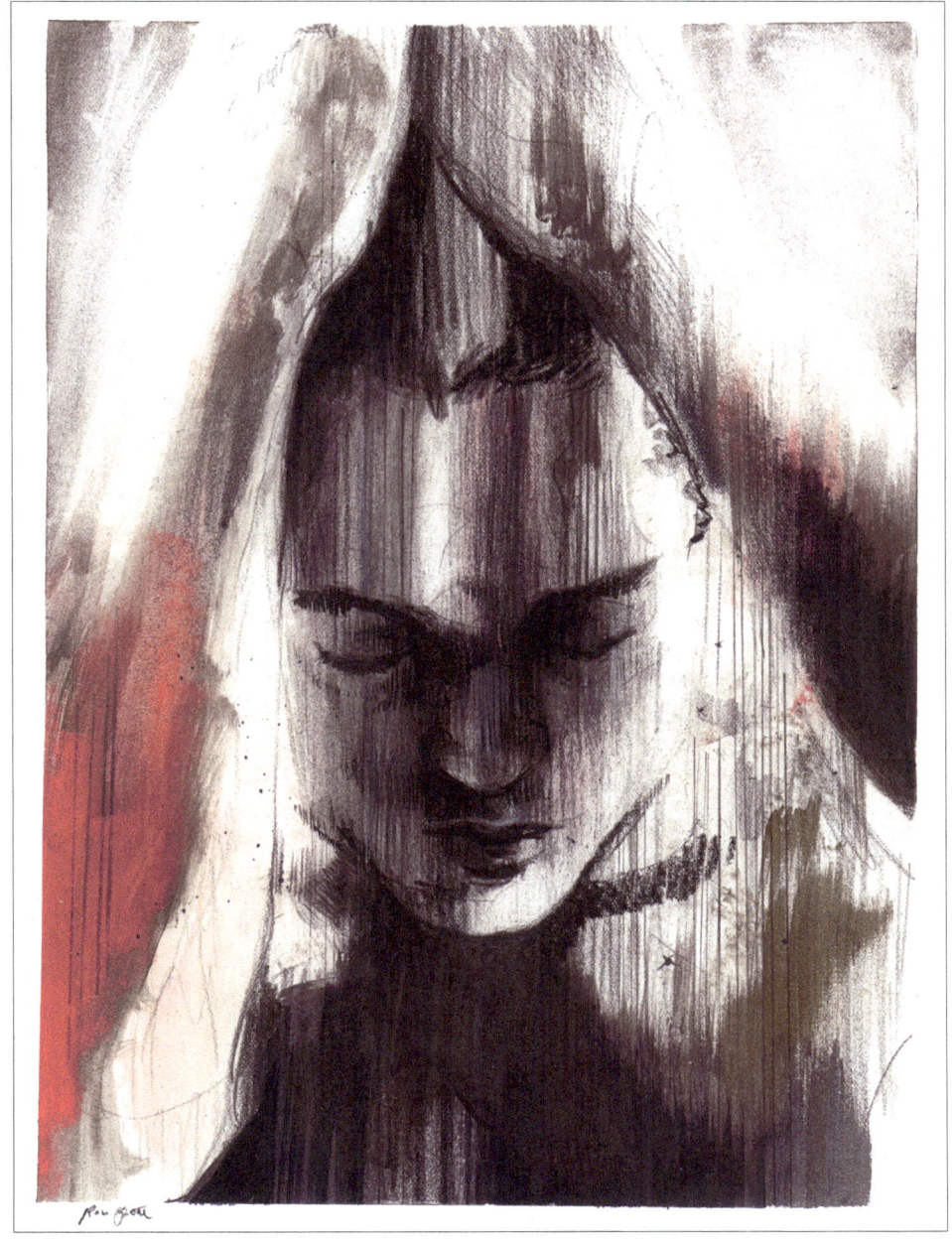

"A Boy Named Stillness" watercolor & color pencil, 9"x12", 2013

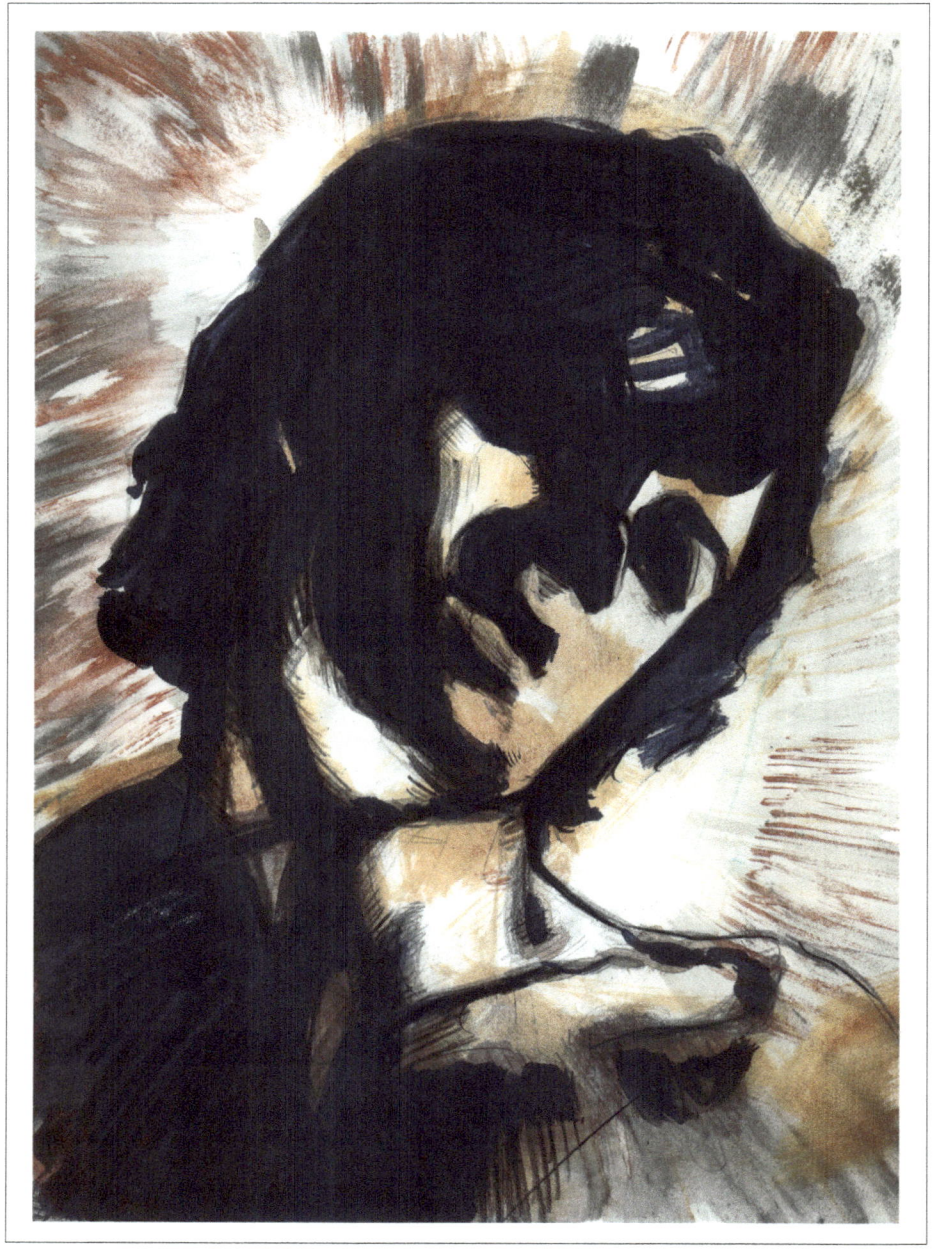

"A Boy Named Autumn" watercolor & ink, 9"x12", 2013

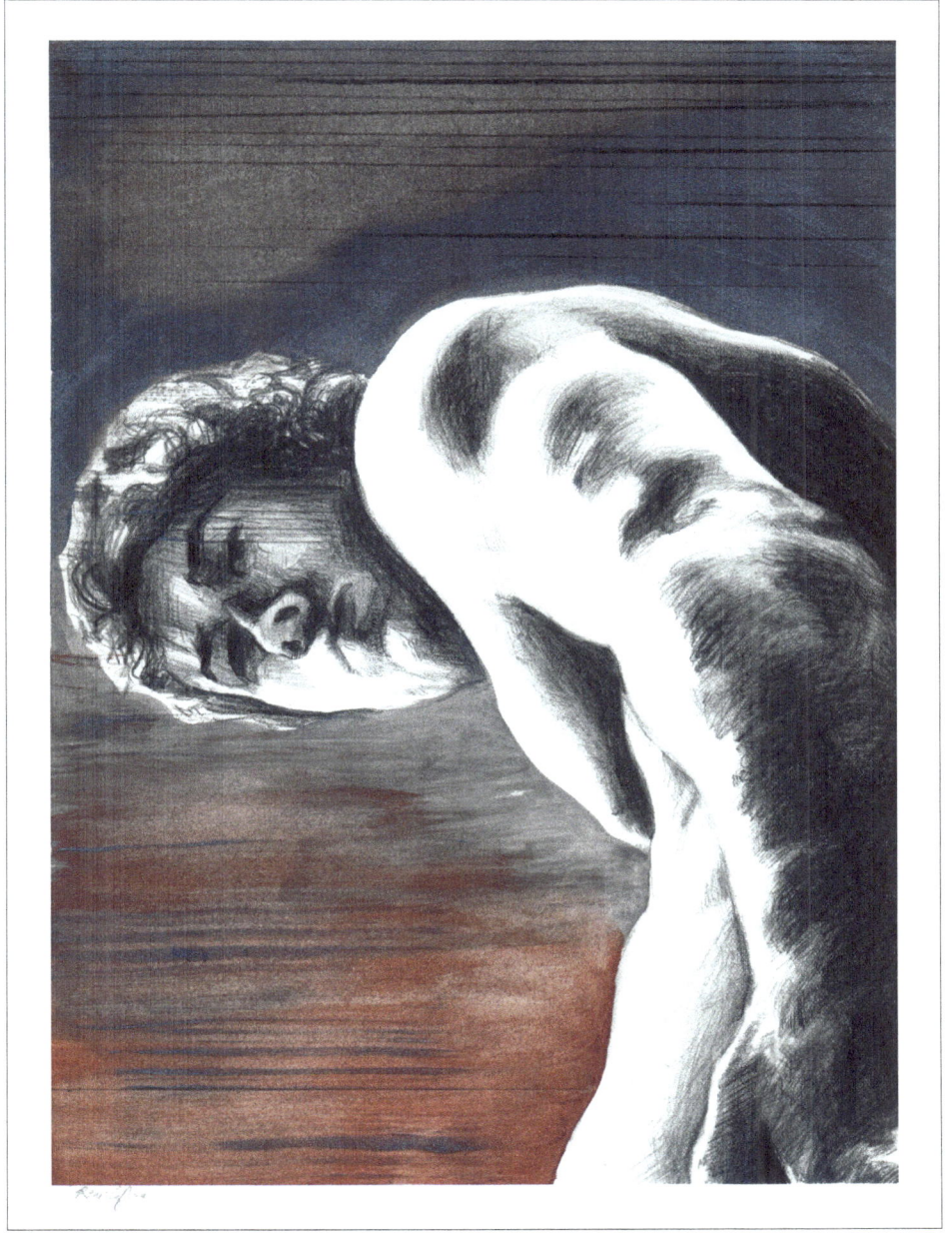

"A Boy Named Sideways" watercolor & pencil, 9"x12", 2013

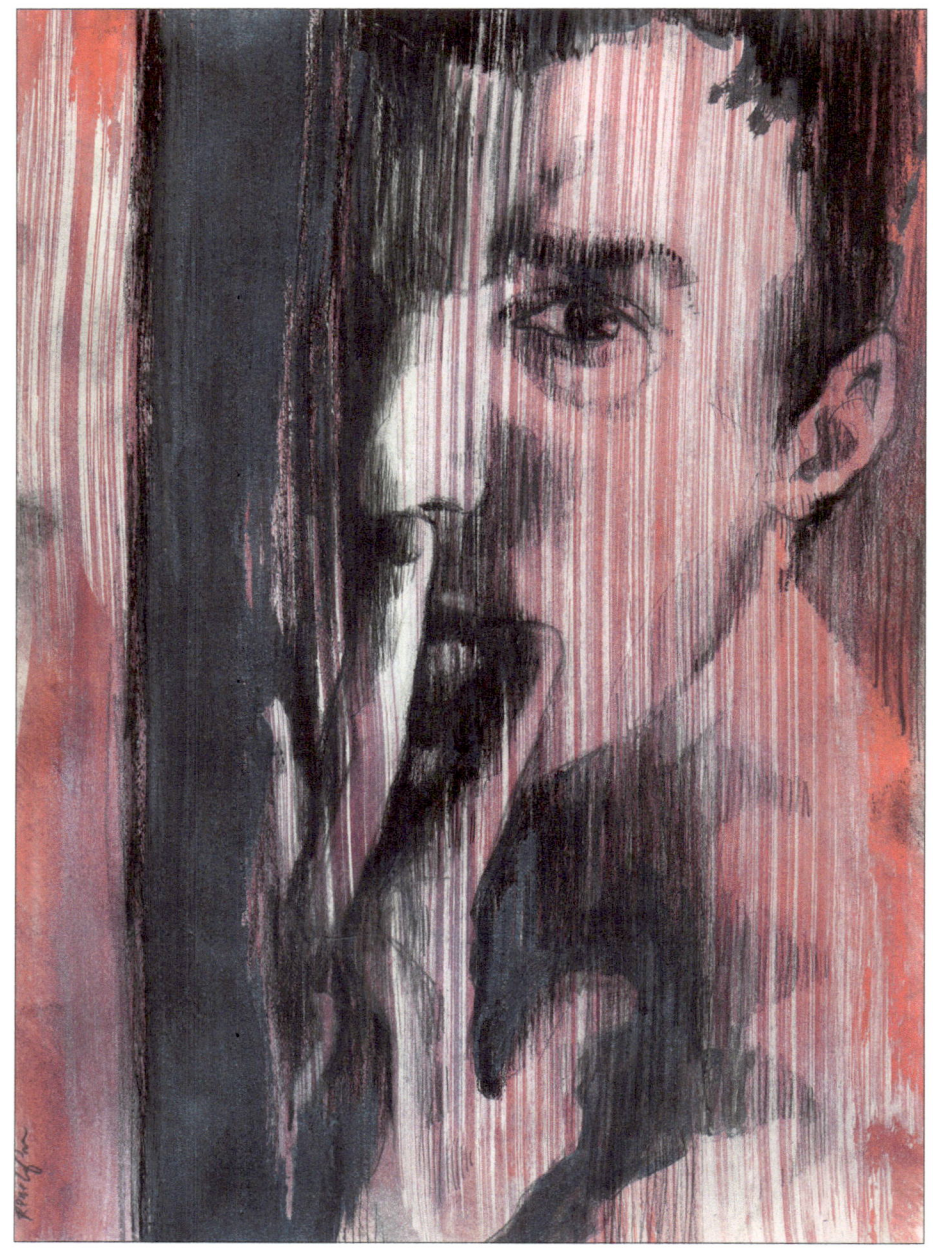

"A Boy Named Silence " watercolor & pencil, 9"x12", 2013

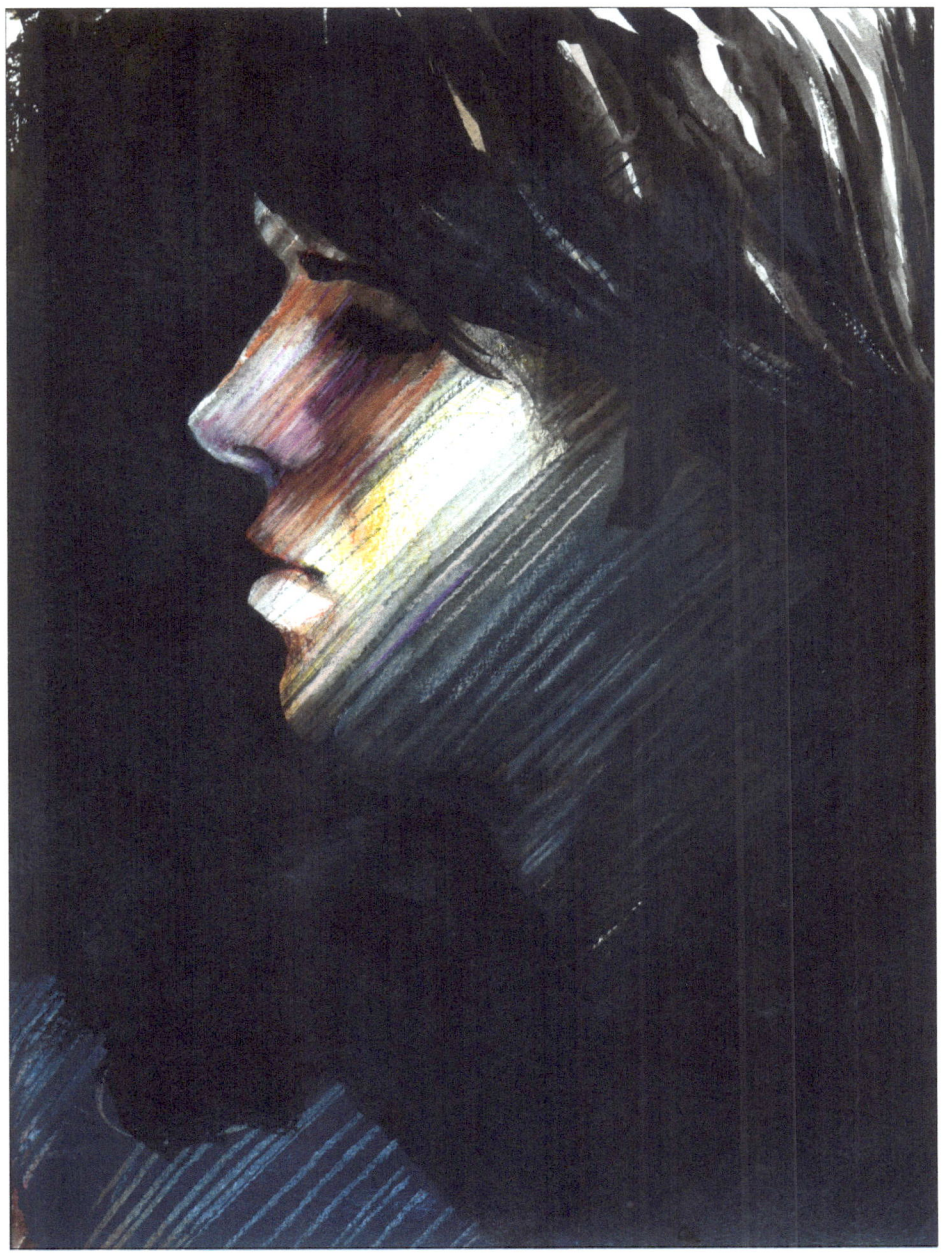

"A Boy Named Rainbow" watercolor & color pencil, 9"x12", 2011

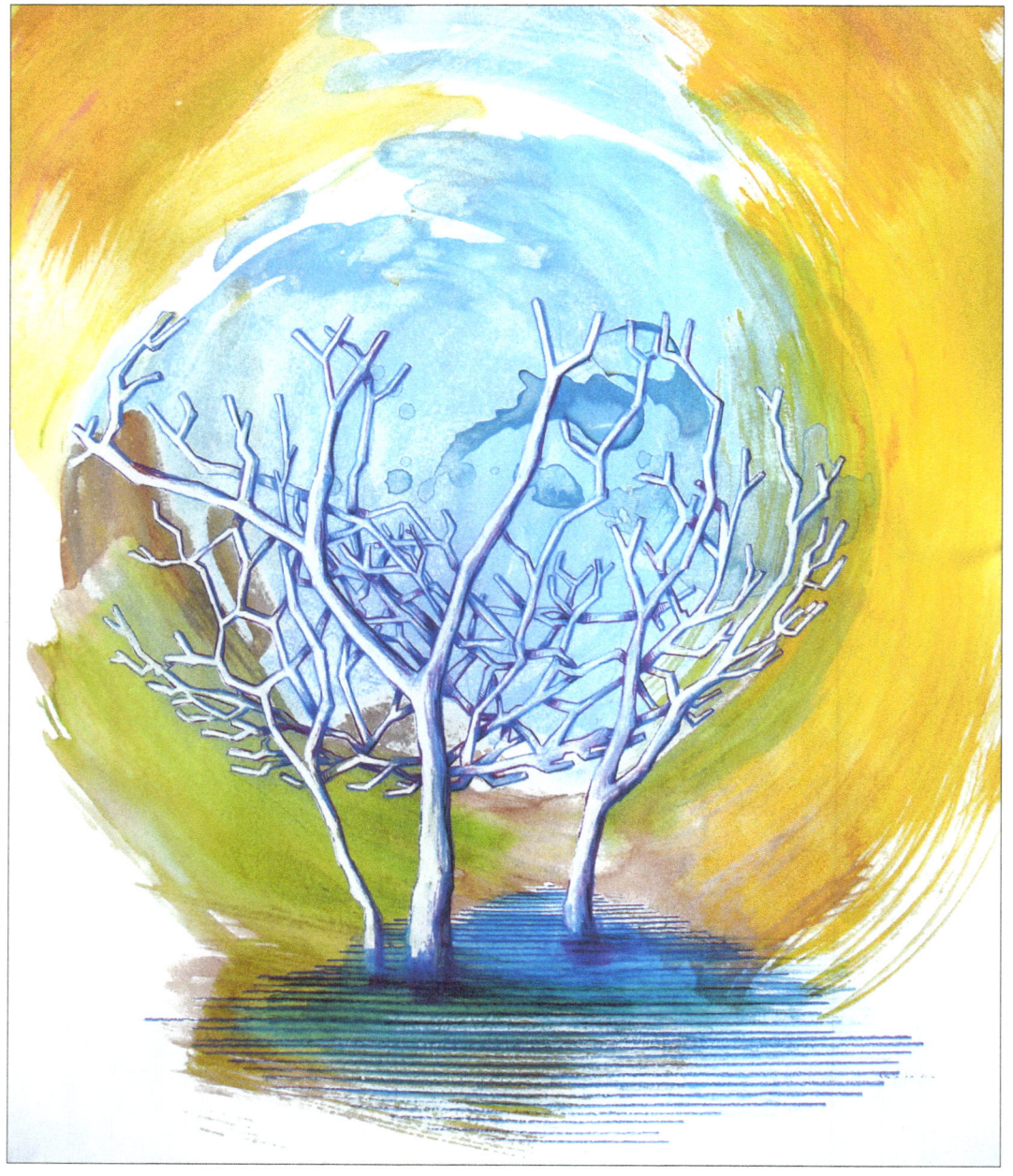

"Beautiful On Purpose" watercolor & color pencil, 18"x24", 2012

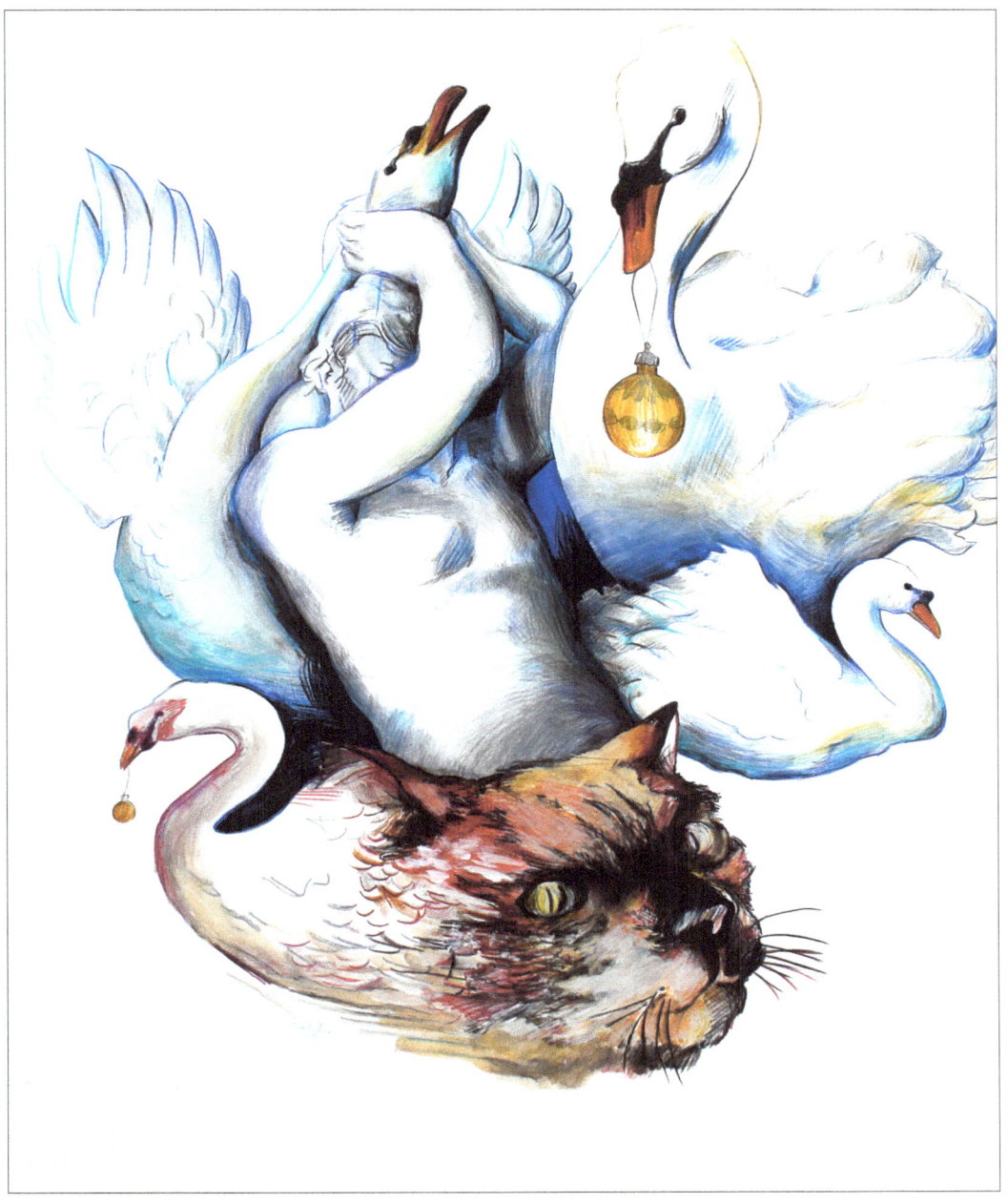

"Cat Scratch Fever" watercolor & color pencil, 22"x30", 2012

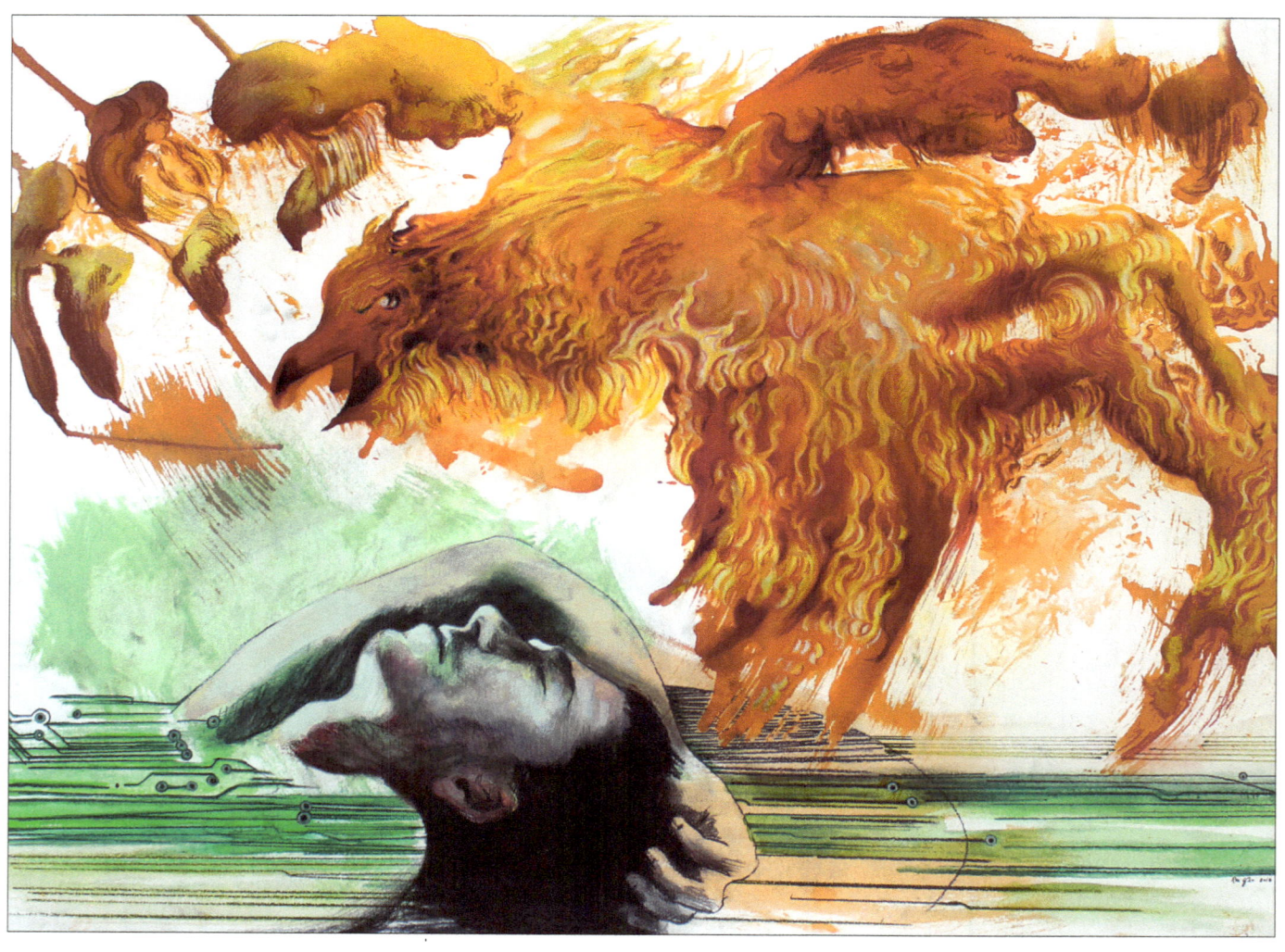

"Digital Phoenix" watercolor & color pencil, 30"x22", 2011

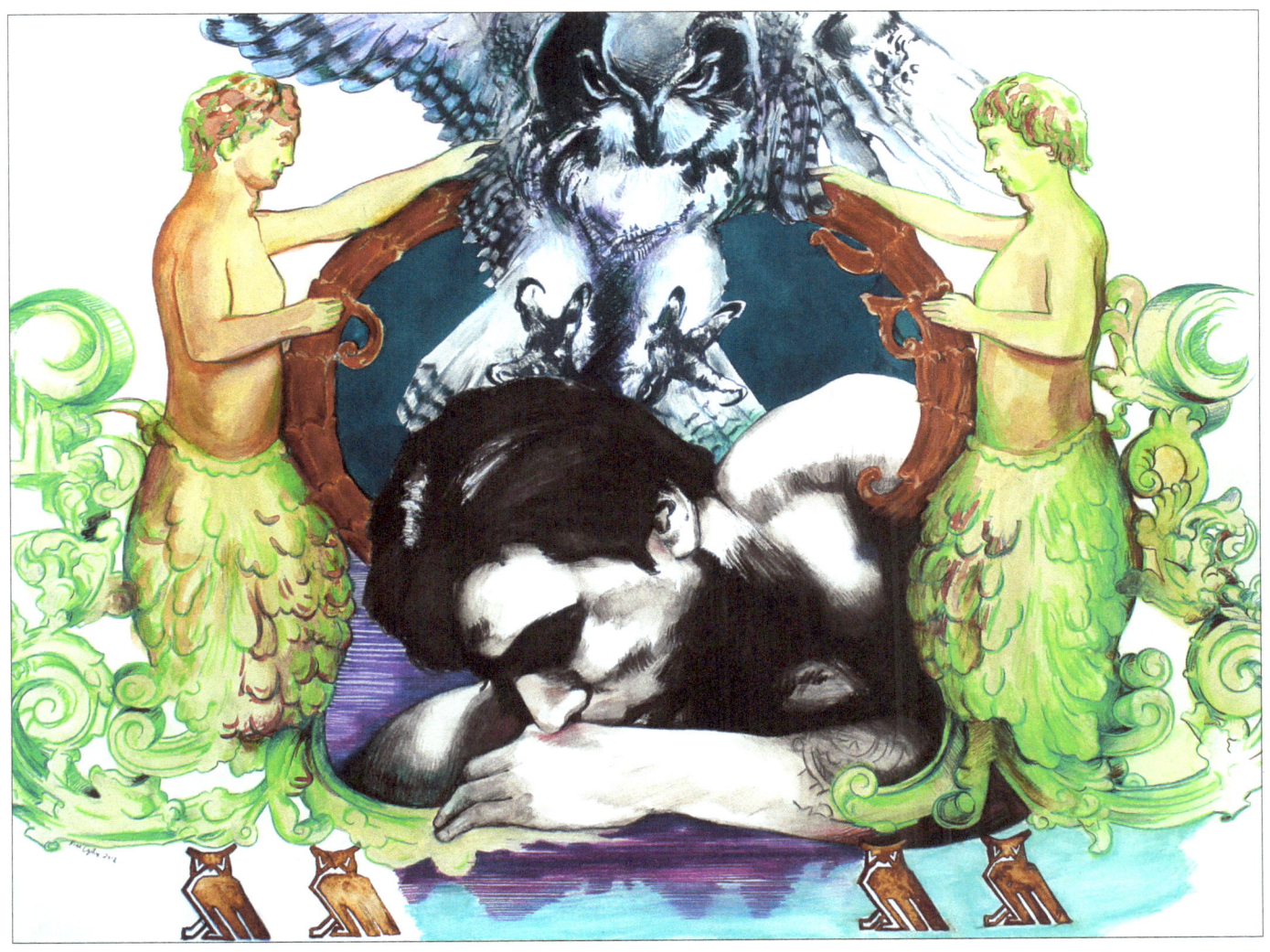

"Awaken" watercolor & color pencil, 30"x22", 2012

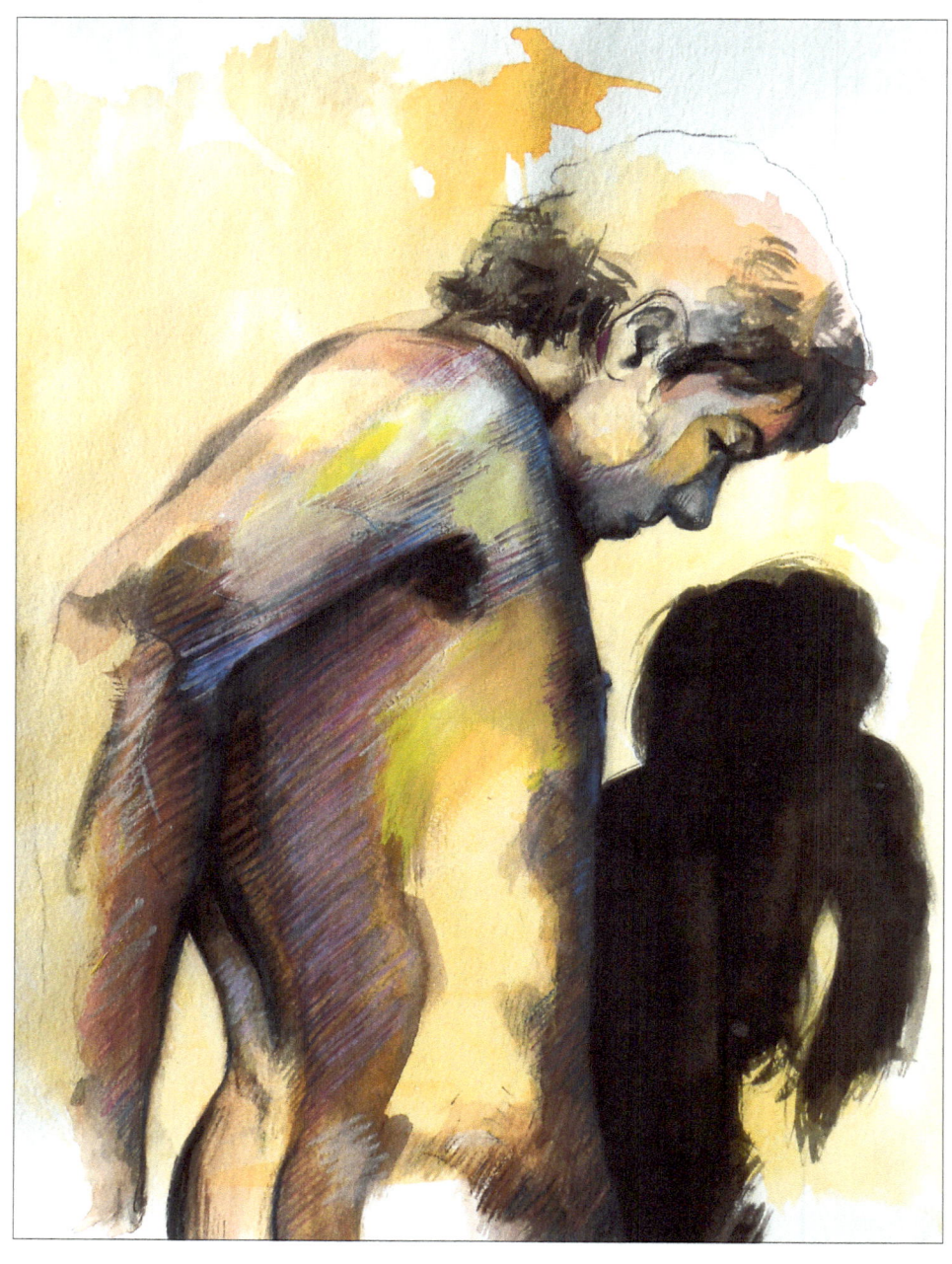

"A Boy Looking for Wisdom" watercolor & color pencil, 12"x19", 2012

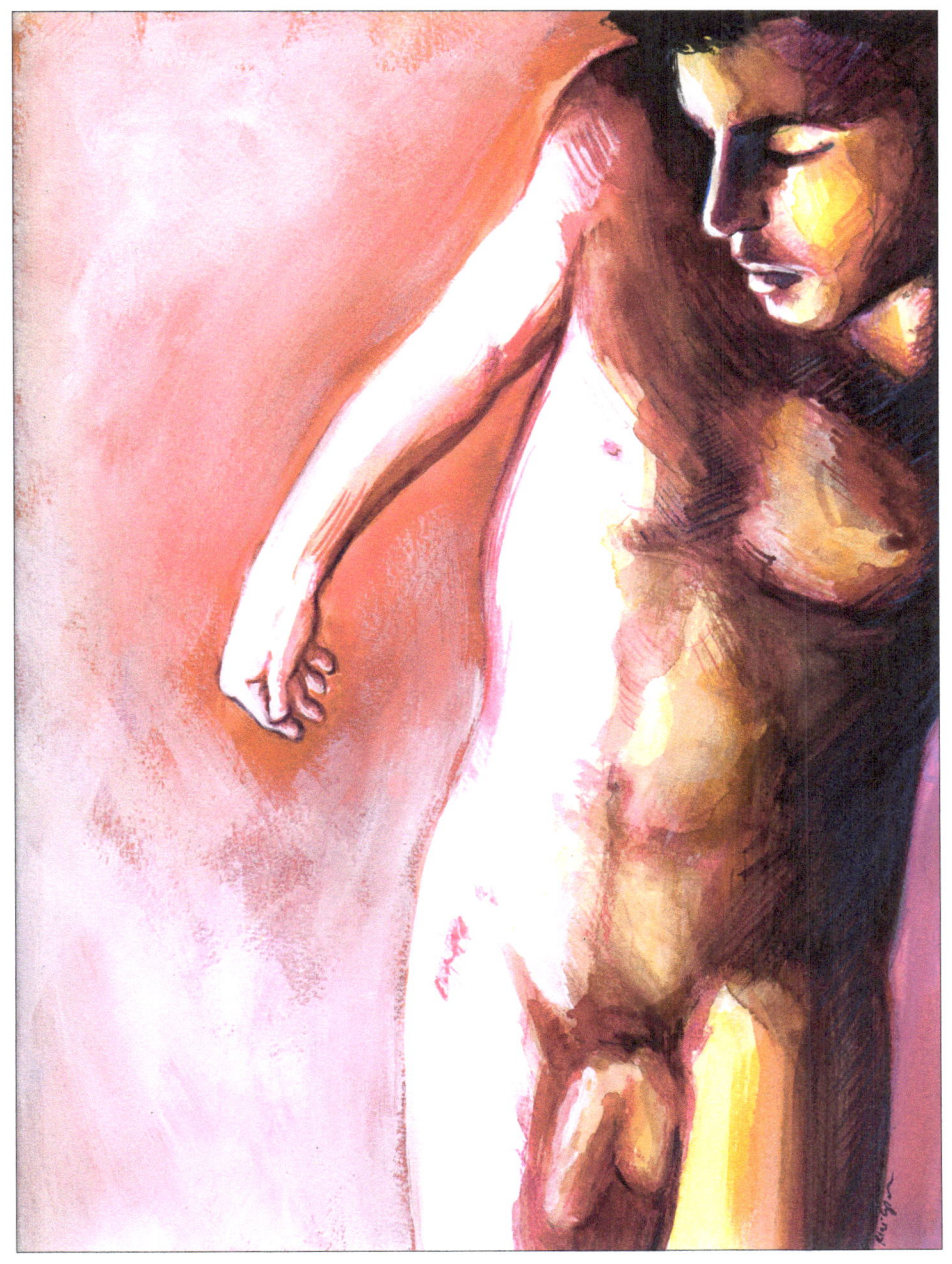

"Wounded #2" watercolor & color pencil, 9"x12", 2011

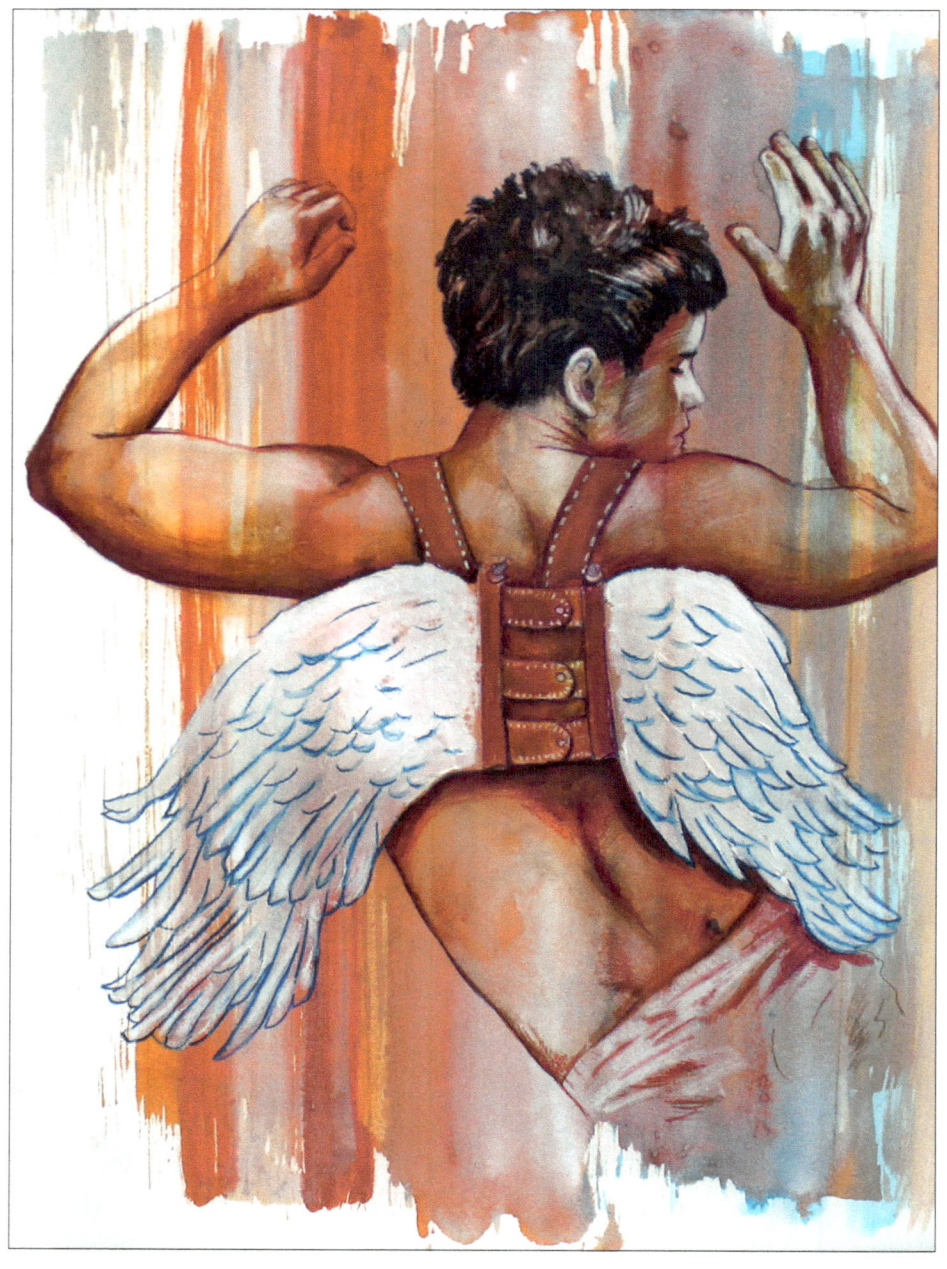

"Icarus' Wings" watercolor & color pencil, 16"x20", 2011

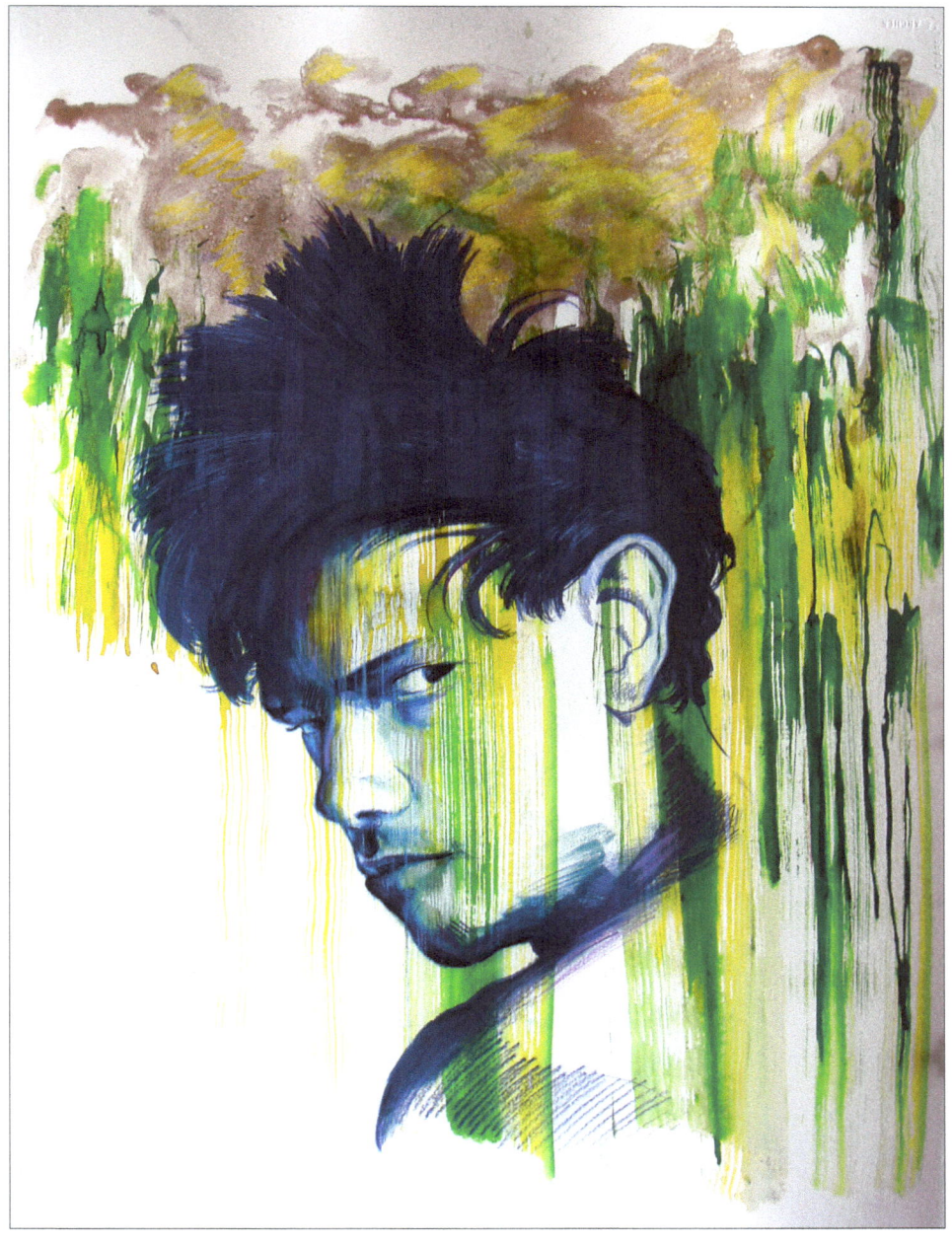

"Icarus" watercolor & color pencil, 22"x30", 2011

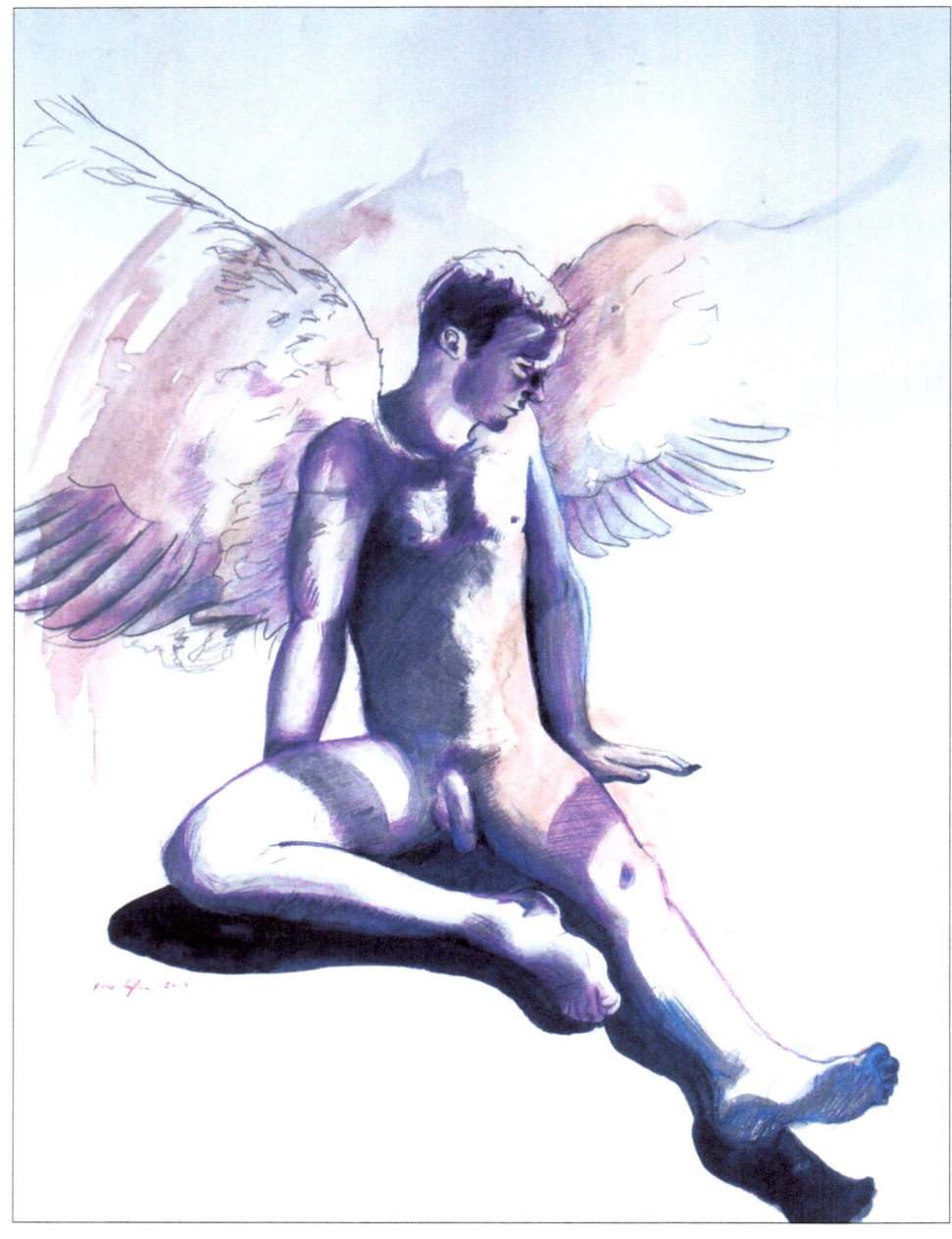

"Faded Angel" watercolor & color pencil, 18"x24", 2012

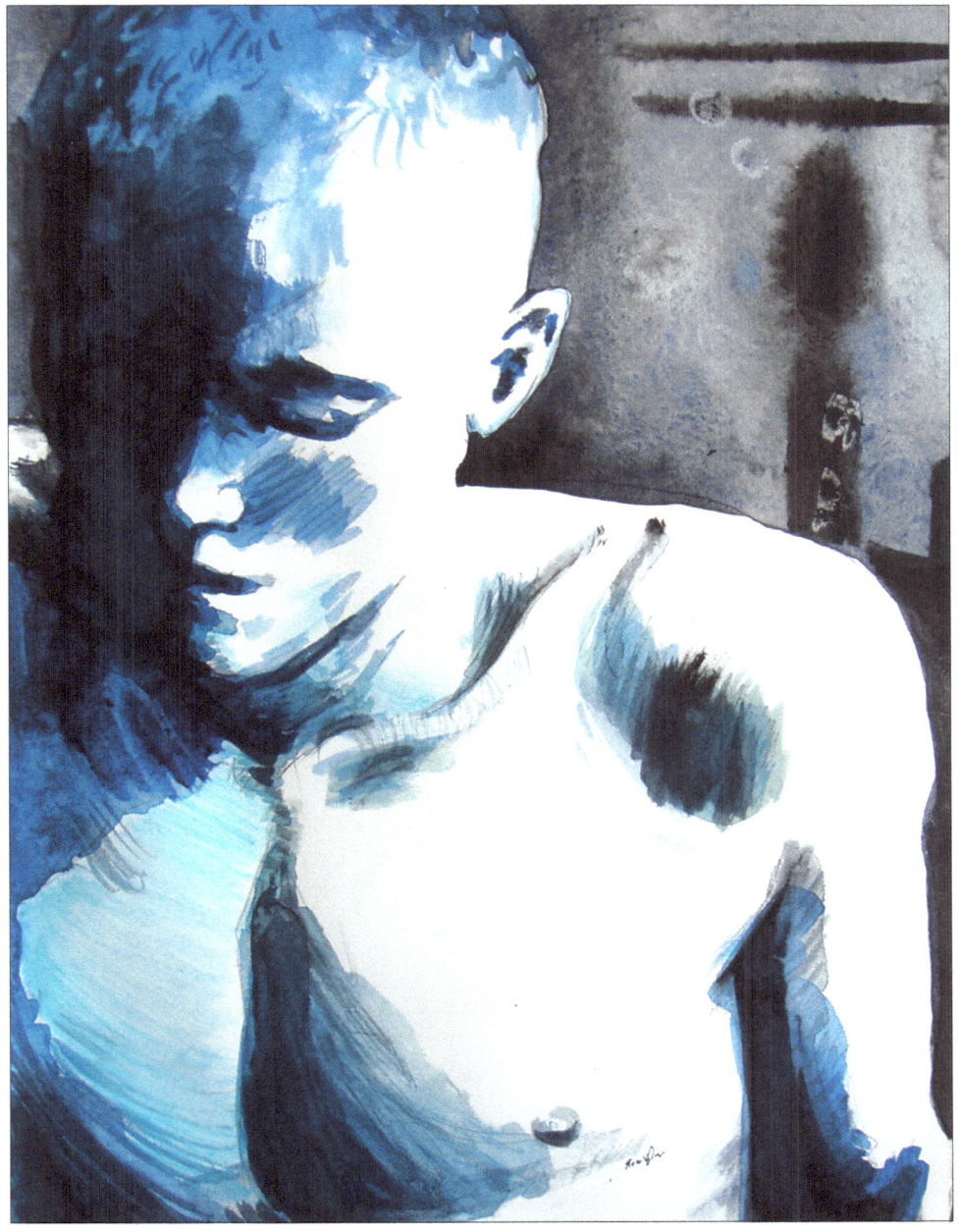

"Hot Child in the City" watercolor, 11"x14", 2011

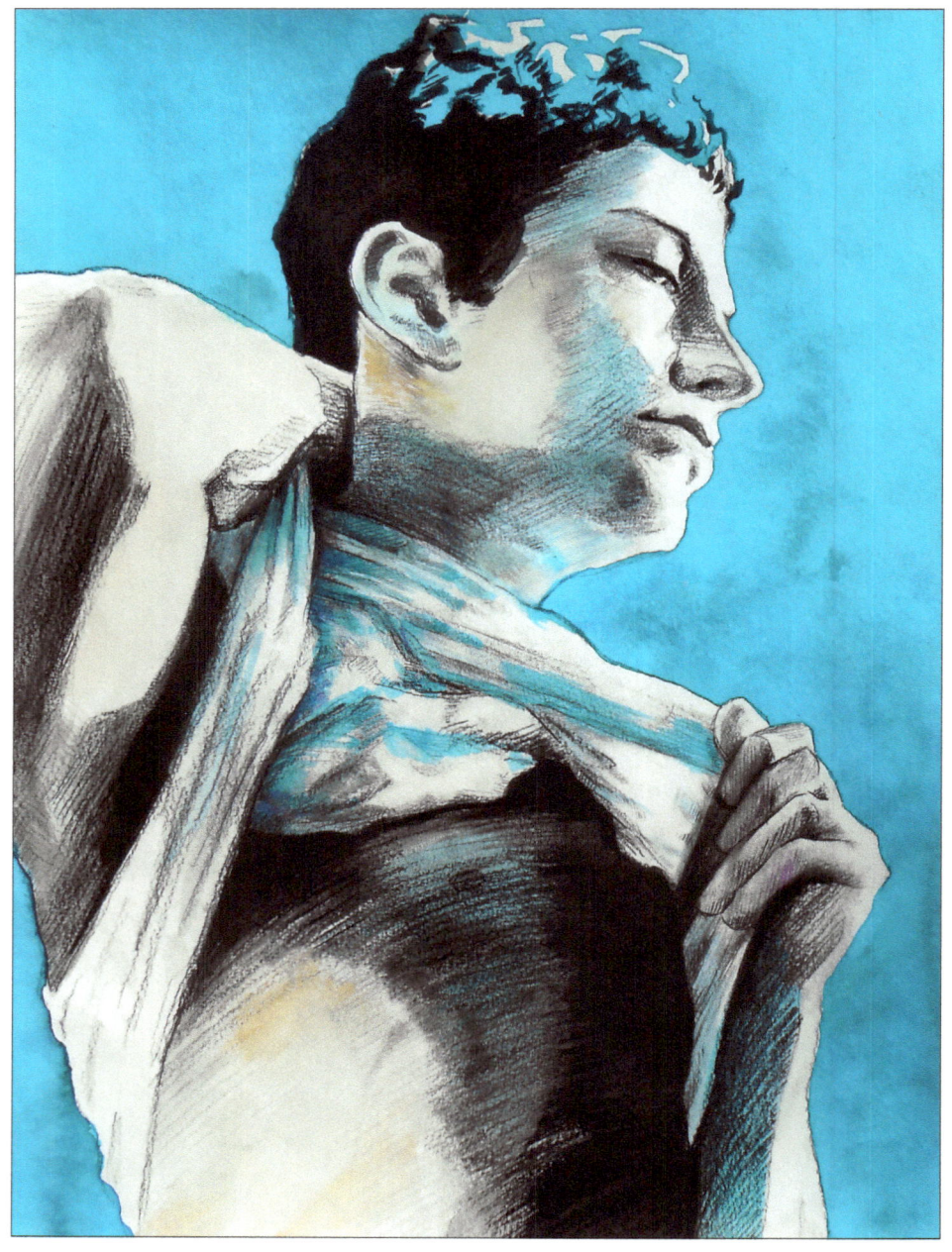

"Twisted & Blue" watercolor & pencil, 12"x19", 2012

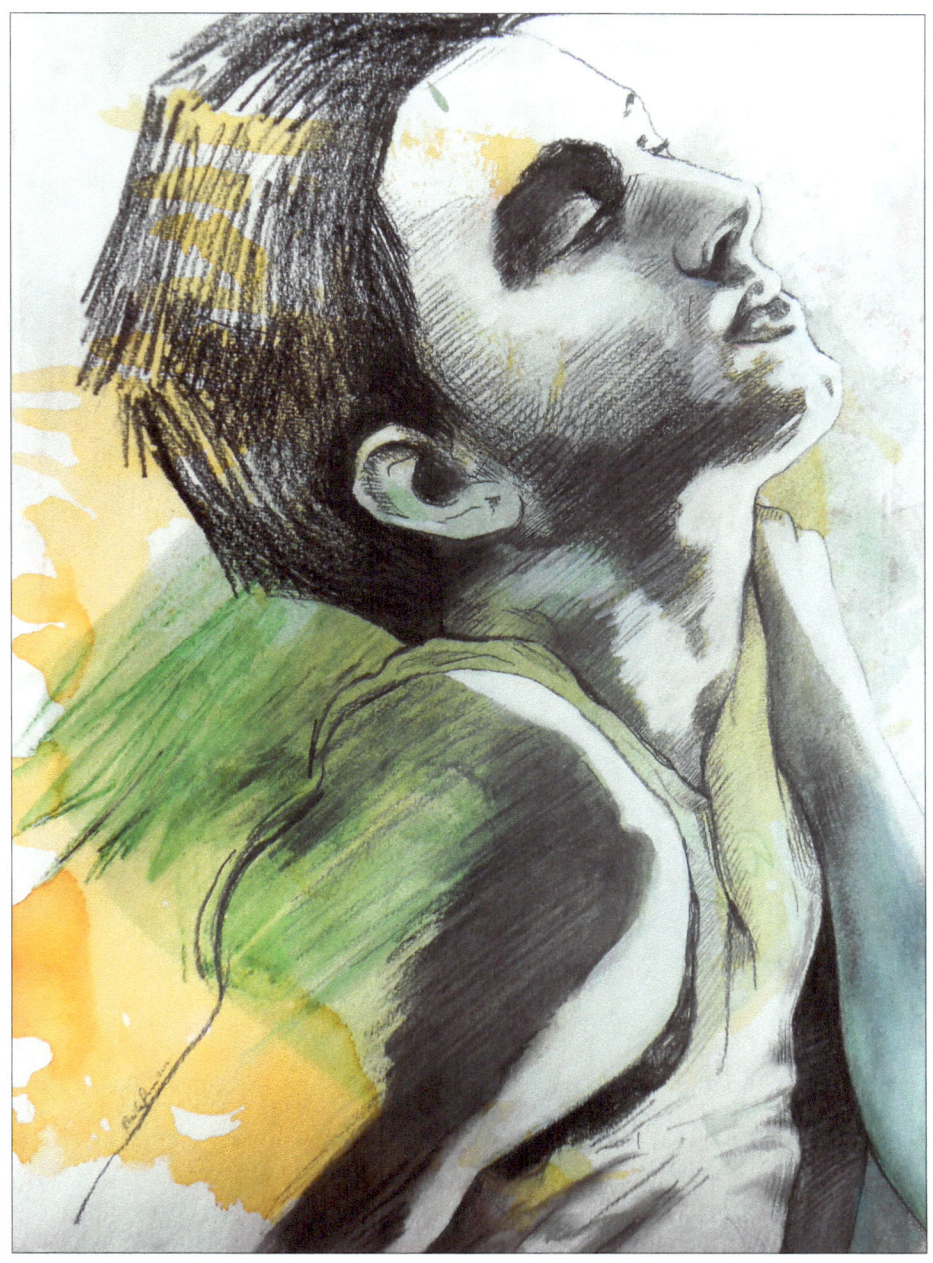

"His Quiet World of Green & Gold" watercolor & pencil, 12"x19", 2012

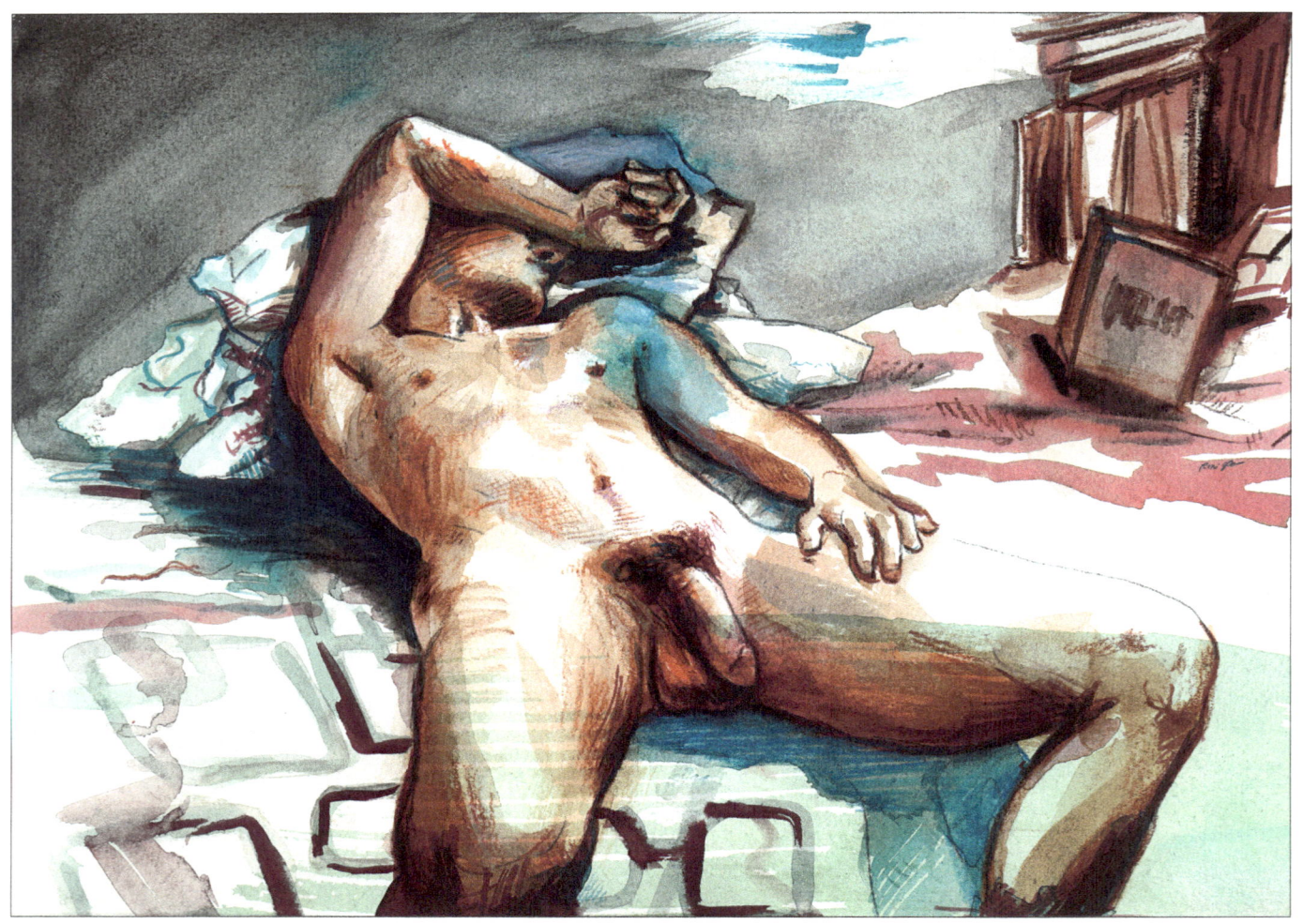

"Recline #1" watercolor & color pencil, 12"x9", 2012

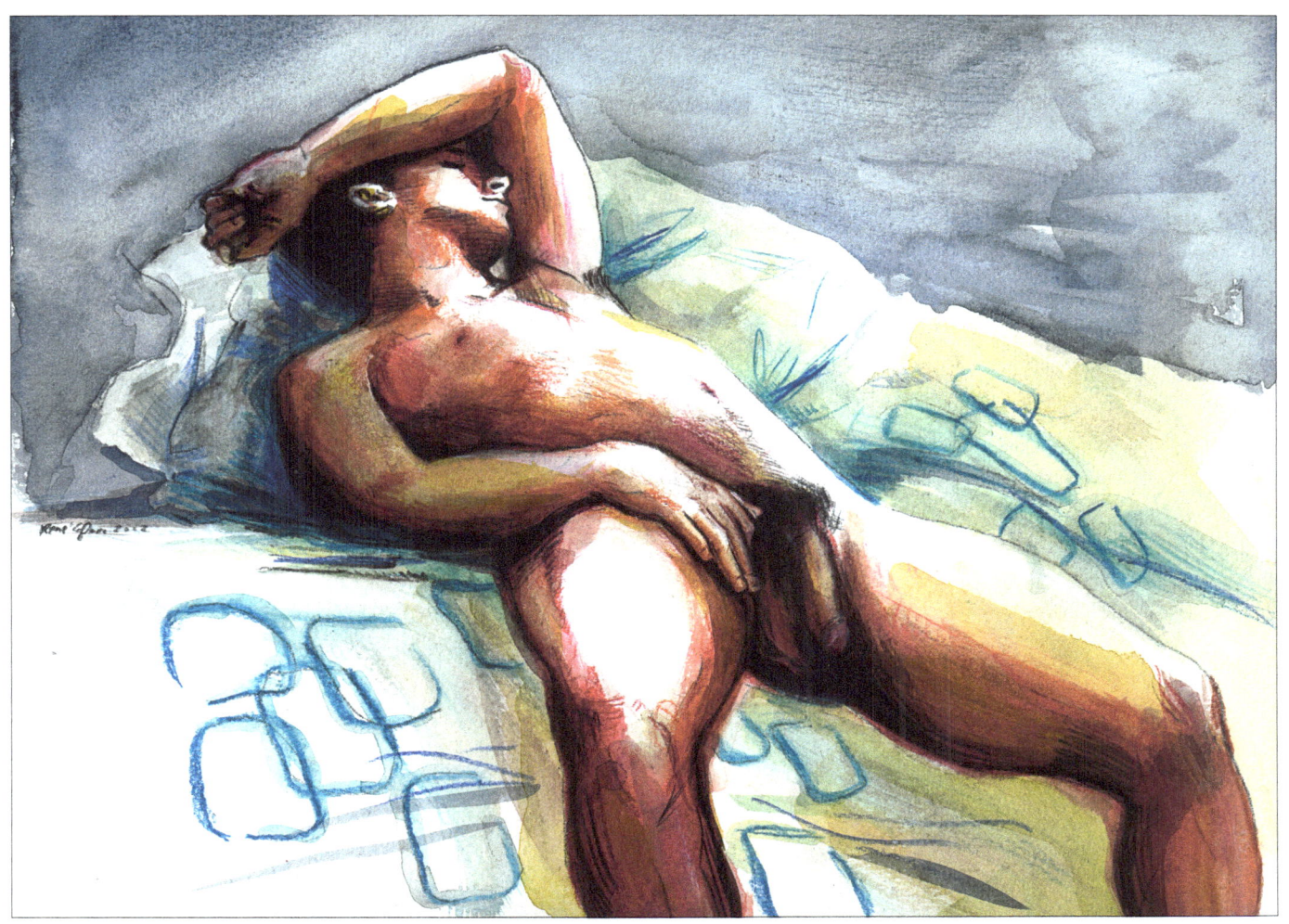

"Recline #2" watercolor & color pencil, 12"x9", 2012

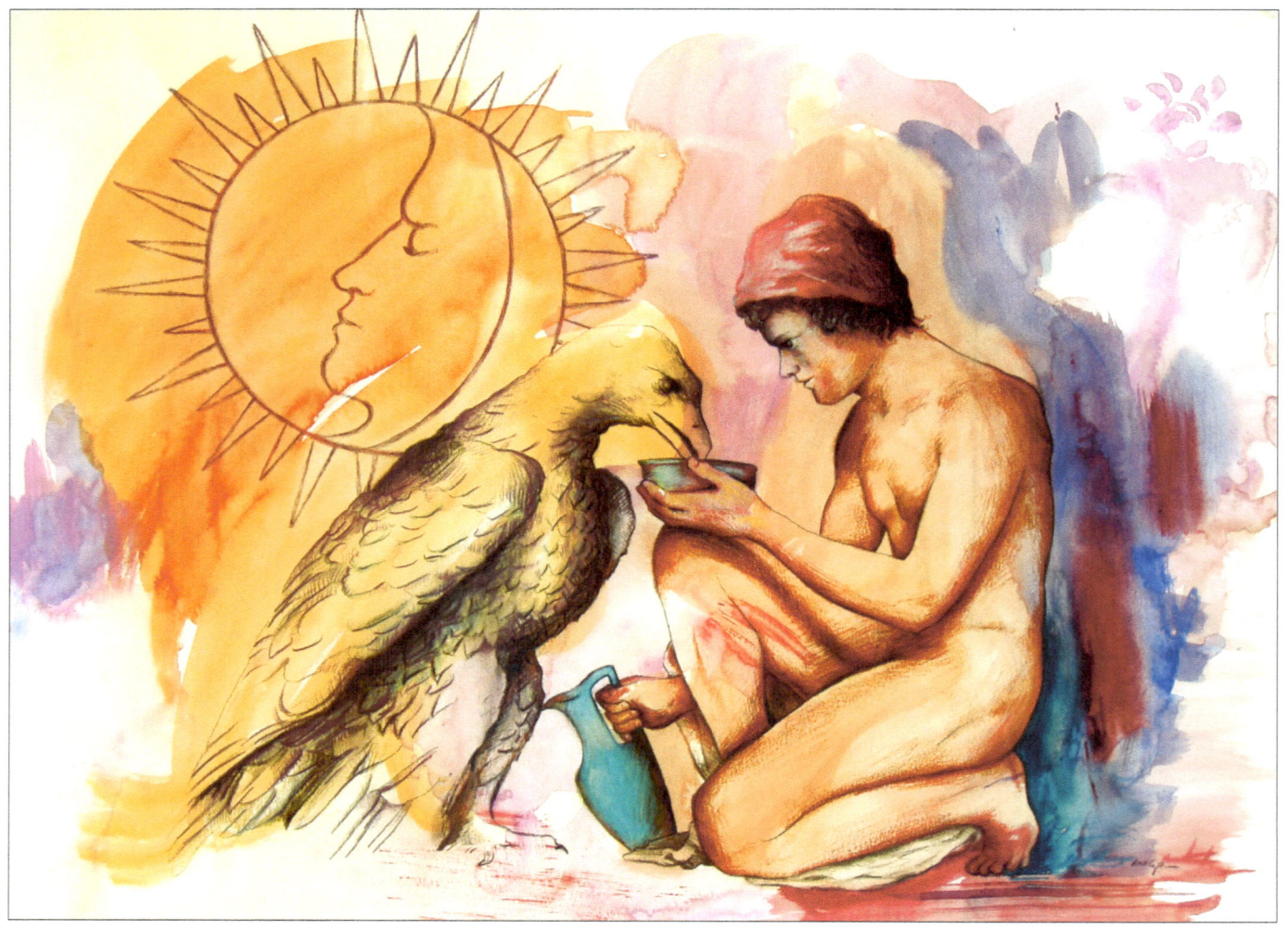

"Ganymede & Zues" watercolor & color pencil, 24"x19", 2012

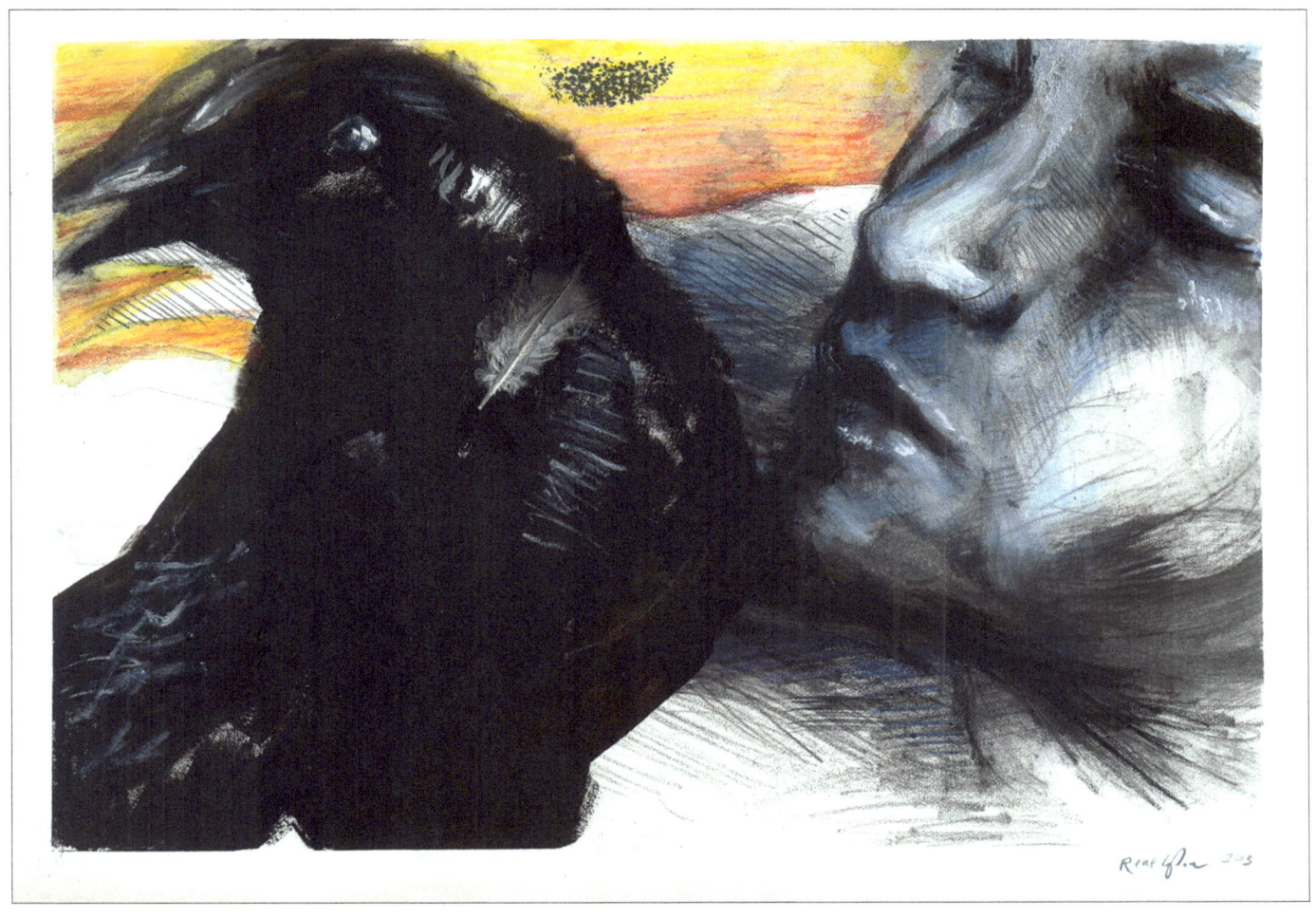

"Outside Your Voodoo" watercolor & color pencil, 12"x9", 2013

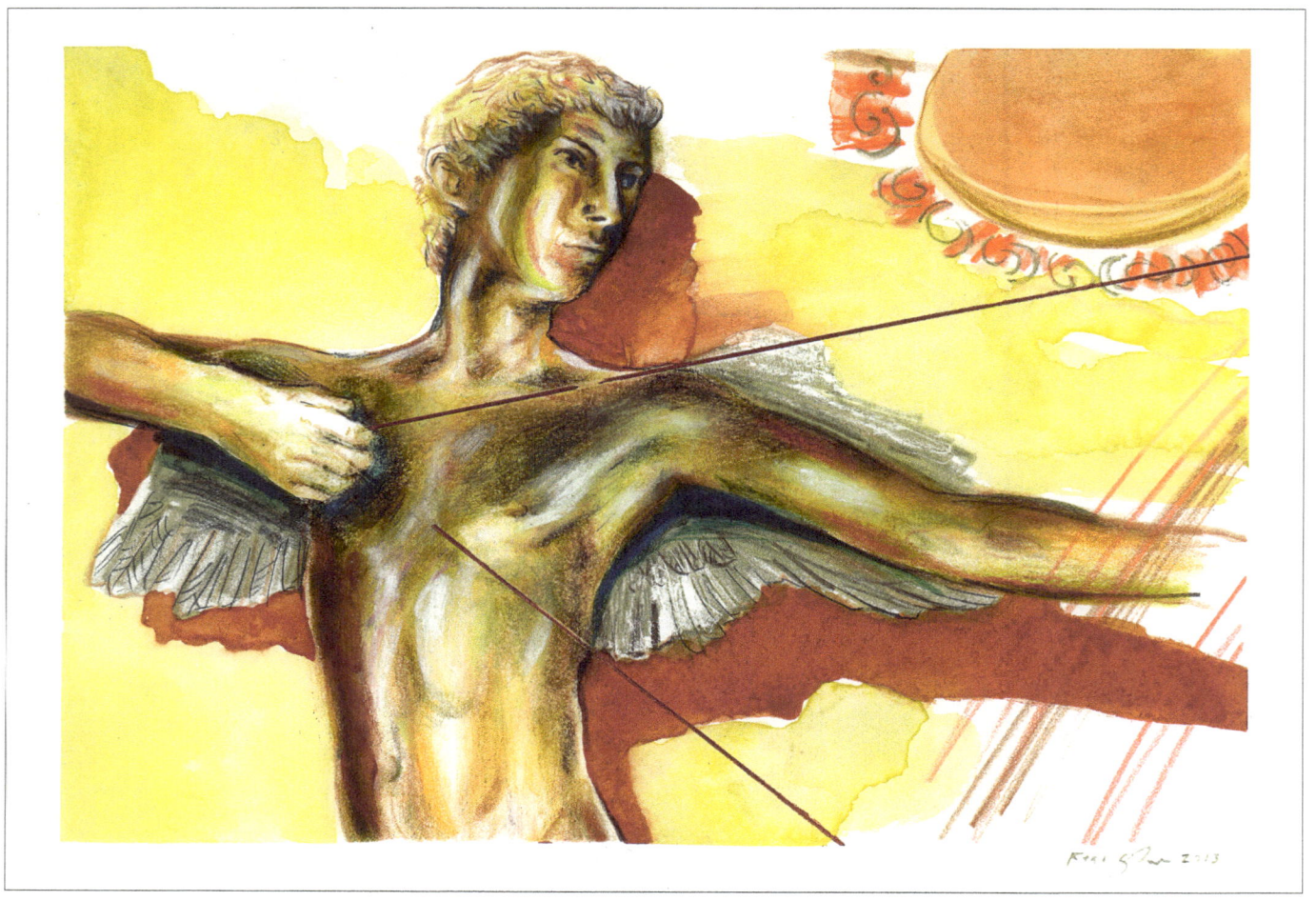

"Sun God" watercolor & color pencil, 12"x9", 2013

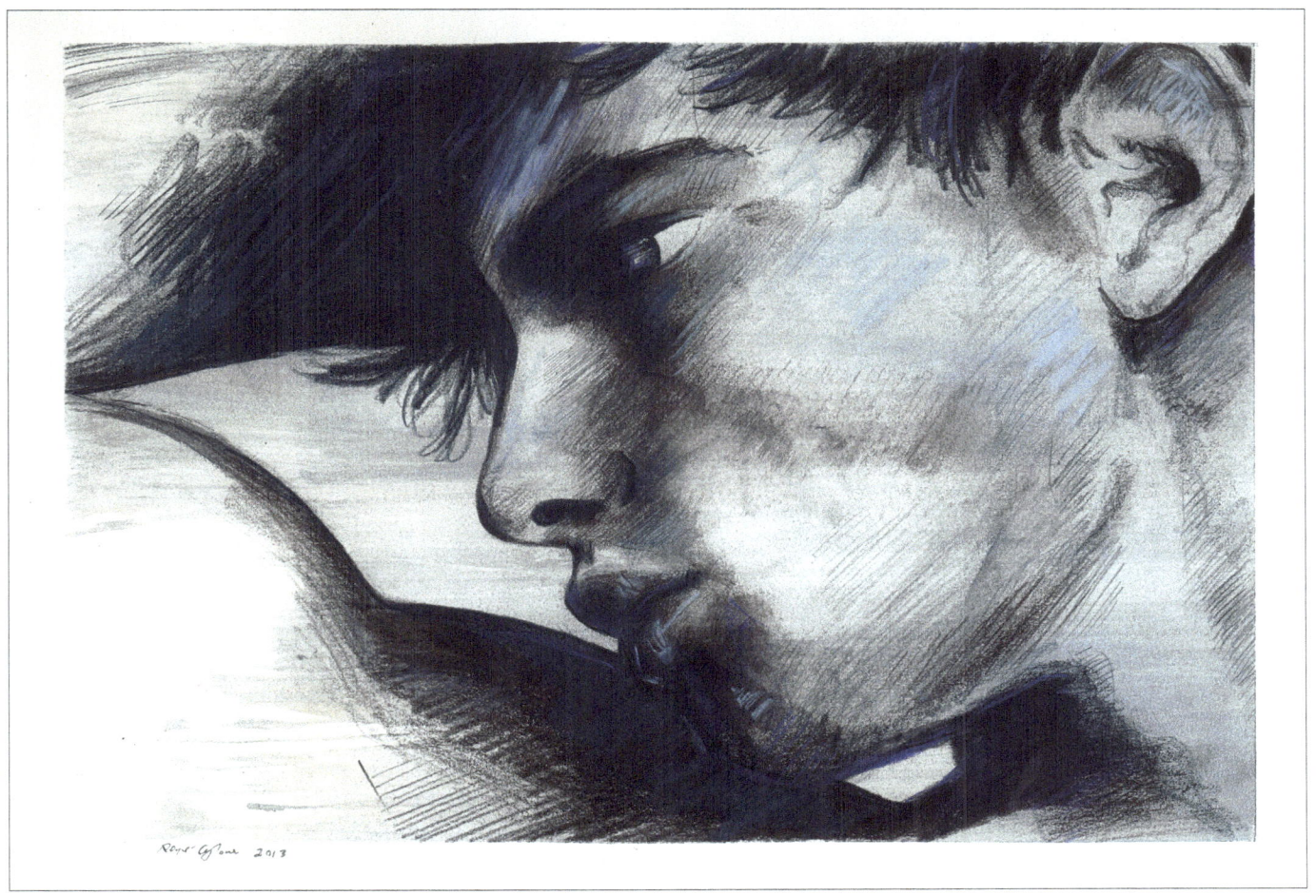

"Silver, Striped & Justified" watercolor & pencil, 12"x9", 2013

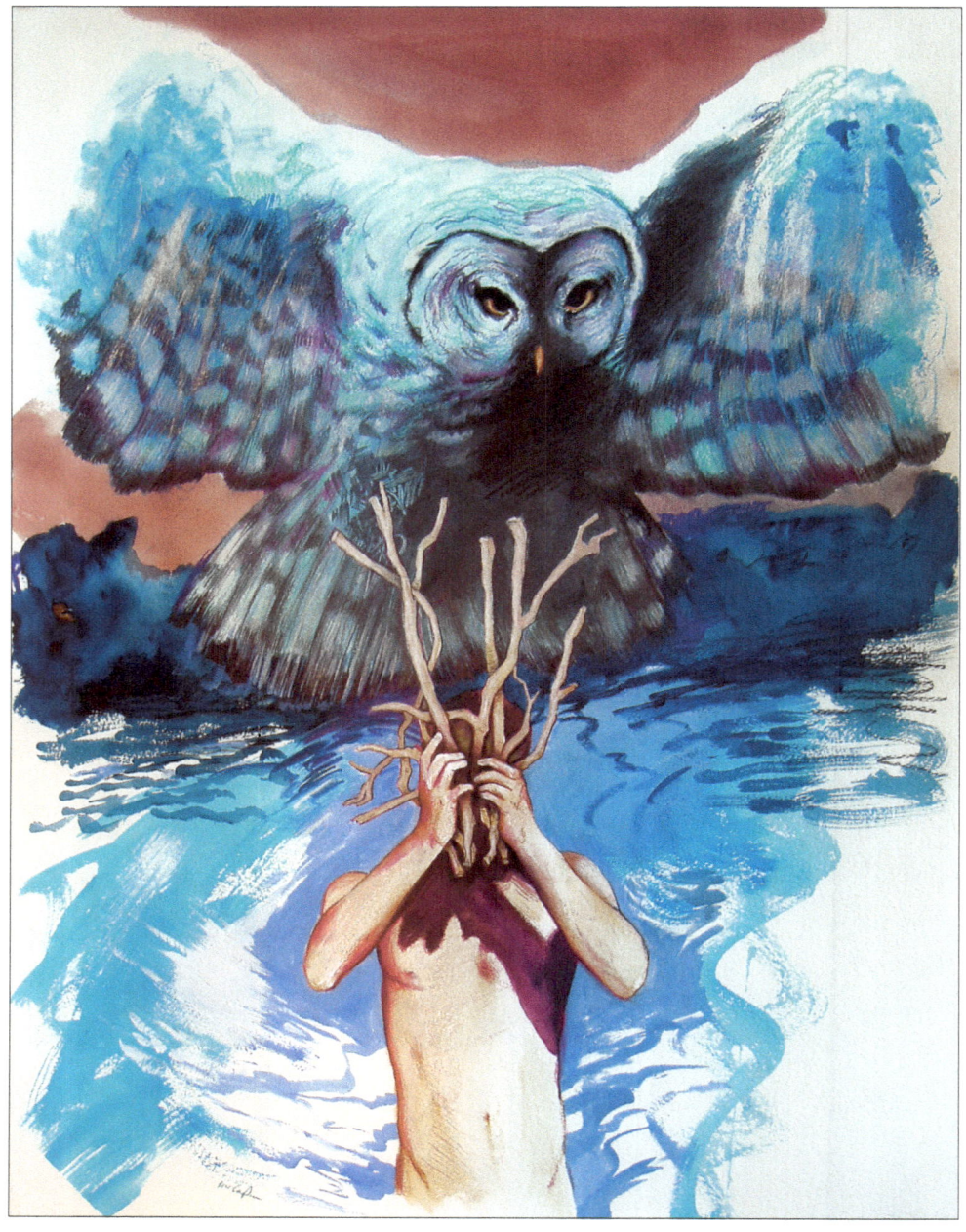

"Hide & Seek" watercolor & color pencil, 22"x30", 2011

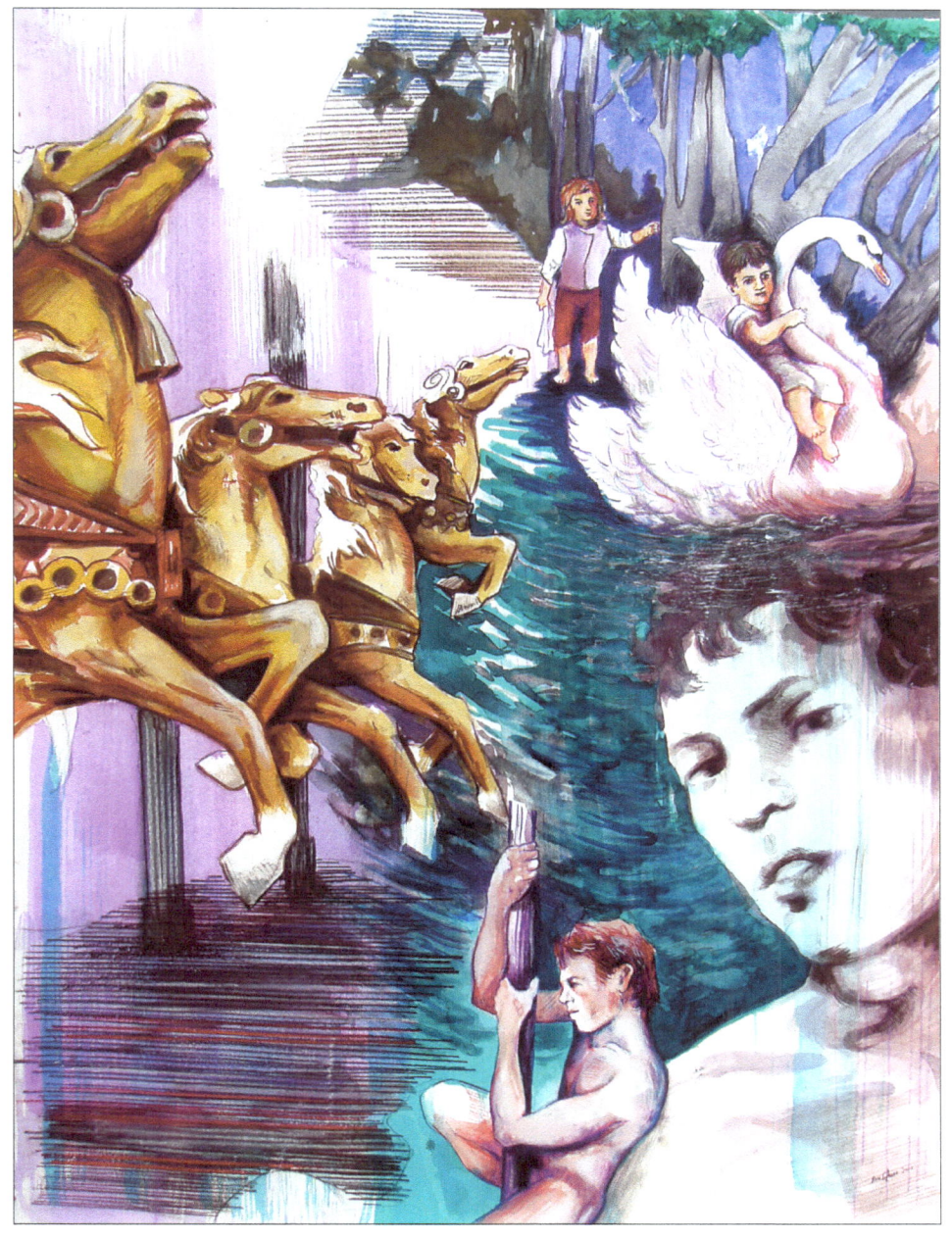

"Escape at Night by Way of Swan, Innocence Lost Twice" watercolor & color pencil, 22"x30", 2012

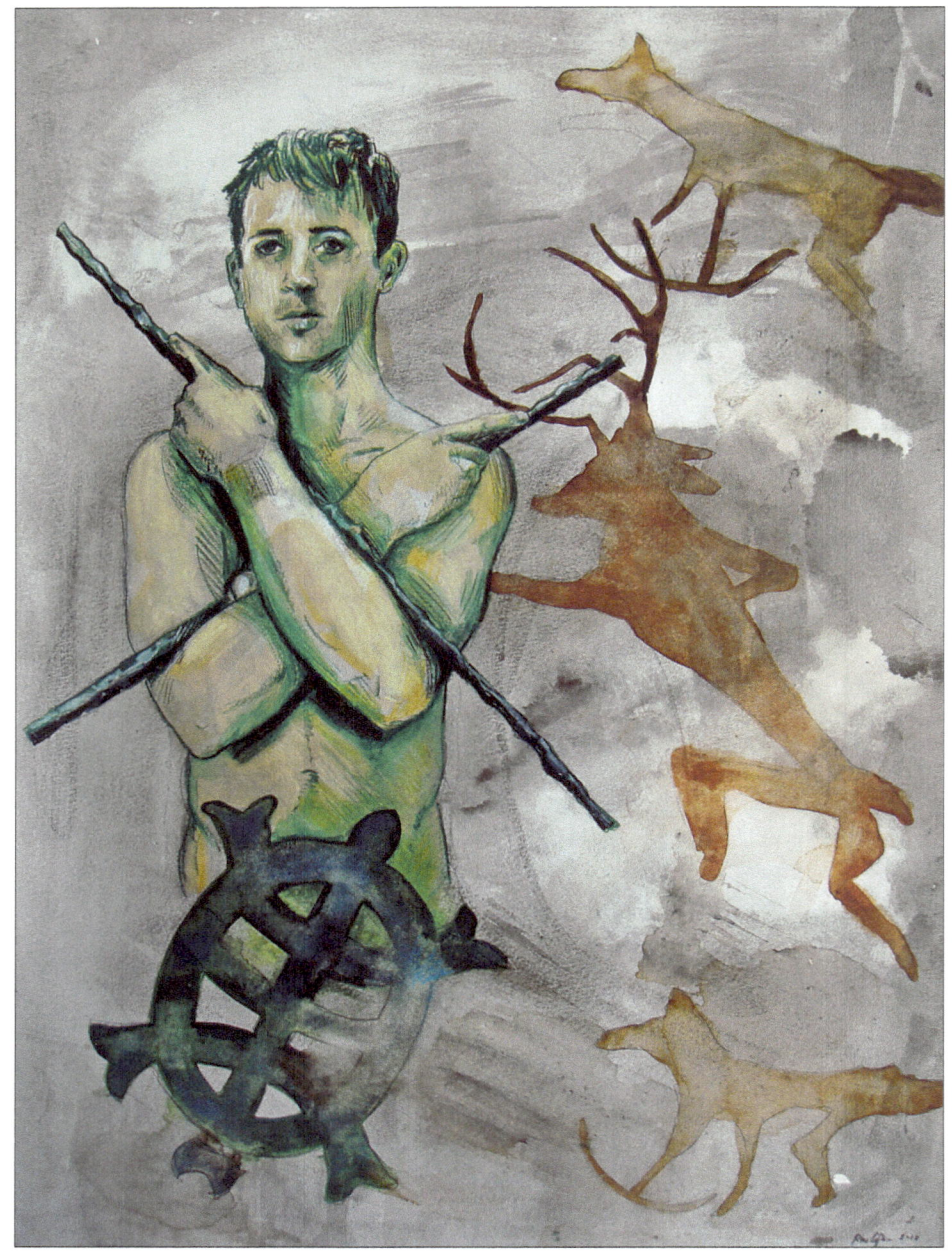

"Hunter" watercolor & pencil, 19"x24", 2011

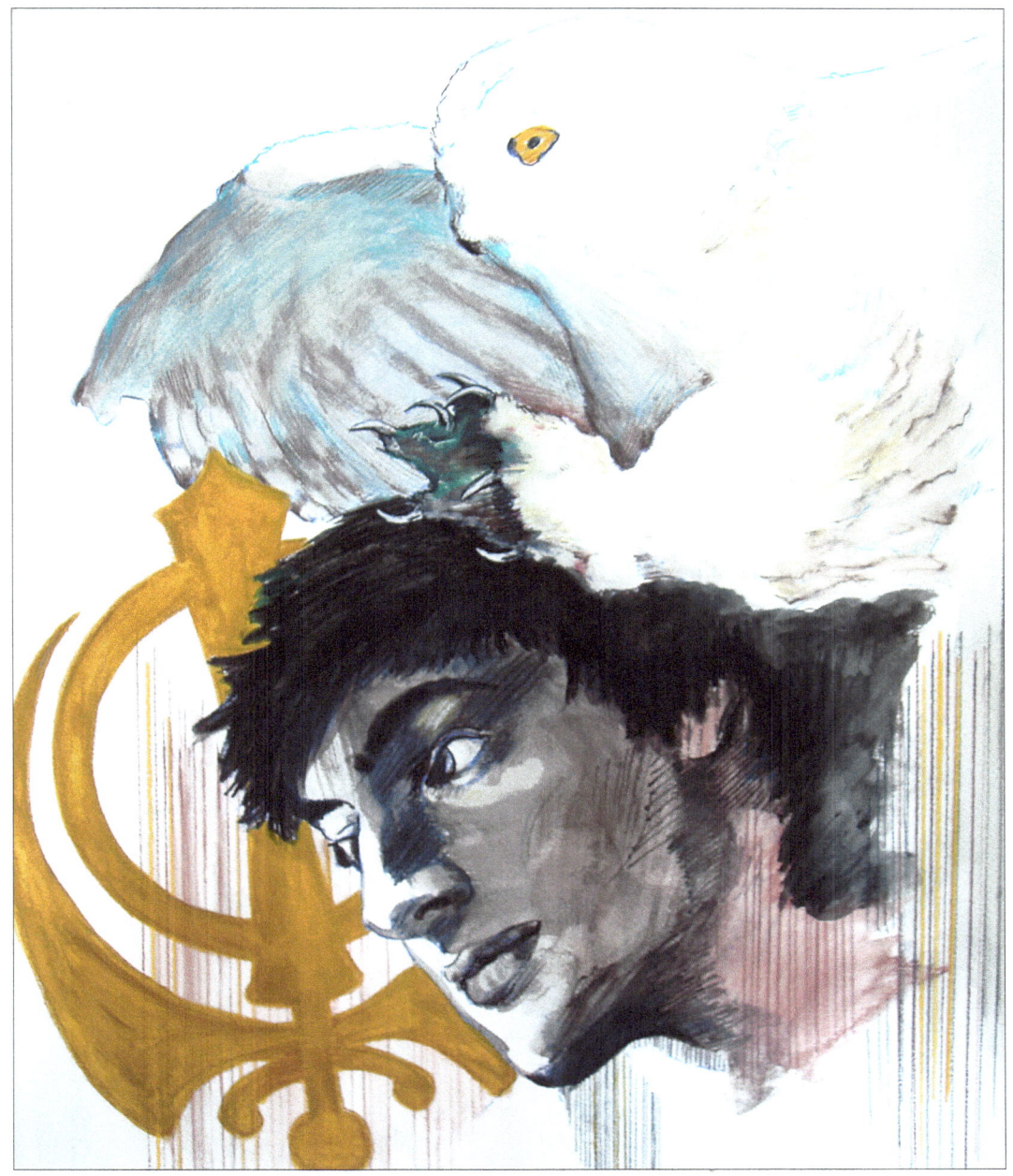

"Owl Illusions" watercolor & color pencil, 20"x24", 2012

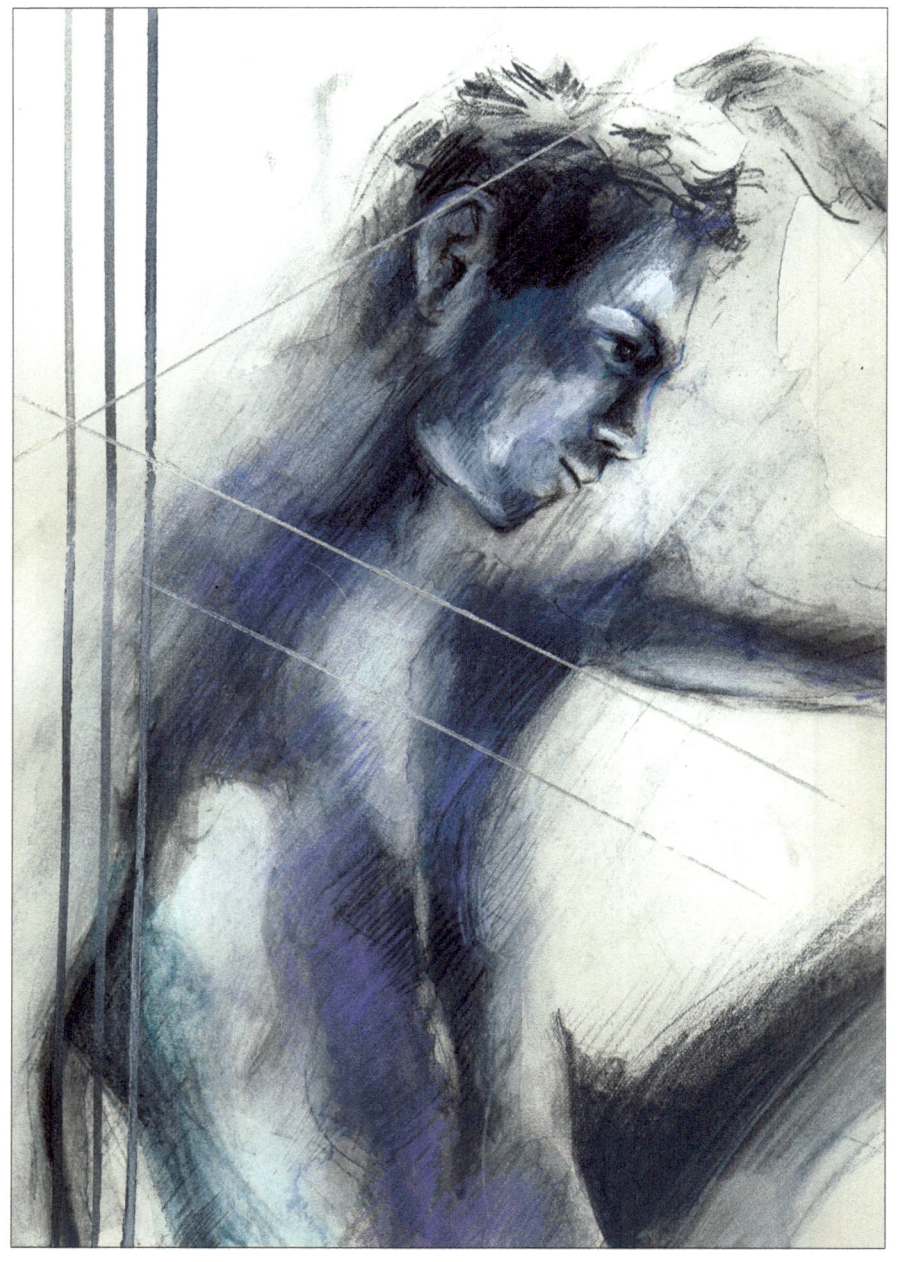

"Morning Mist" watercolor & color pencil, 11"x14", 2013

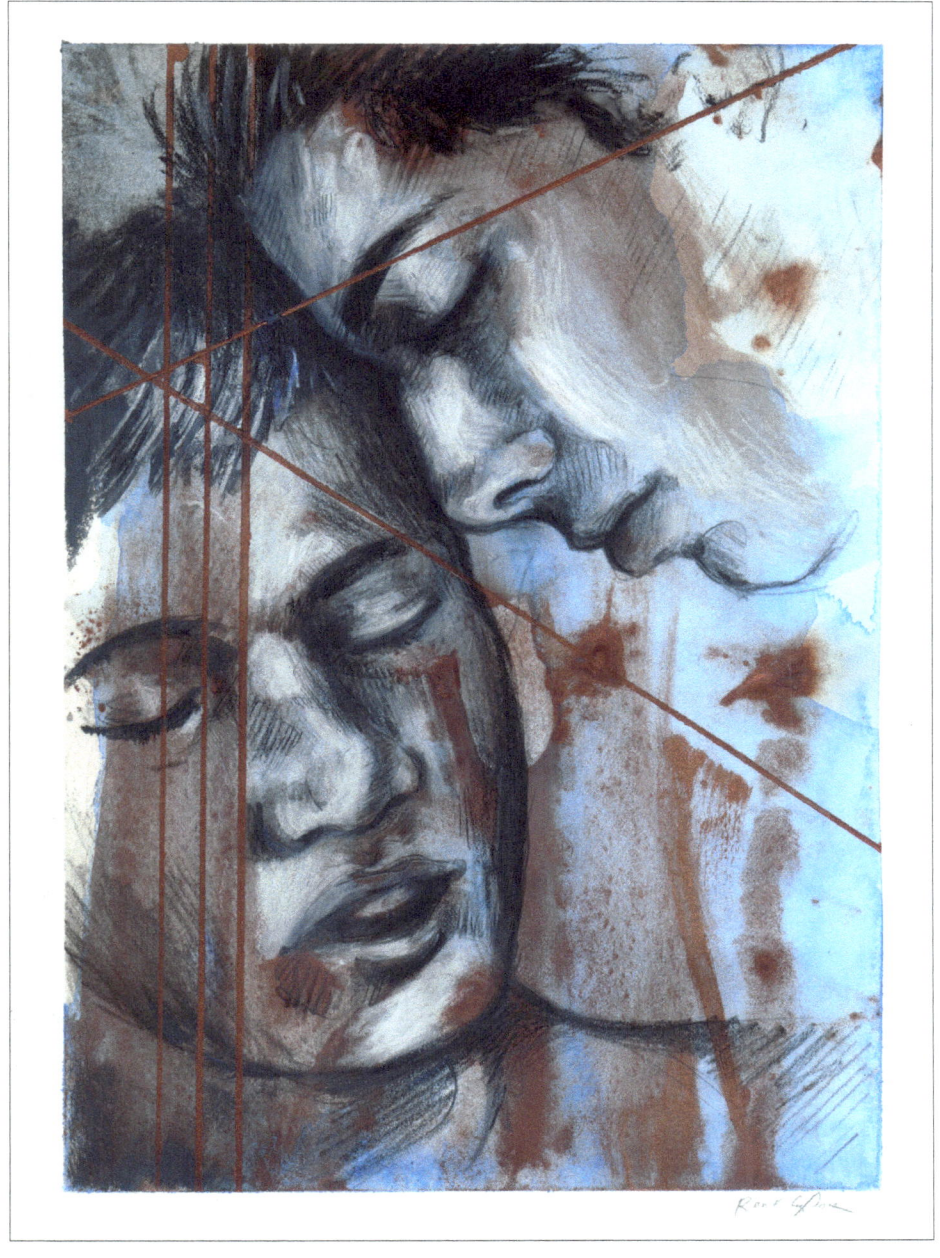

"Broken Languages" watercolor & color pencil, 9"x12", 2013

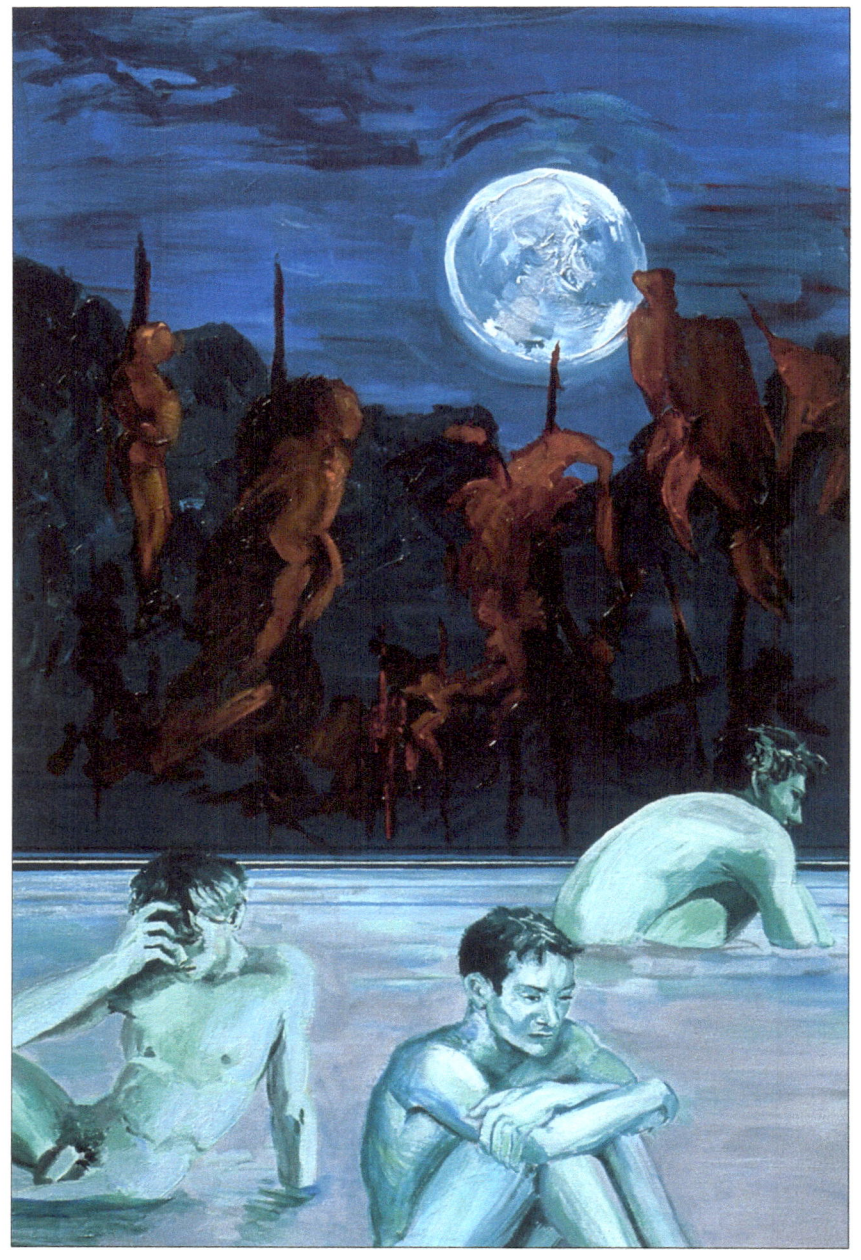

"Reflections of the War" acrylic, 24"x36", 2003

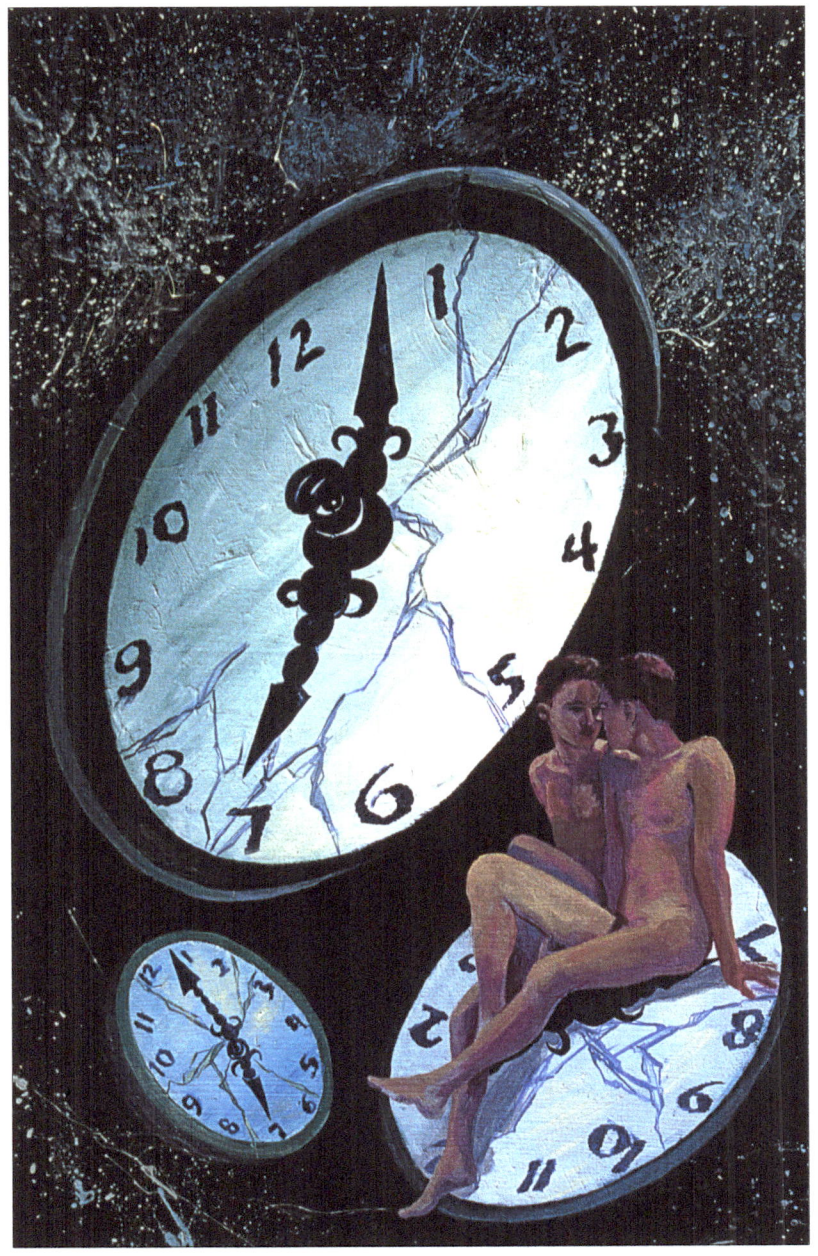

"Not Enough Time" acrylic, 24"x36", 2005

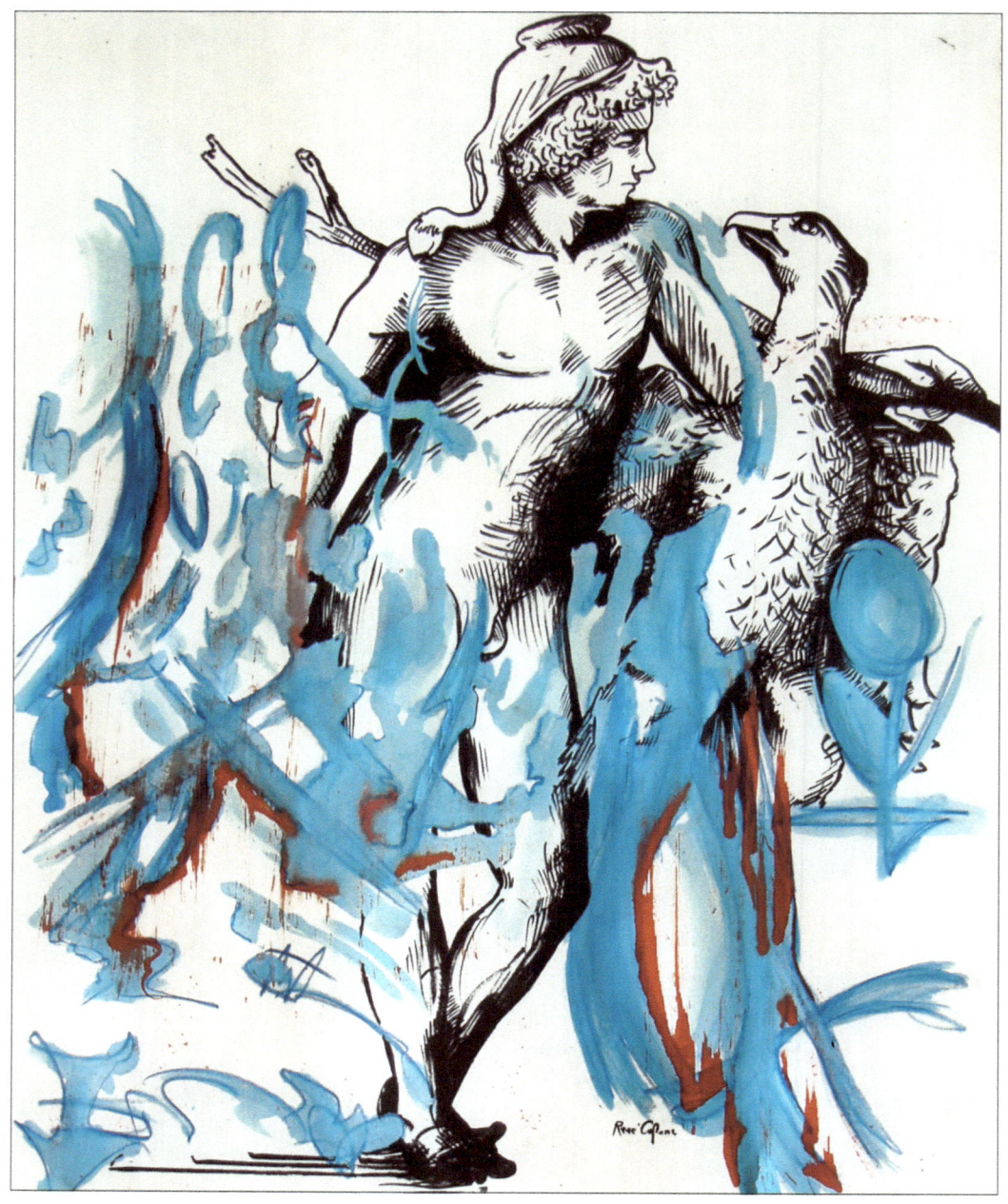

"Ganymede" watercolor & ink, 18"x24", 2012

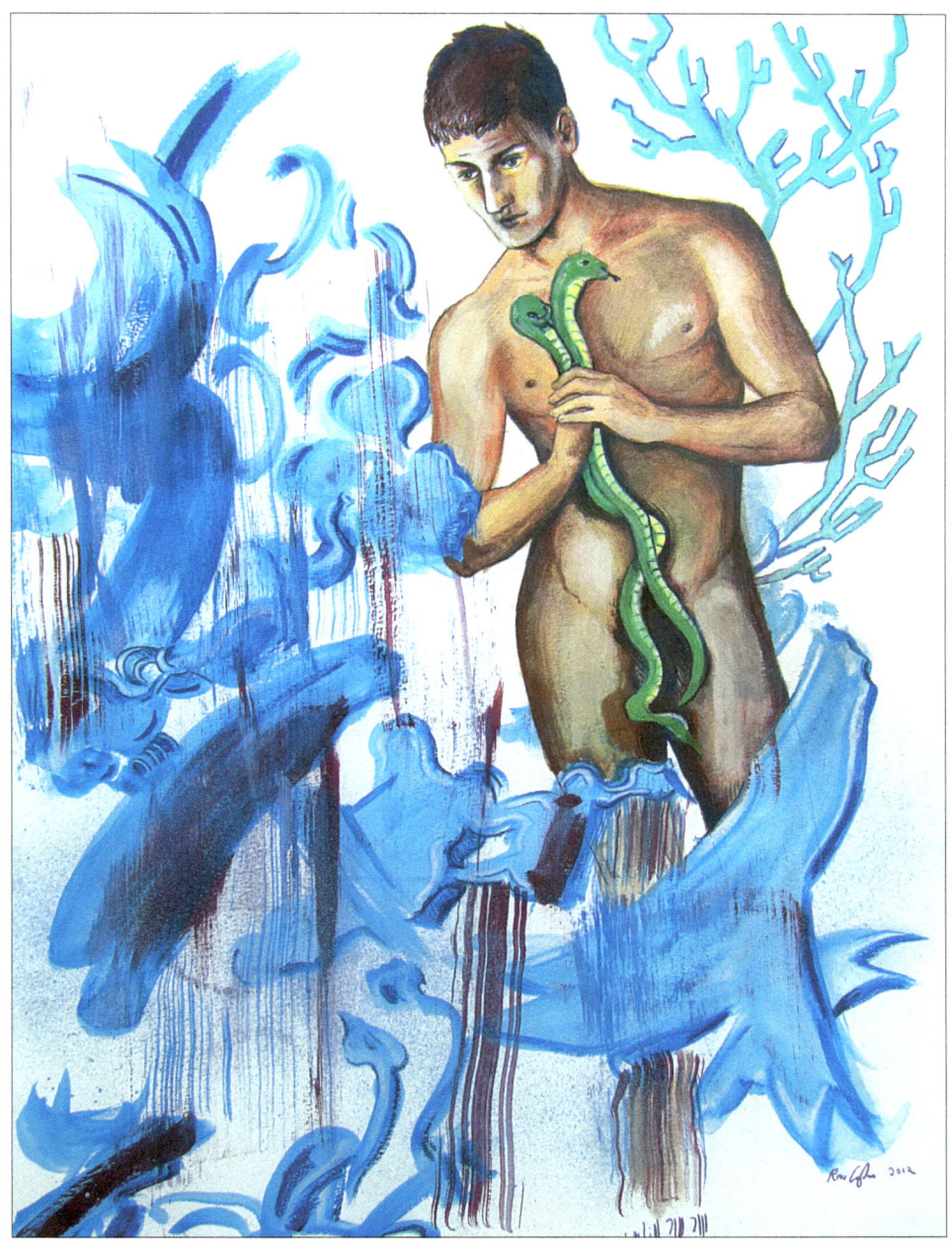

"Coral & Snakes" (for Mr. Fisher) watercolor & color pencil, 18"x24", 2012

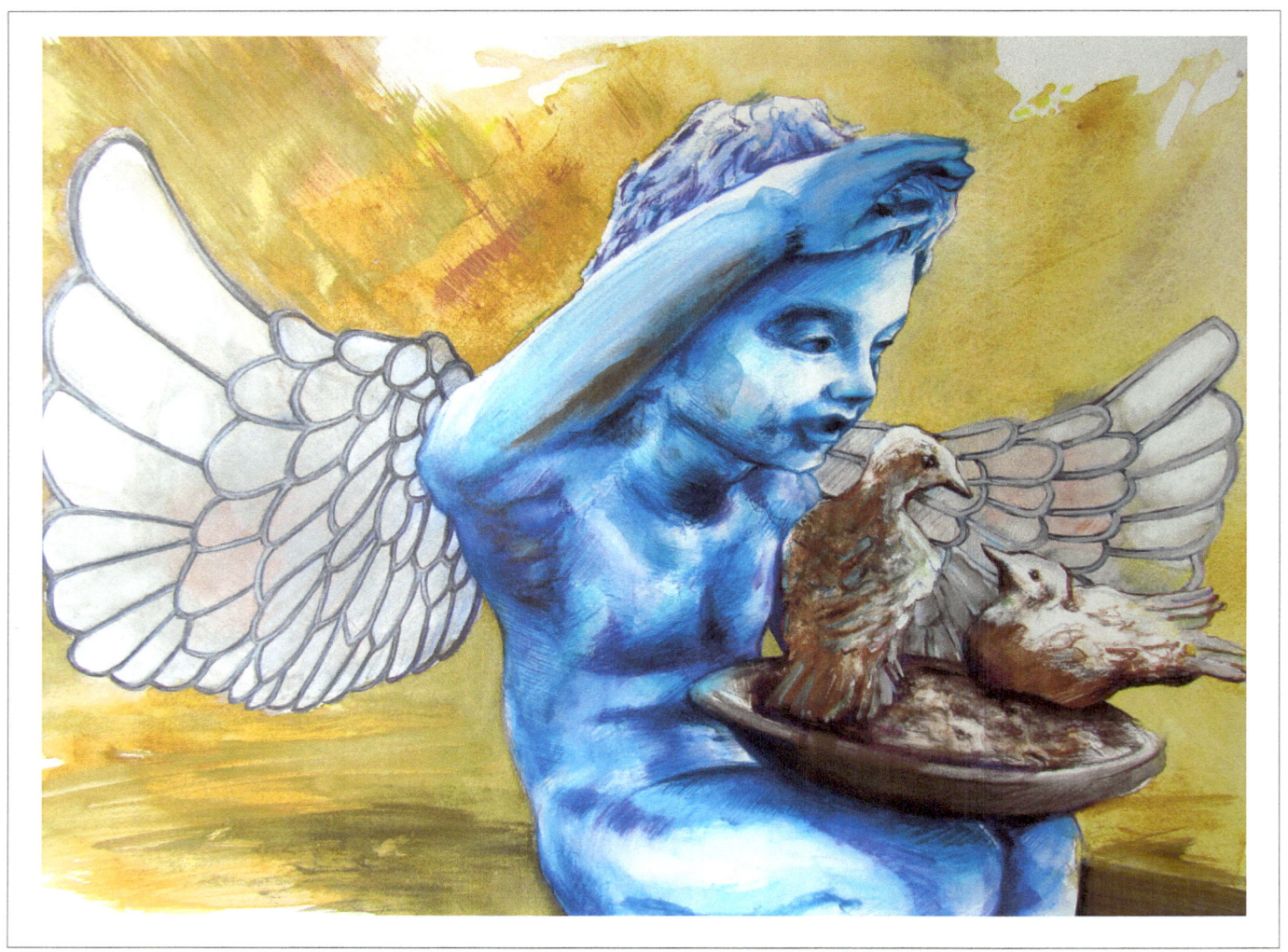

"An Opalescent Boy" watercolor & color pencil, 30"x22", 2013

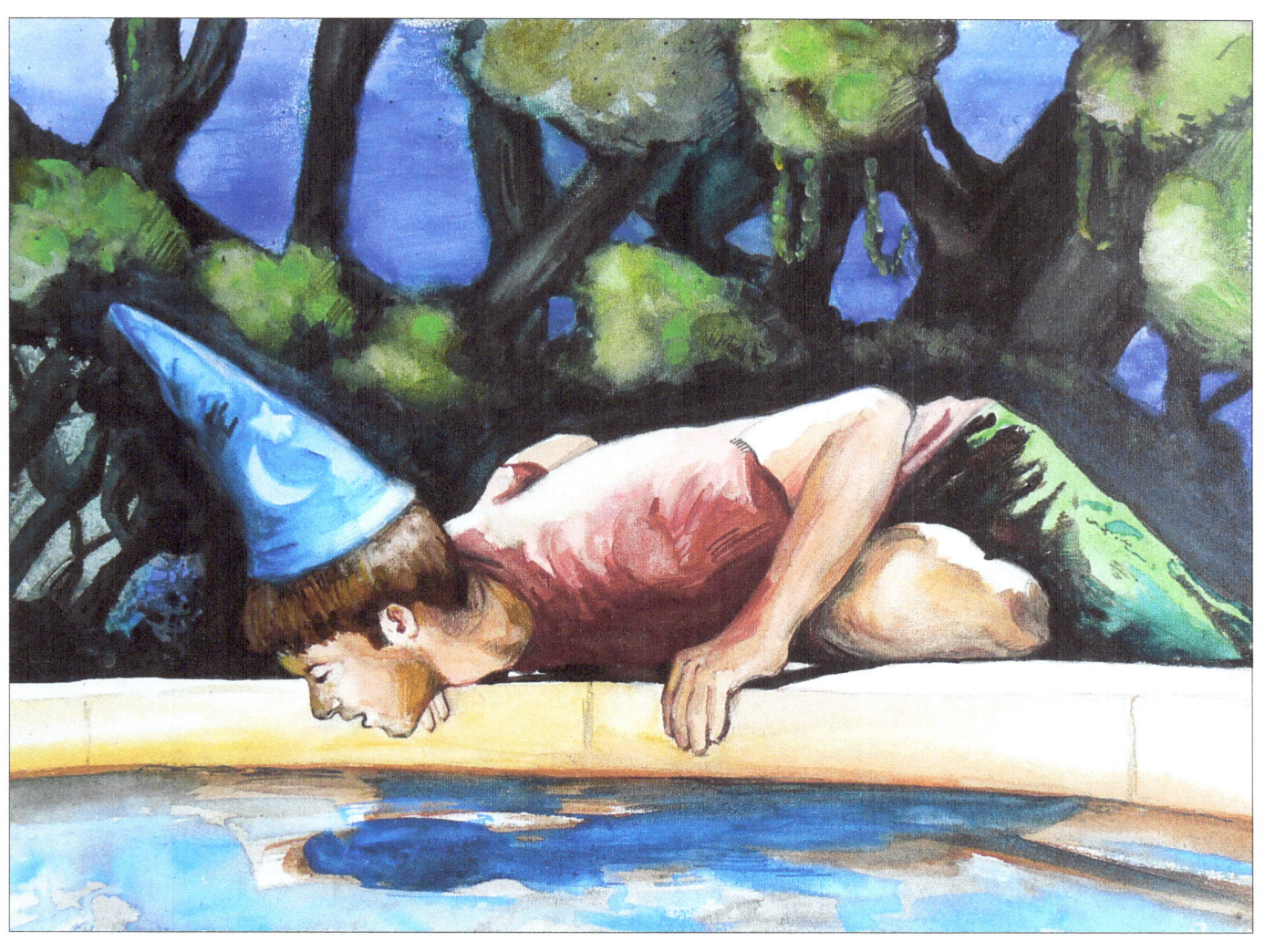

"If You Believe In Magic 2" watercolor, 12"x9", 2012

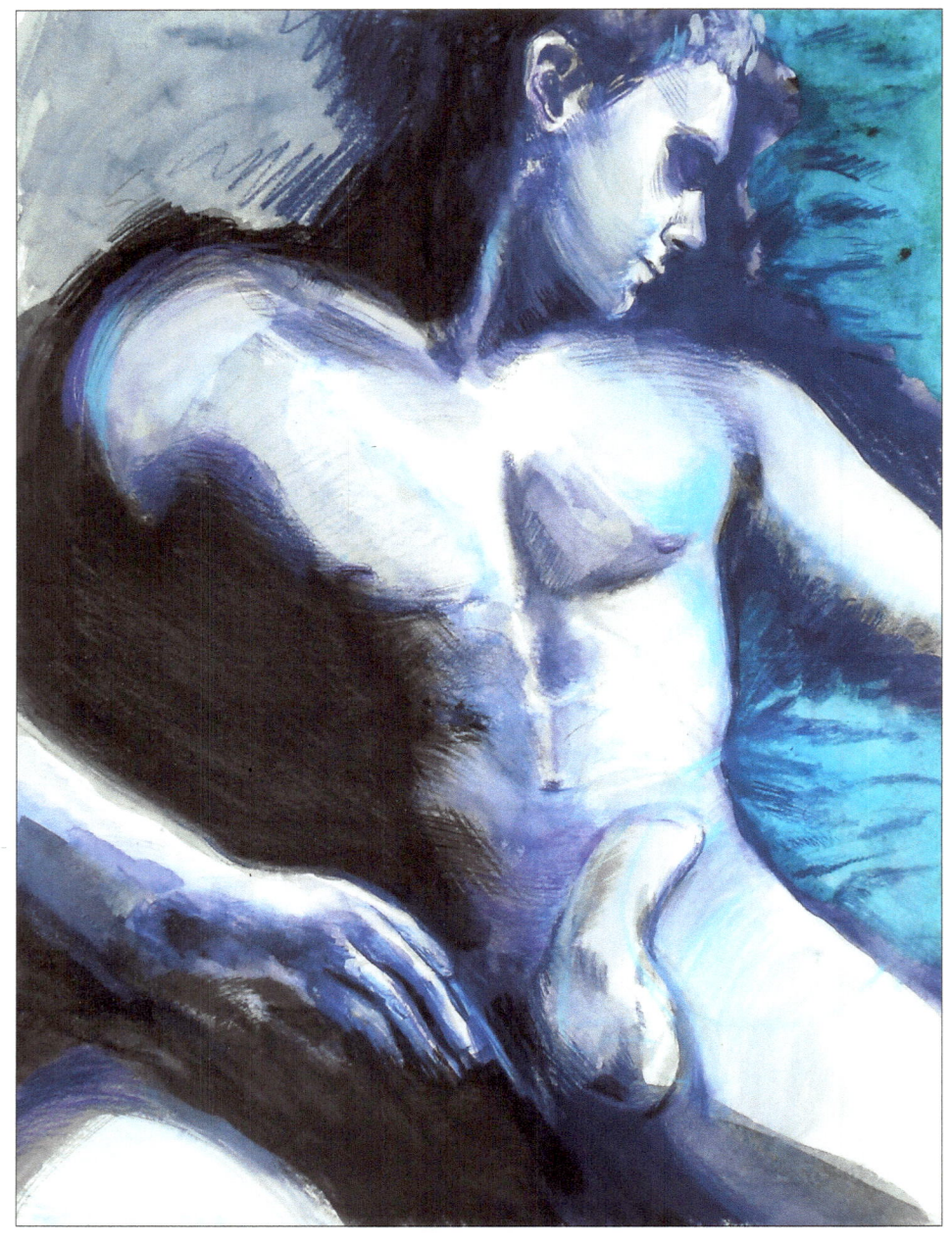

"Boy's Blues" watercolor & color pencil, 16"x20", 2012

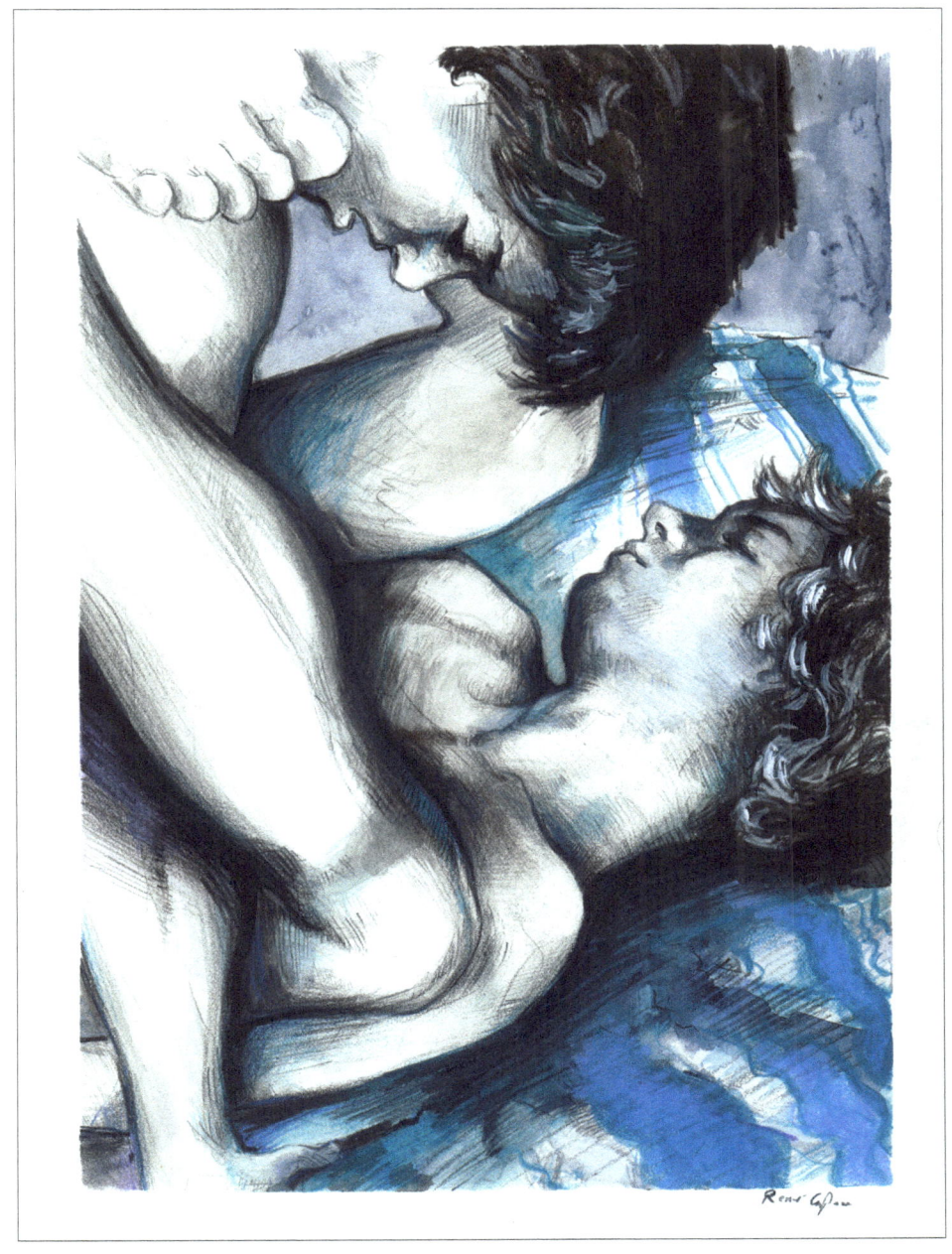

"Boys" watercolor & color pencil, 9"x12", 2013

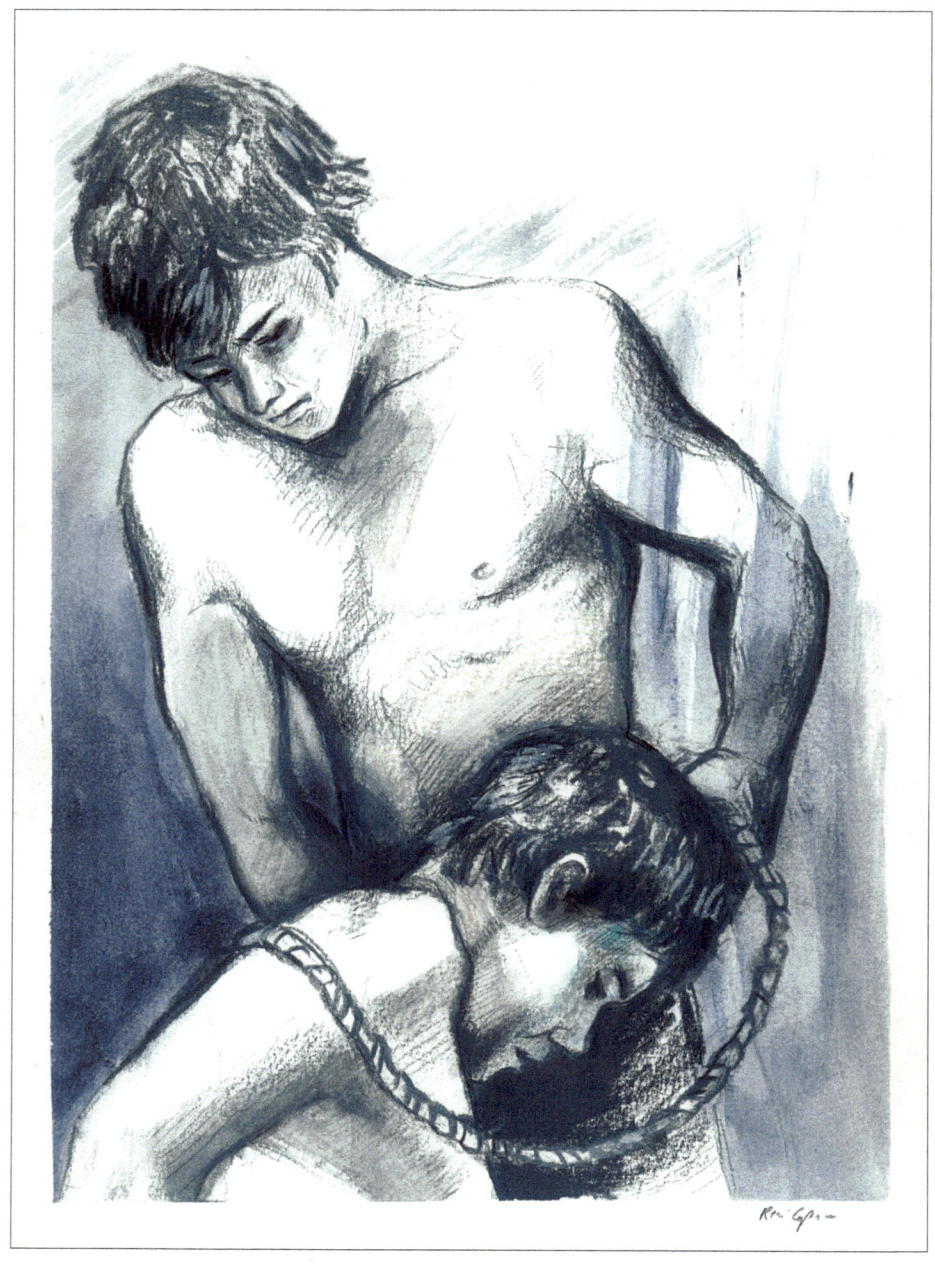

"Bound to You" watercolor & color pencil, 9"x12", 2013

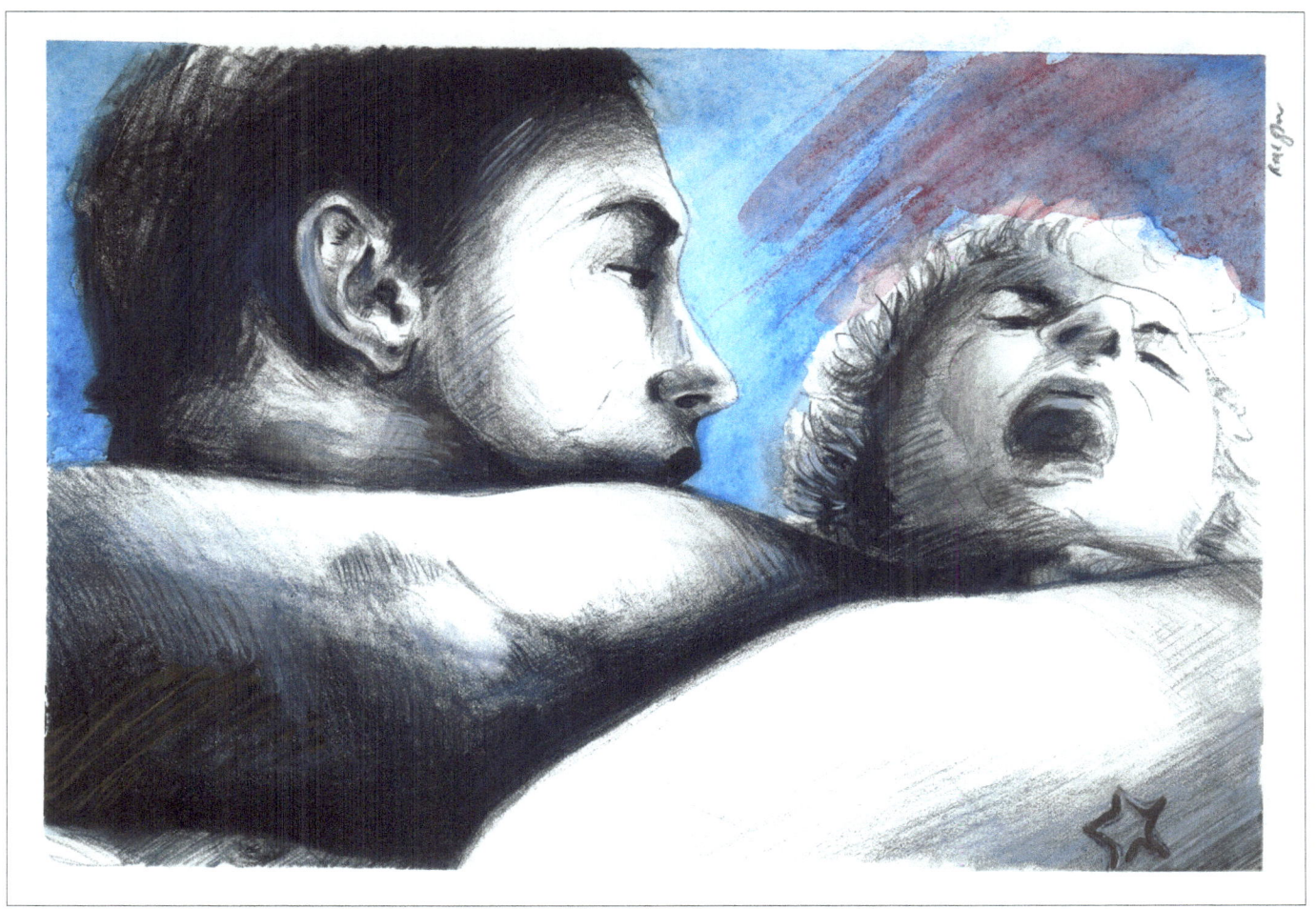

"Panic Attack" watercolor & pencil, 12"x9", 2013

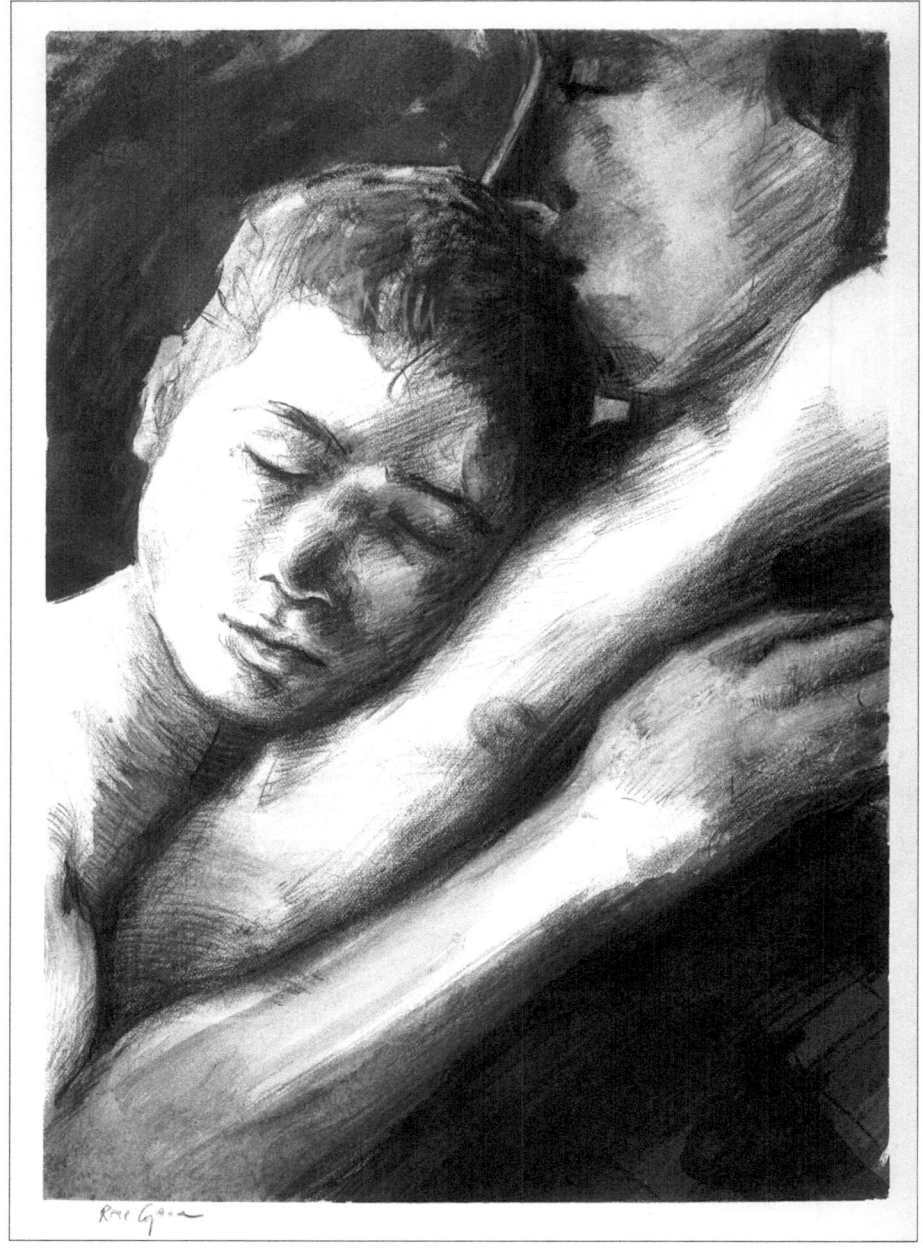

"Tenderness" watercolor & pencil, 9"x12", 2013

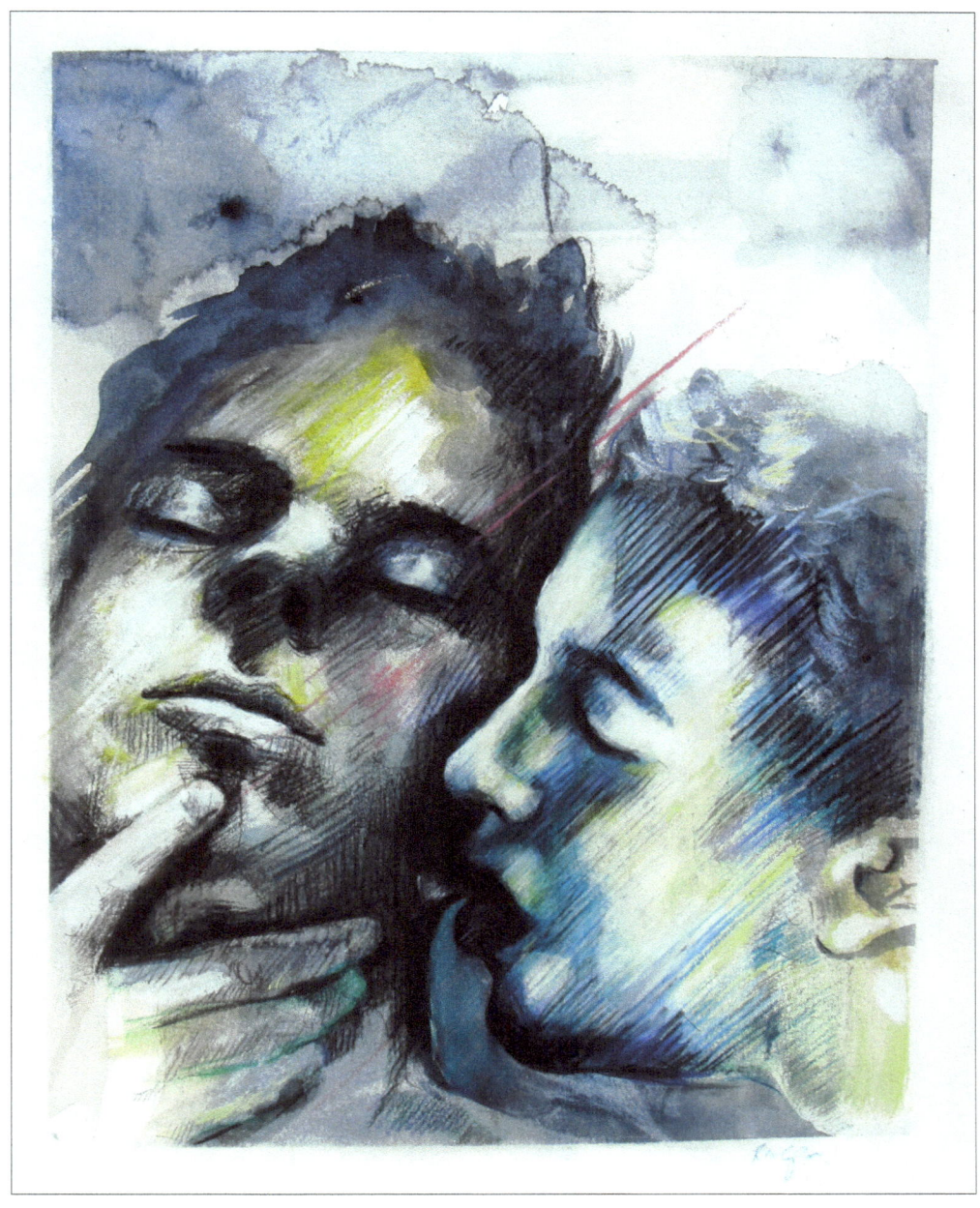

"Aquatic Dreams" watercolor & pencil, 11"x14", 2013

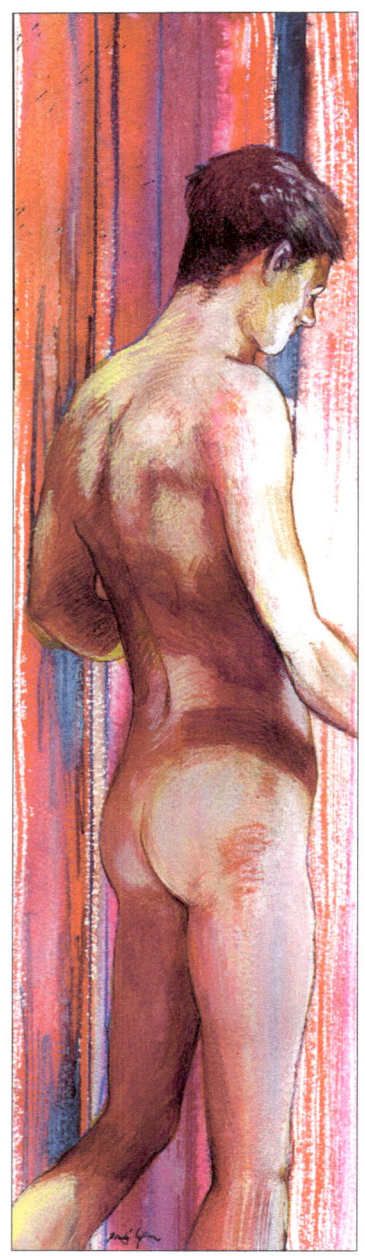

"Vertical" watercolor, 2"x12", 2013 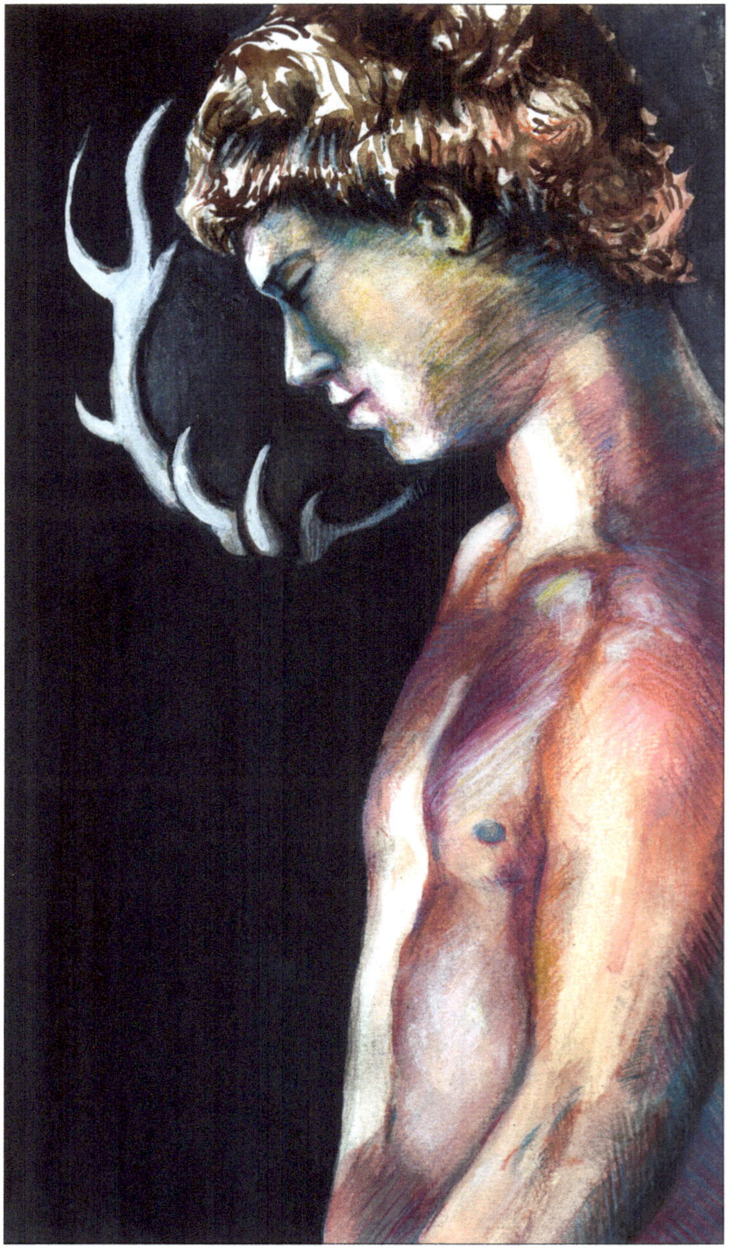   "Buck" watercolor & color pencil, 5"x12", 2013

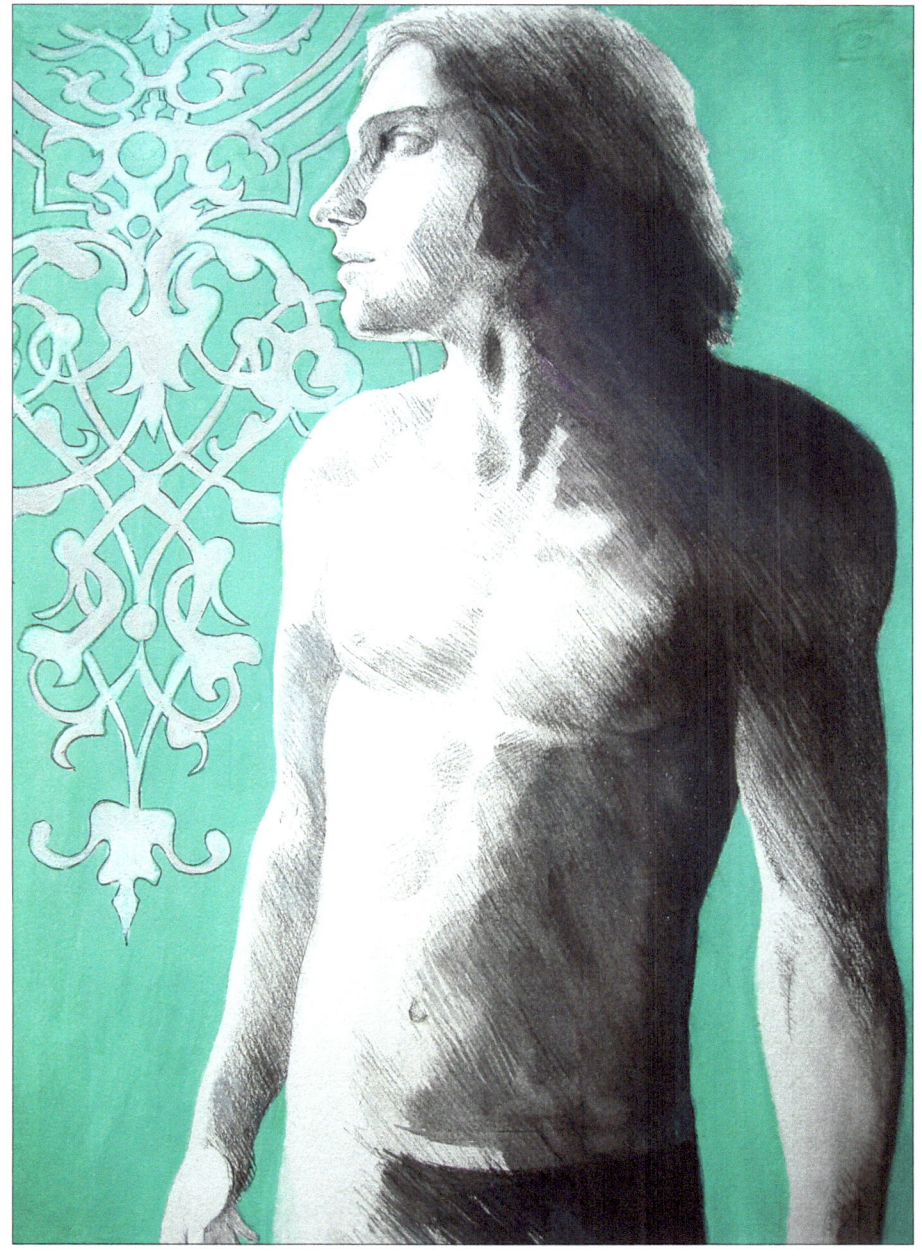

"Dorian Grey" watercolor & pencil, 11"x16", 2012

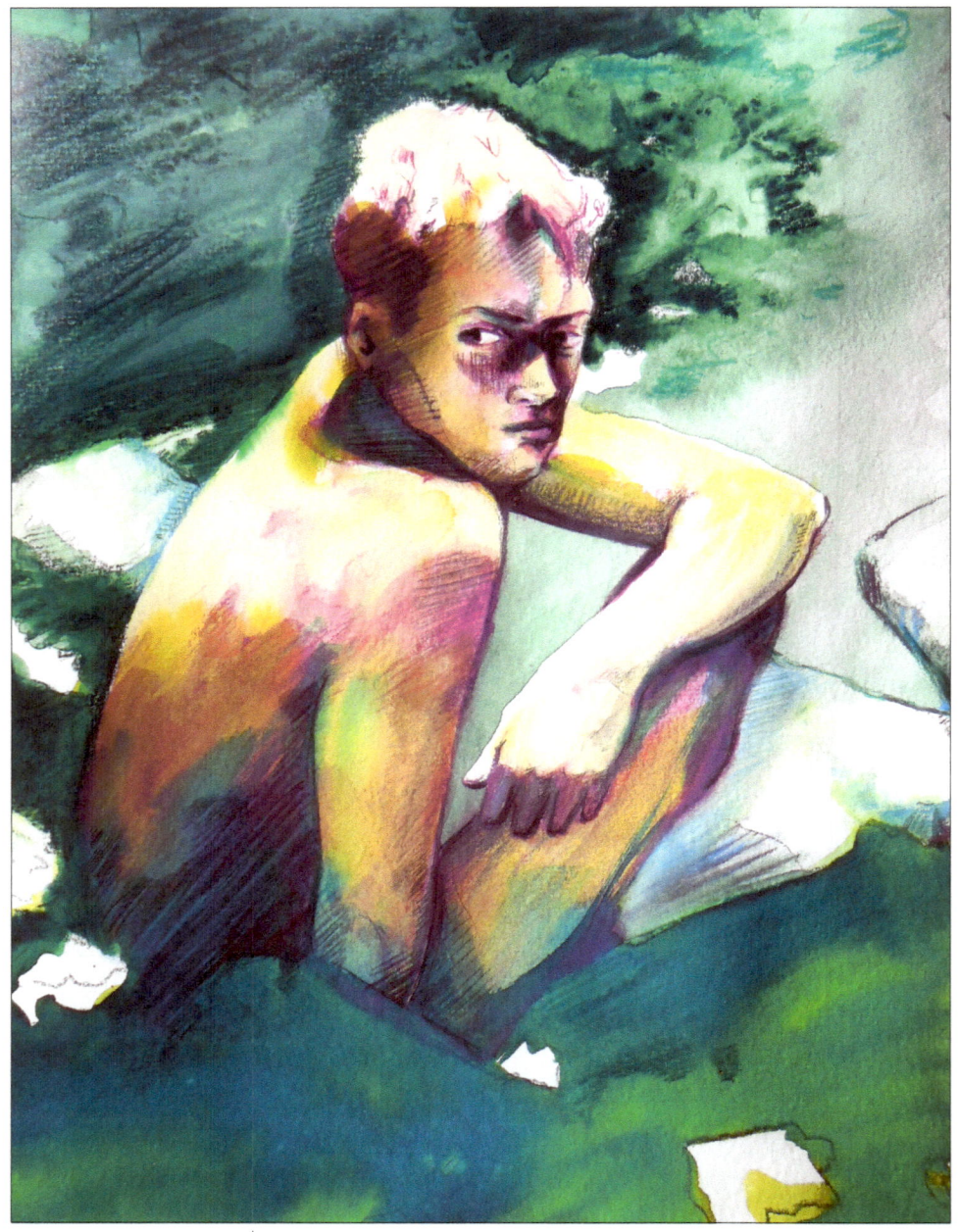

"California Sun" watercolor, 9"x12", 2012

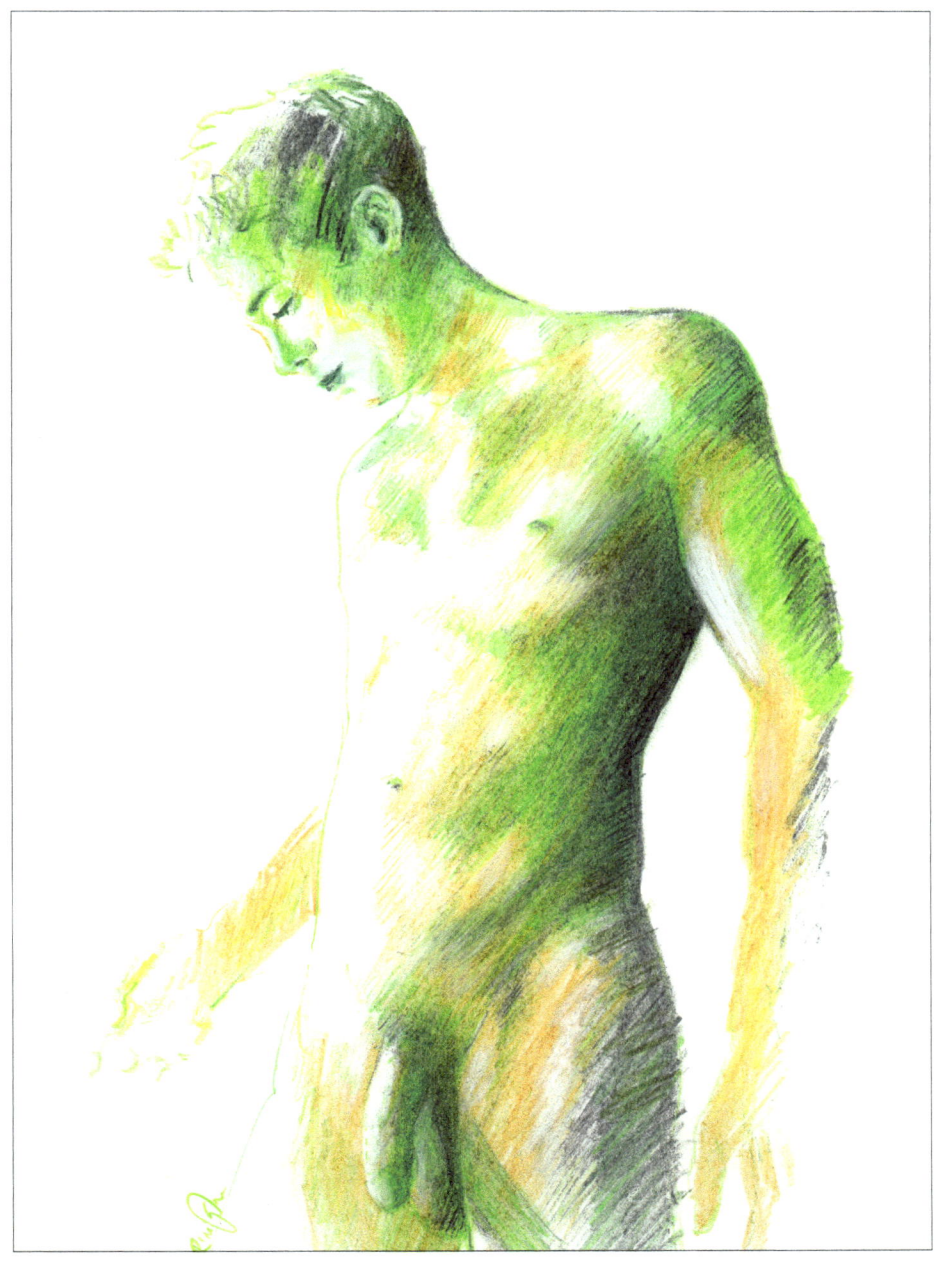

"Bathed In Green Light" watercolor & pencil, 9"x12", 2013

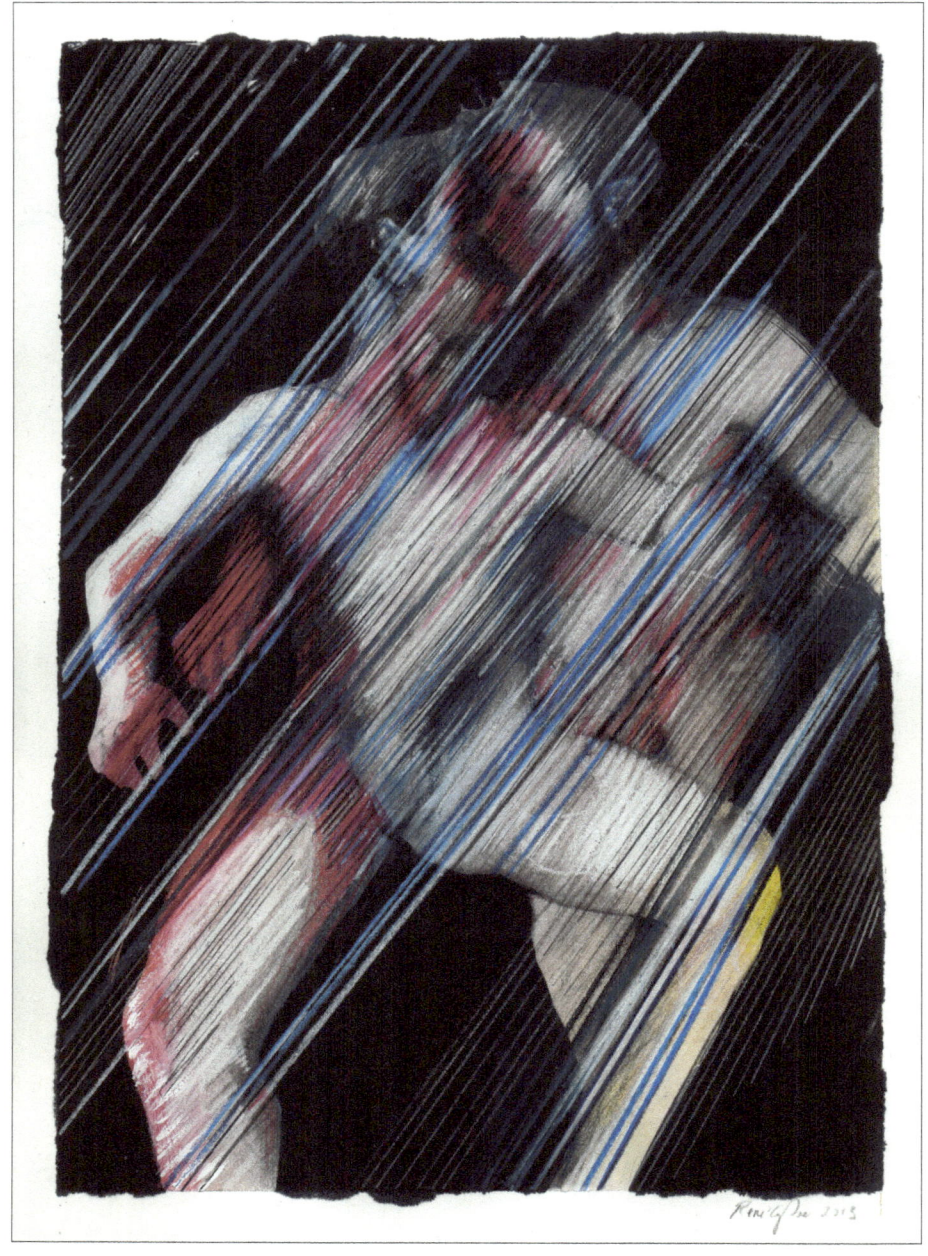

"Love Seen Through Streaked Glass" watercolor & pencil, 9"x12", 2013

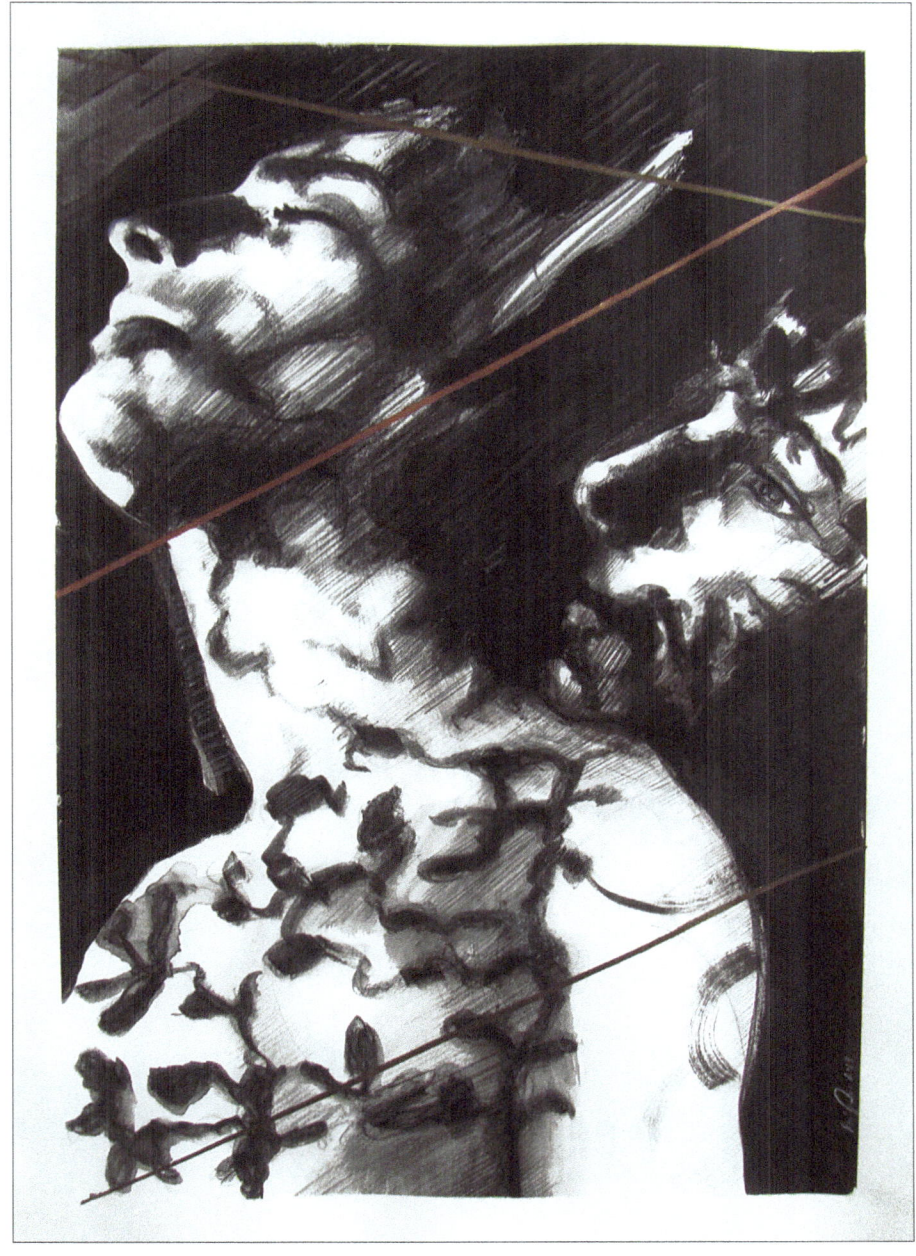

"Dangerous Beautiful Things" acrylic & pencil, 14"x20", 2013

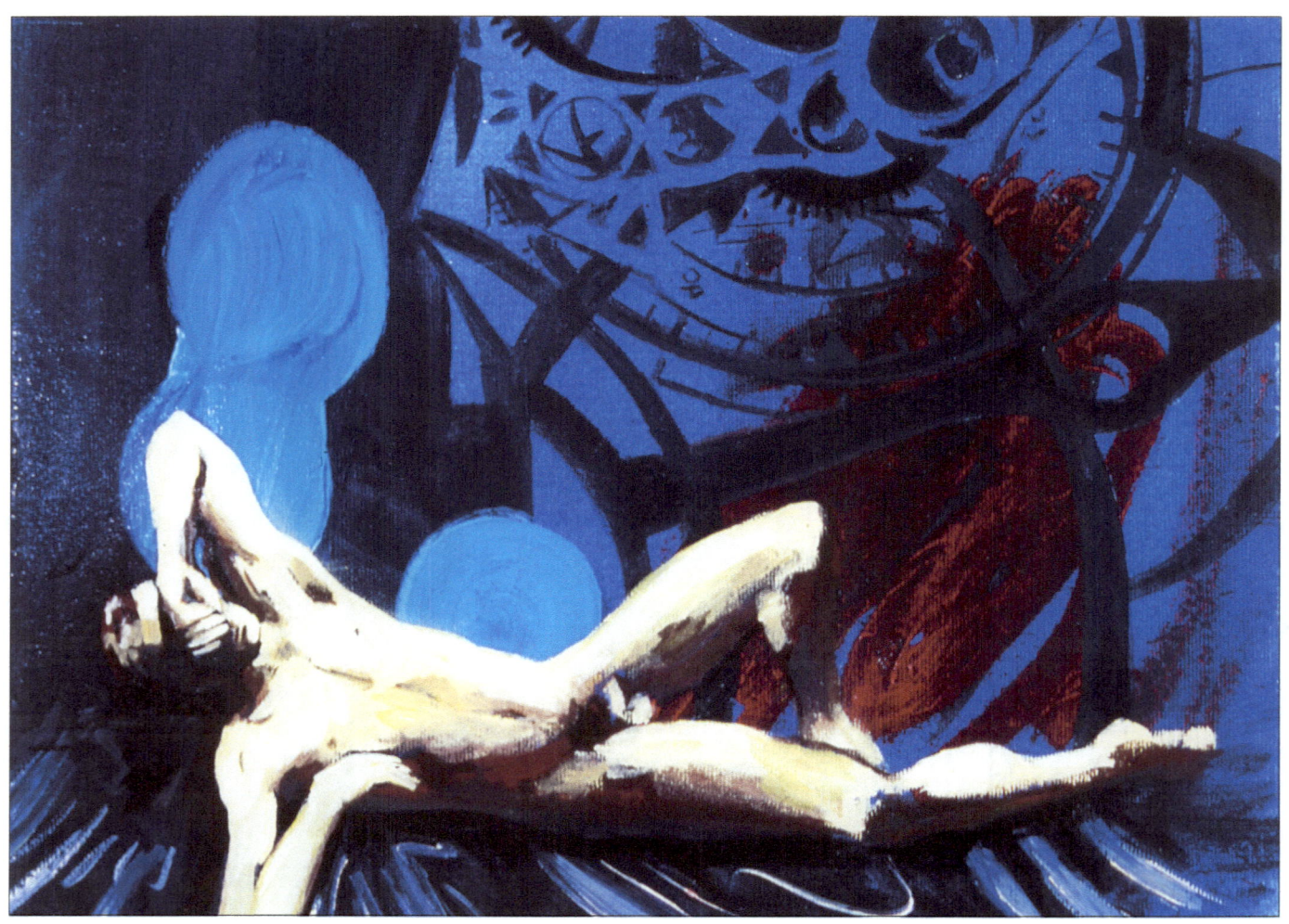

"Measure of Blindness" acrylic, 10"x8", 2004

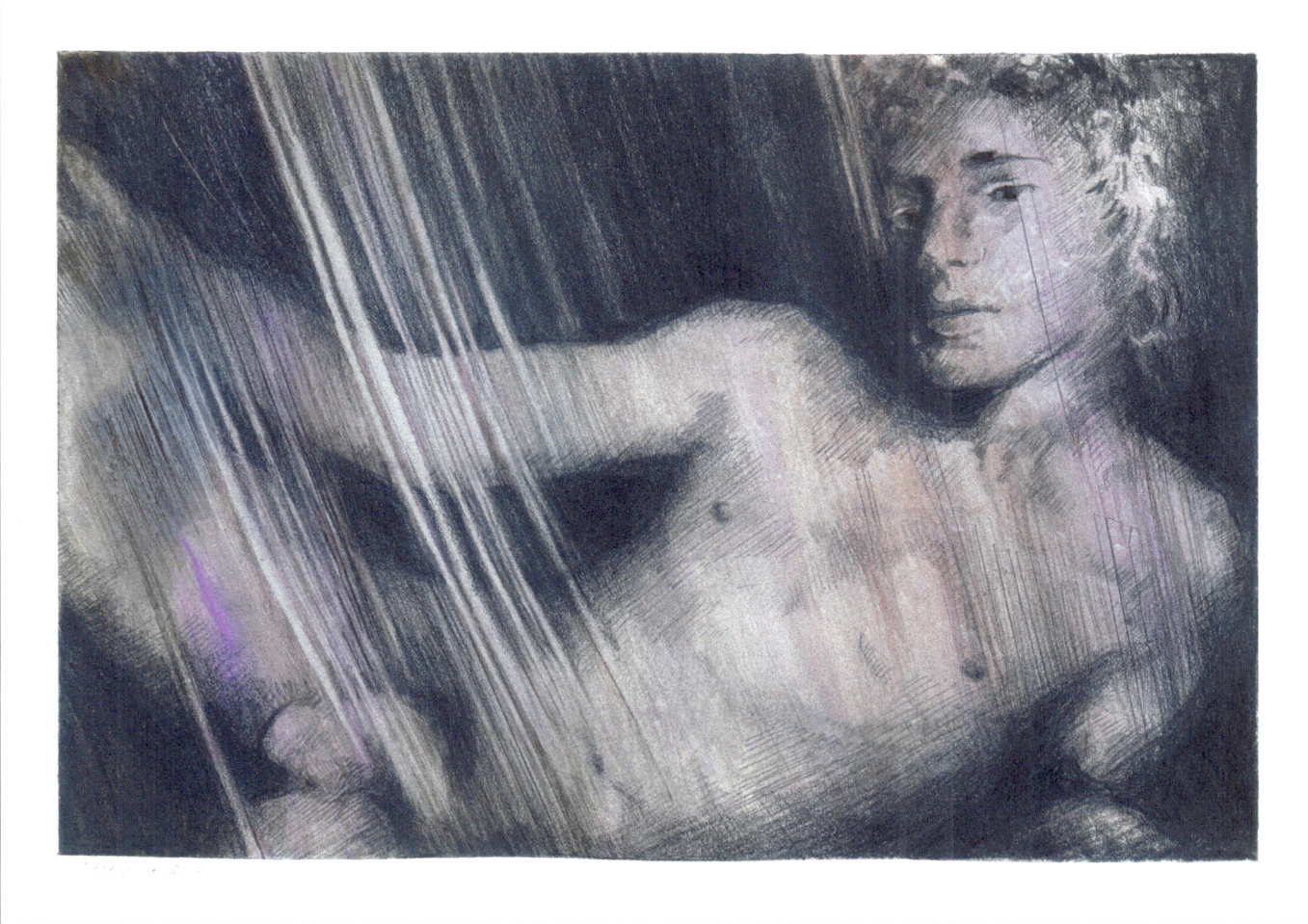

"California Boy" watercolor & color pencil, 12"x9", 2013

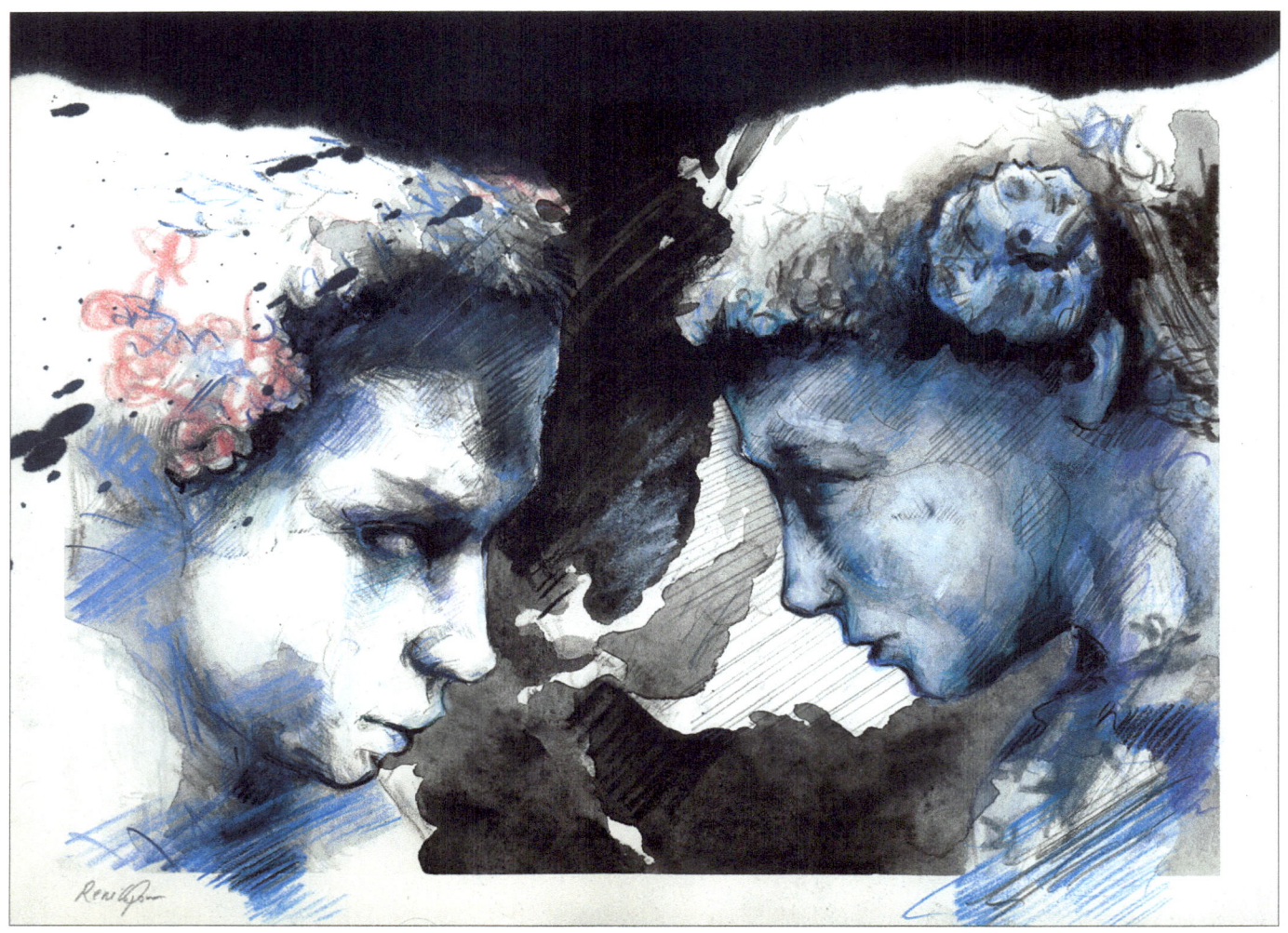

"Law of Attraction" watercolor & color pencil, 12"x9", 2013

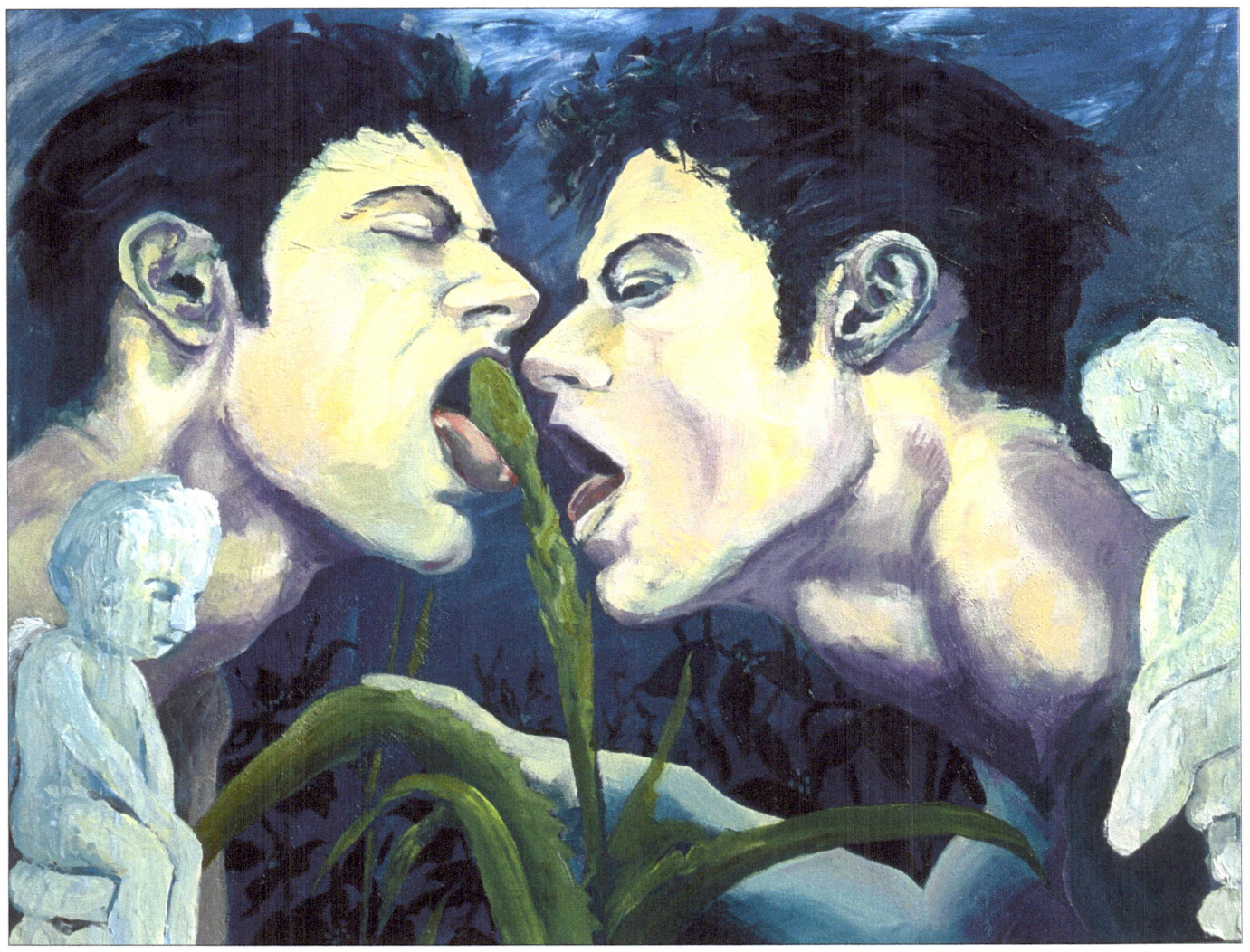

"Whisper Me a New Harvest" watercolor and color pencil, 30"x28", 2002

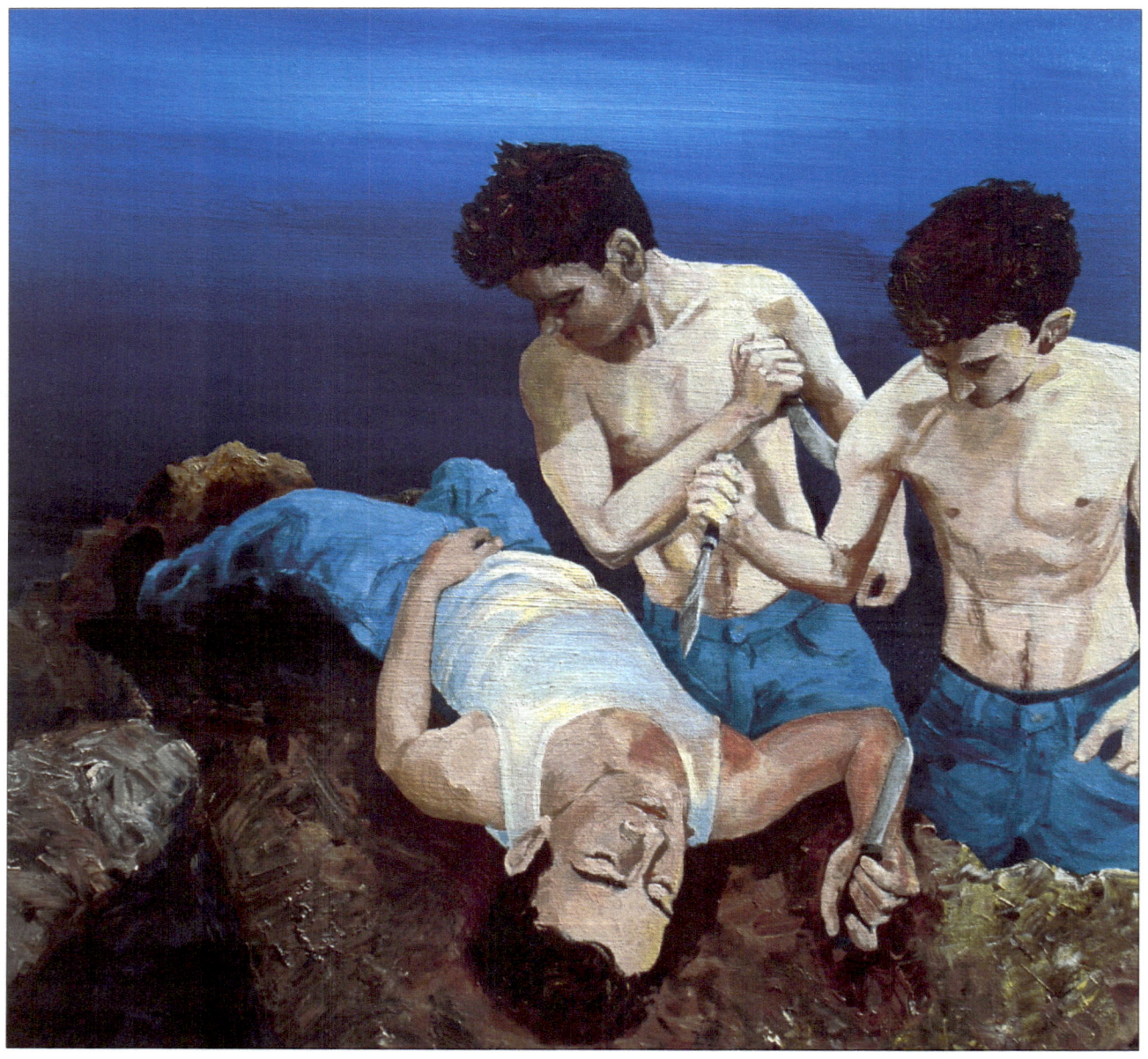

"Who Is It, When Did It Happen & Where?" acrylic, 24"x24", 2005

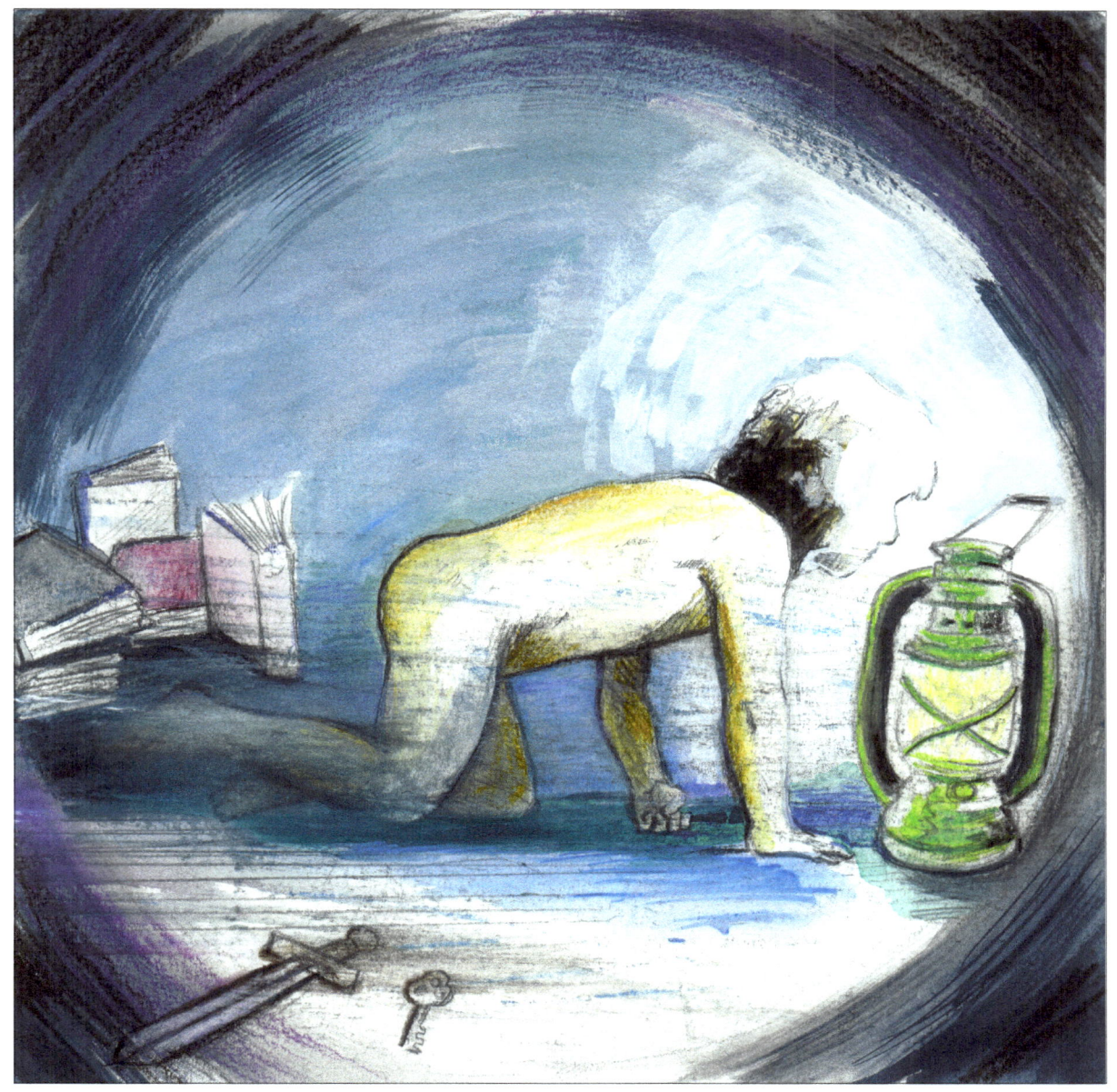

"Escape with Knowledge" watercolor & color pencil, 12"x12", 2012

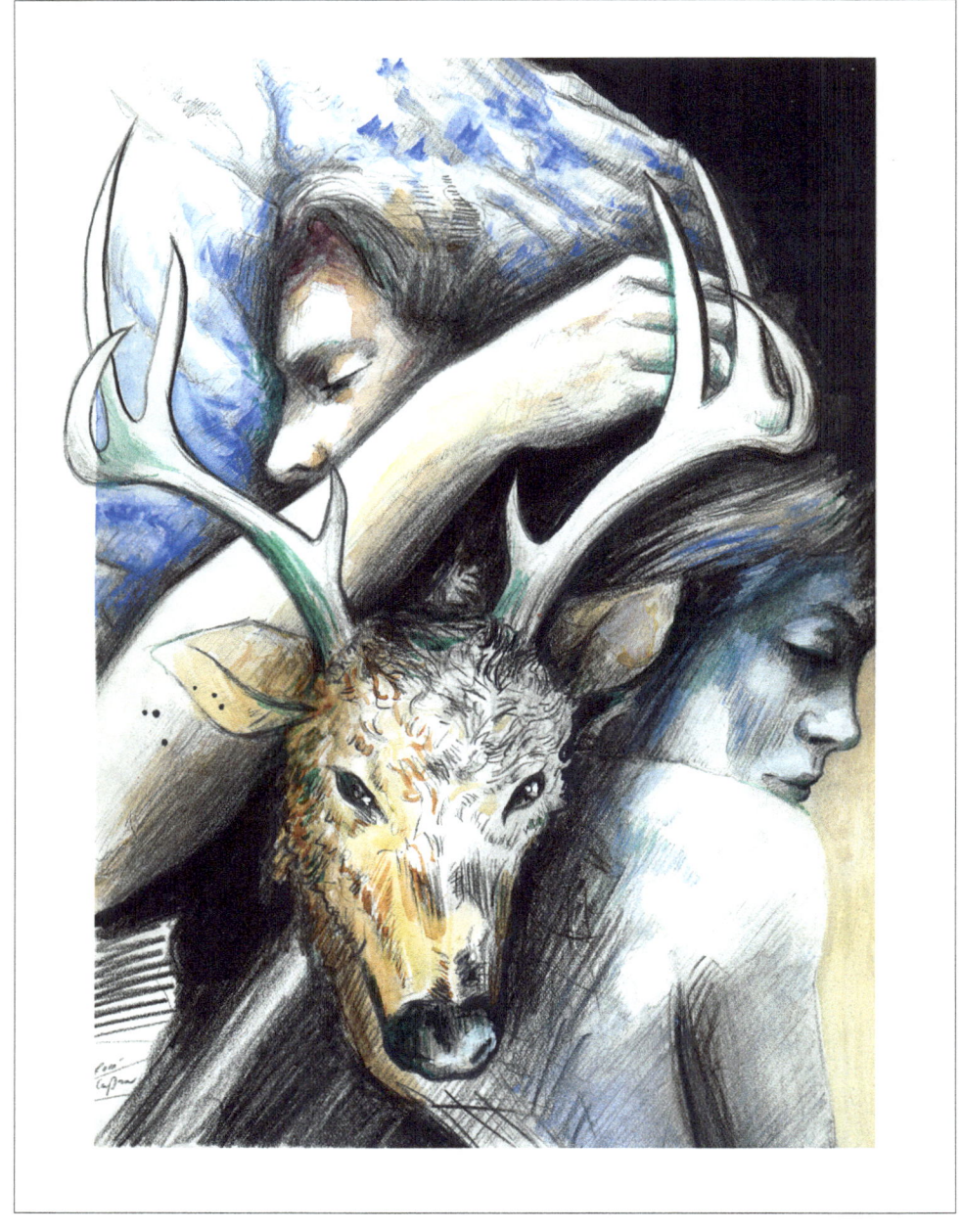

"Spring's Eternal Love Affair with the Ice Princess" watercolor, 9"x12", 2013

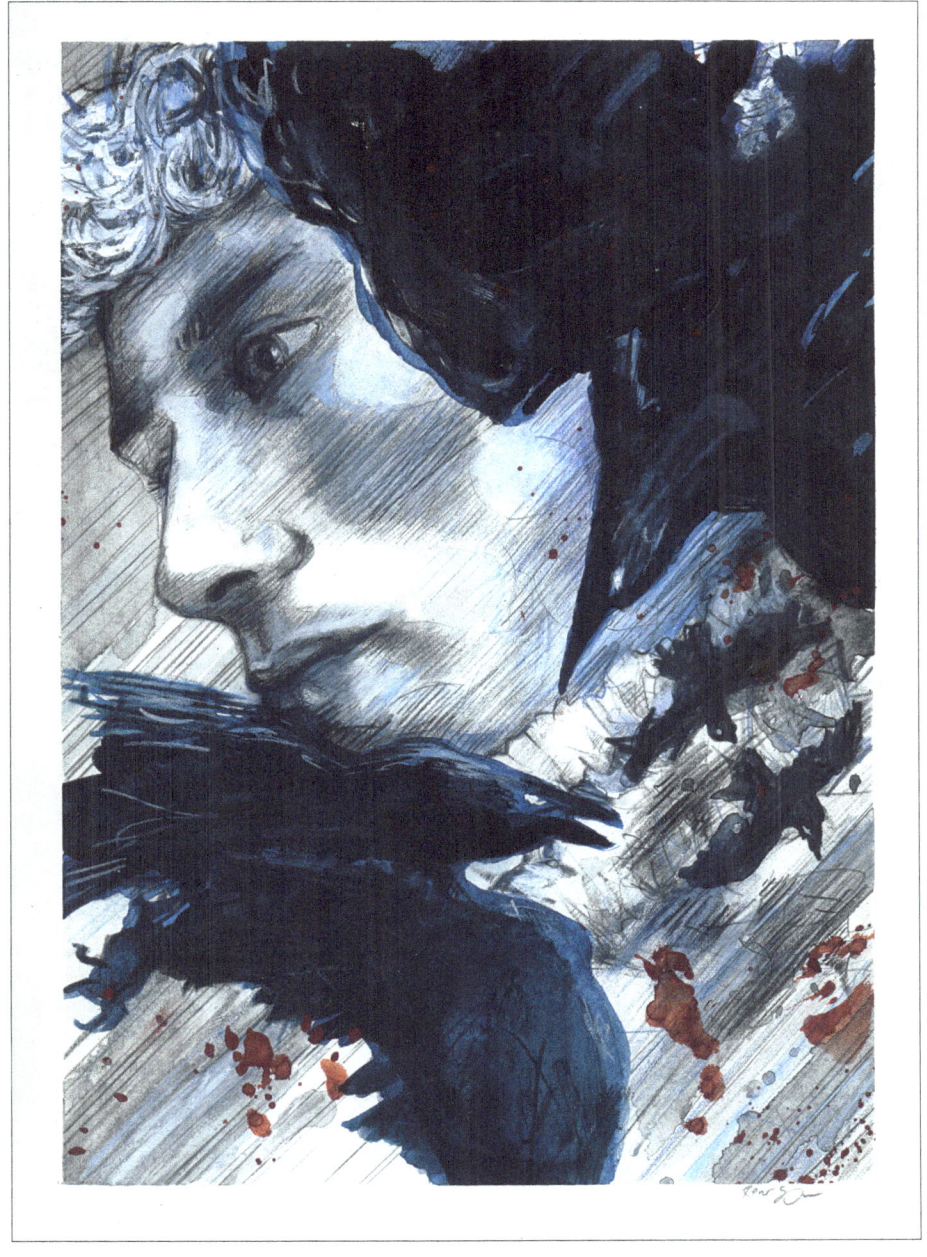

"Two Crows" watercolor & color pencil, 9"x12", 2013

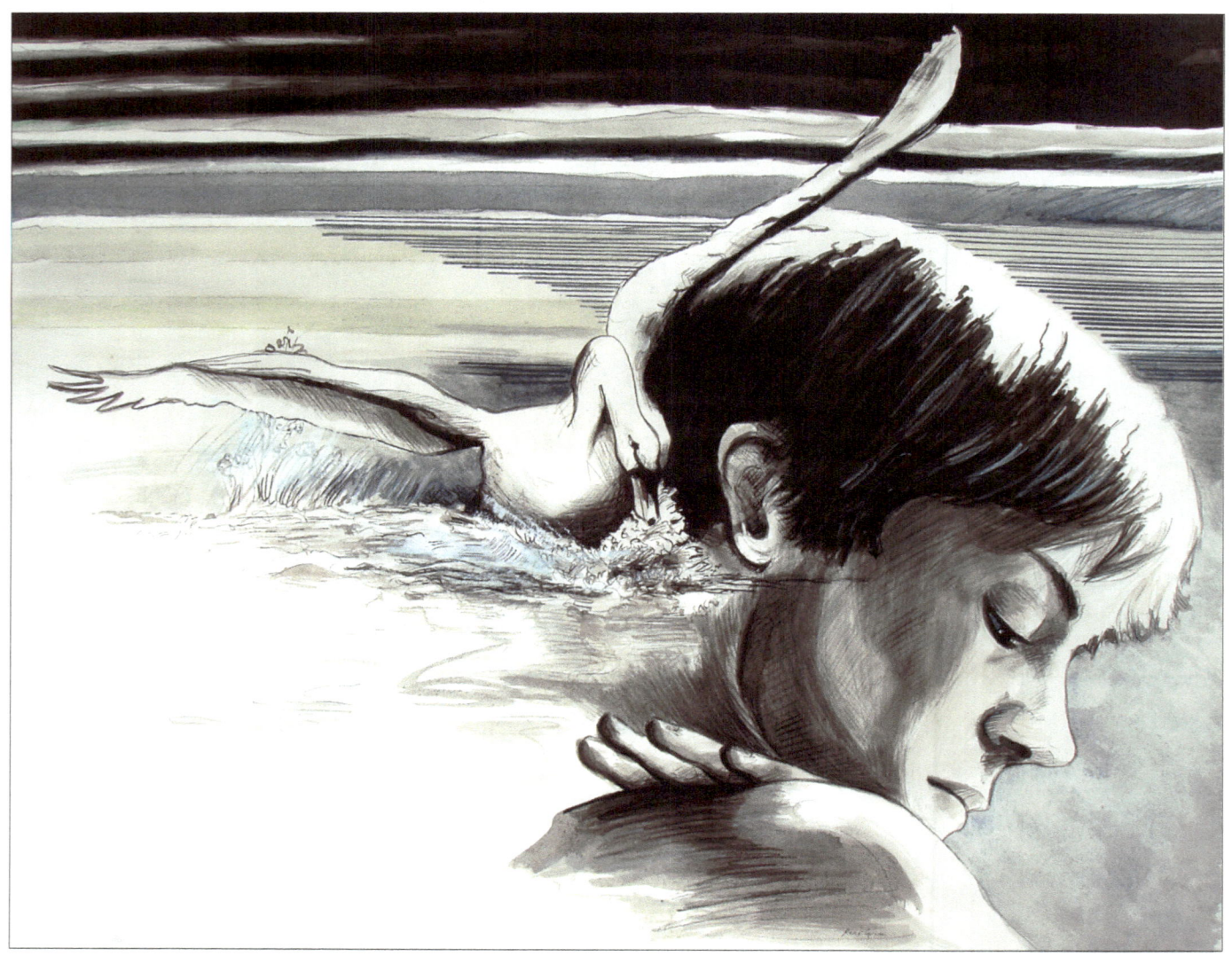

"Stroke" watercolor & pencil, 30"x22", 2012

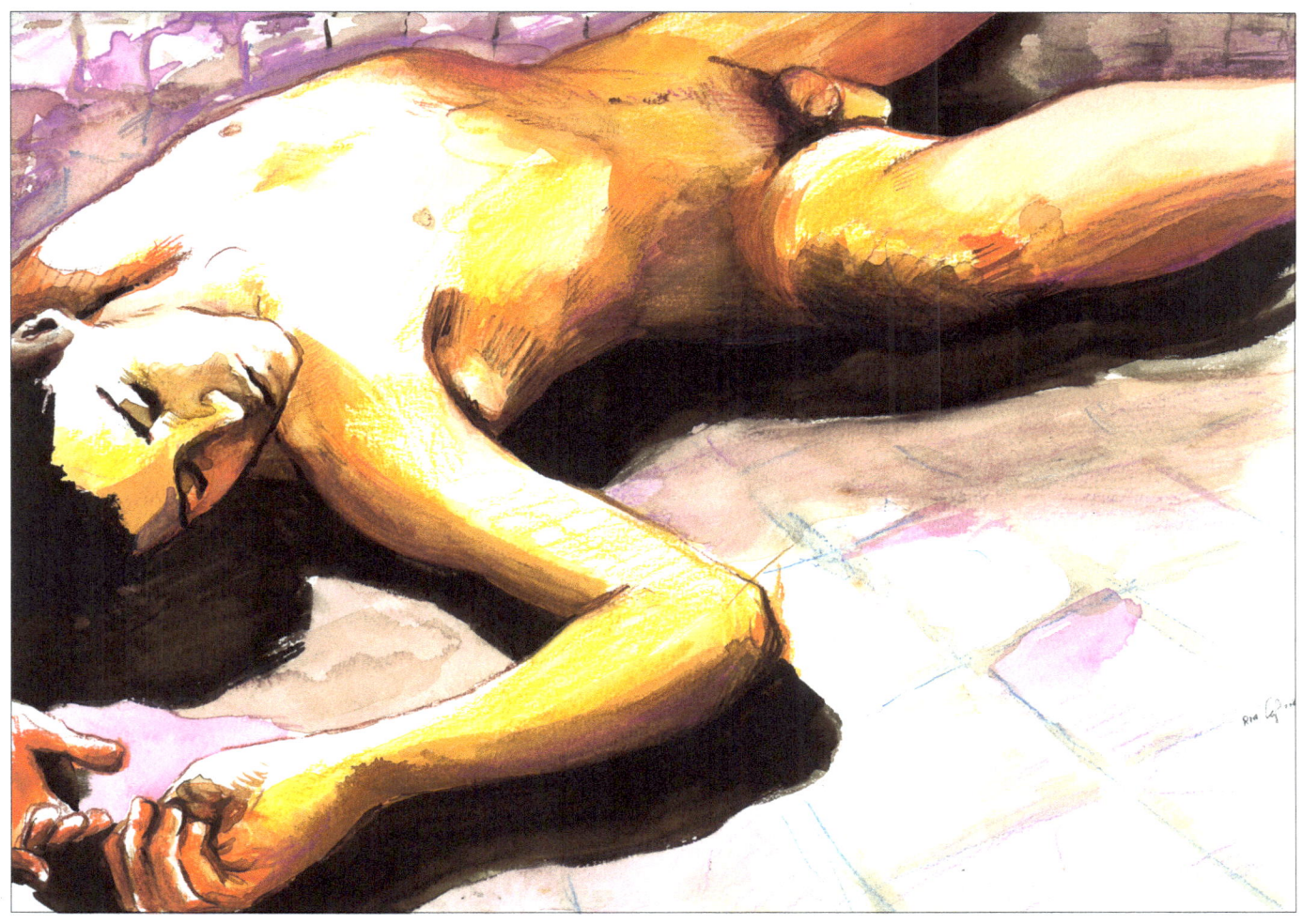

"To Kill a Dead Boy #2" watercolor & color pencil, 12"x9", 2012

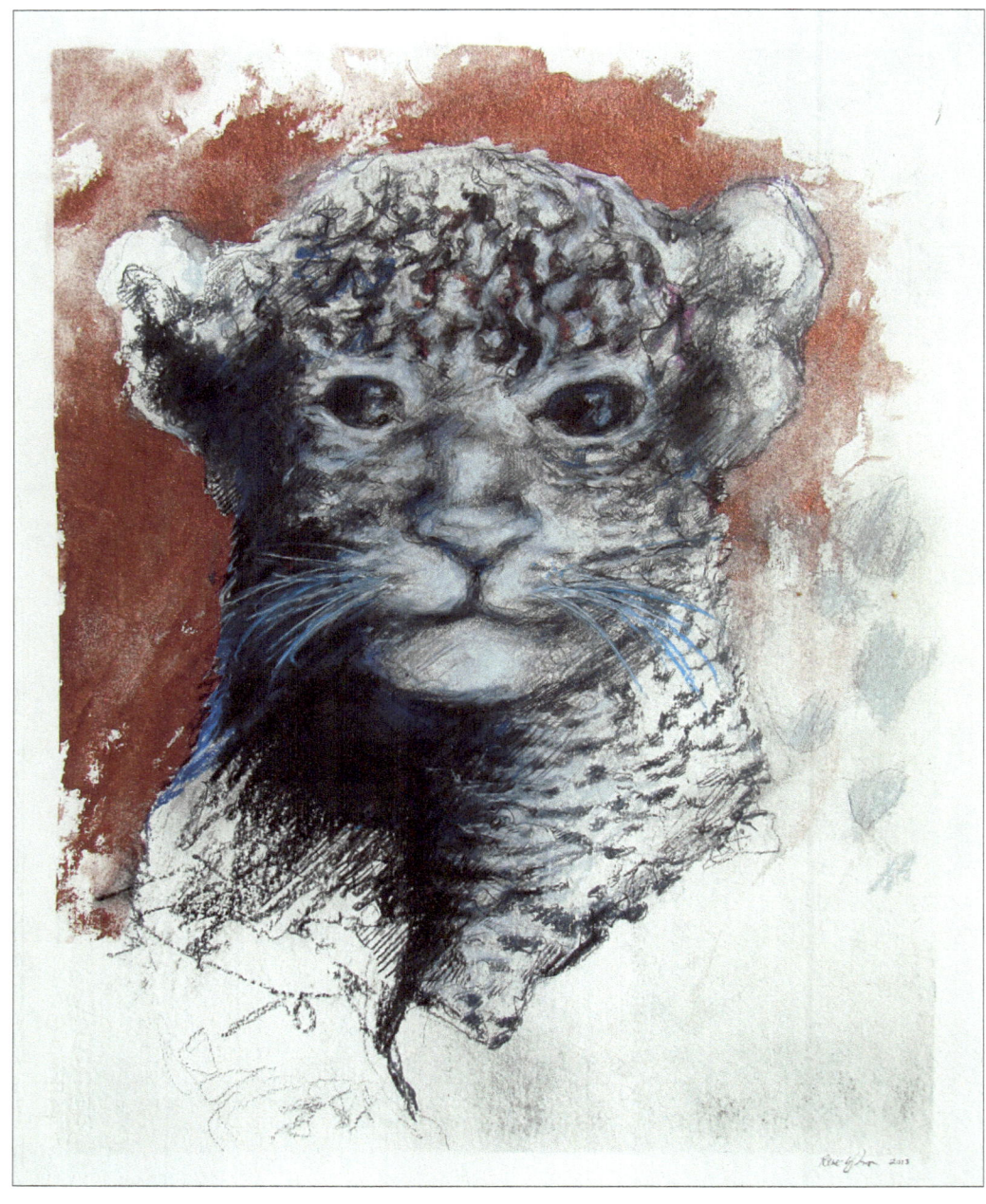

"Kitty" watercolor & color pencil, 16"x20", 2013

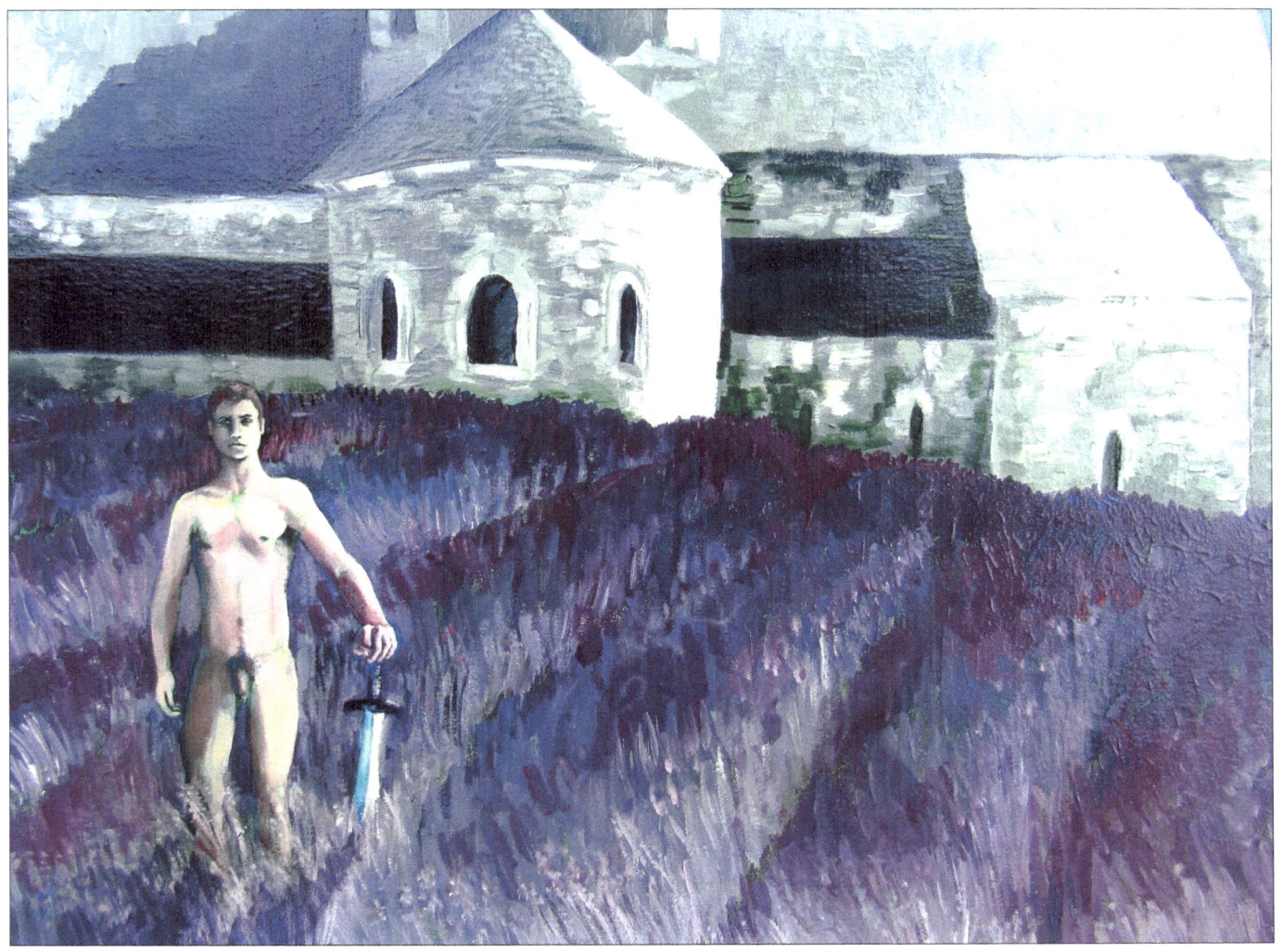

"Lavender" acrylic, 20"x16", 2005

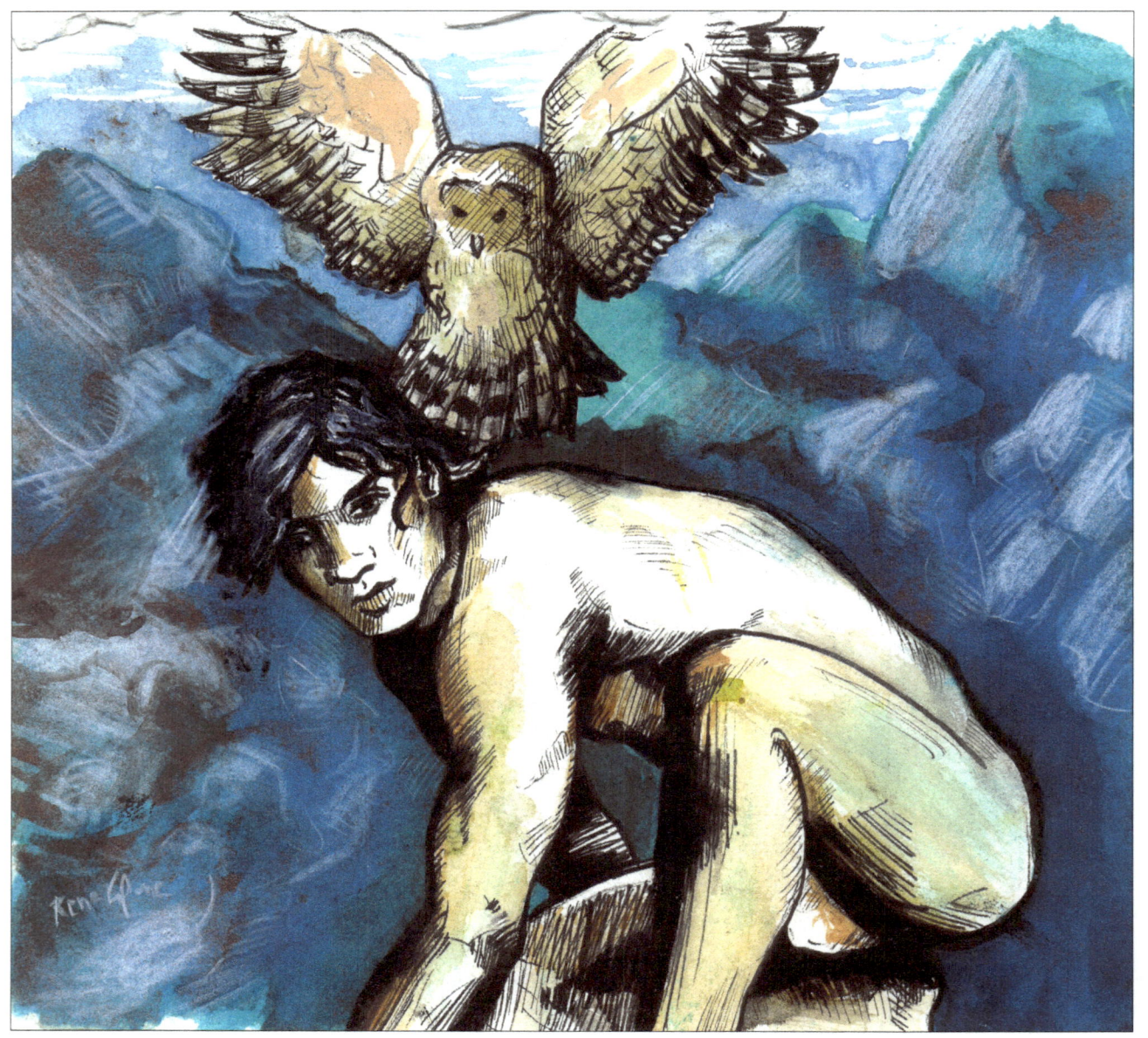

"Nightly Visitors" watercolor & color pencil, 8"x8", 2012

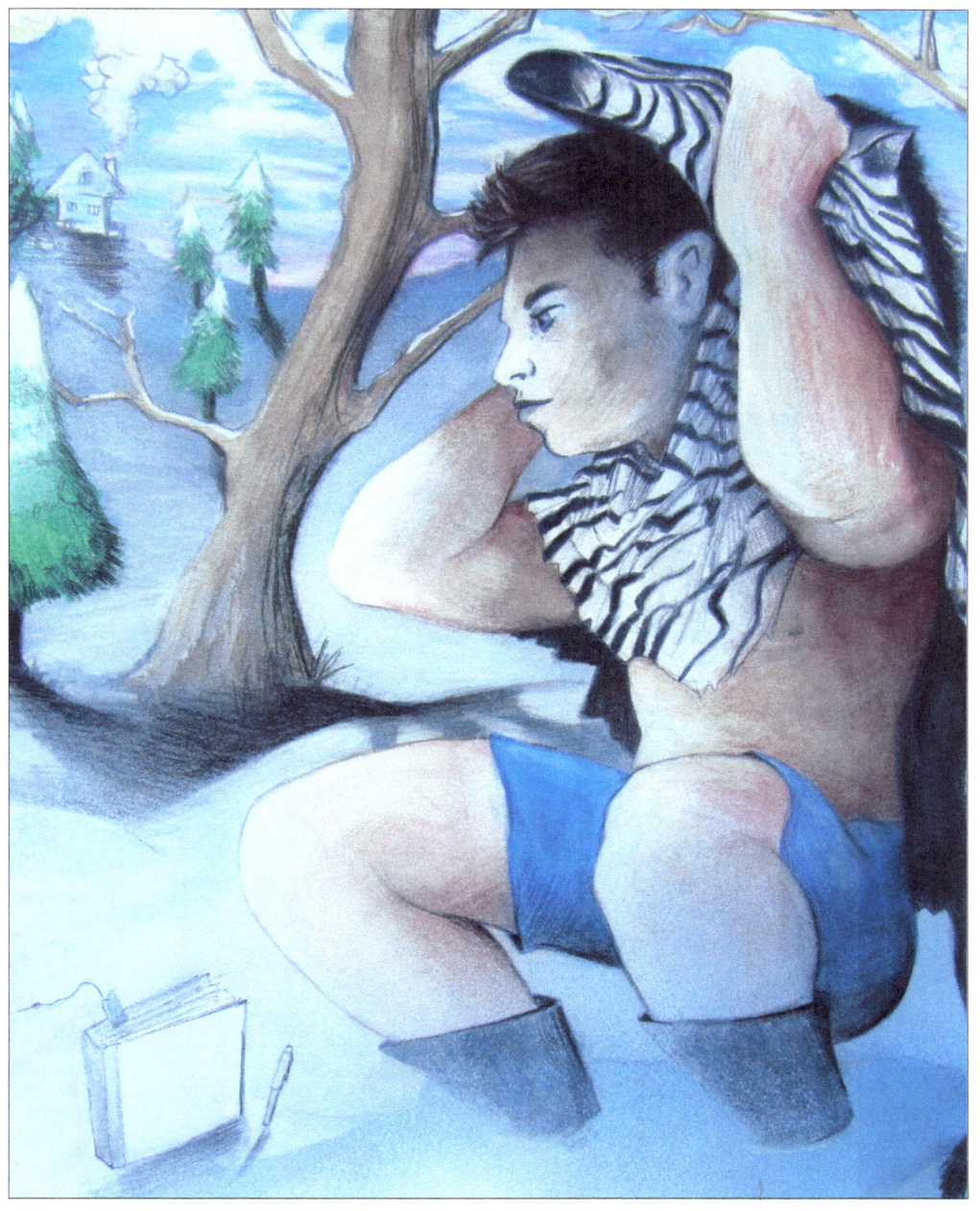

"Zebra Boy" watercolor & color pencil, 16"x19", 2011

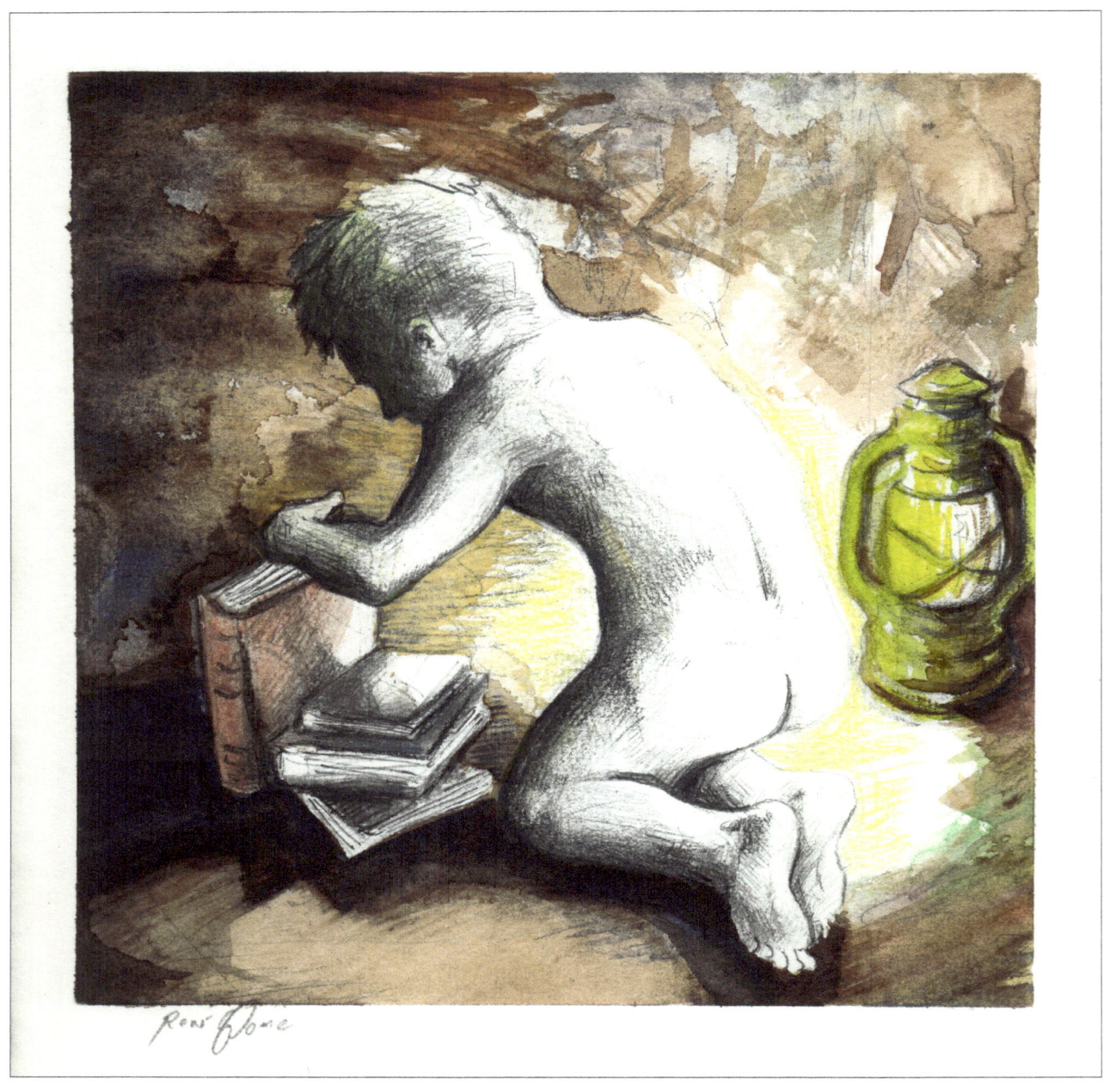

"Light My Way #1" watercolor & pencil, 8"x8", 2012

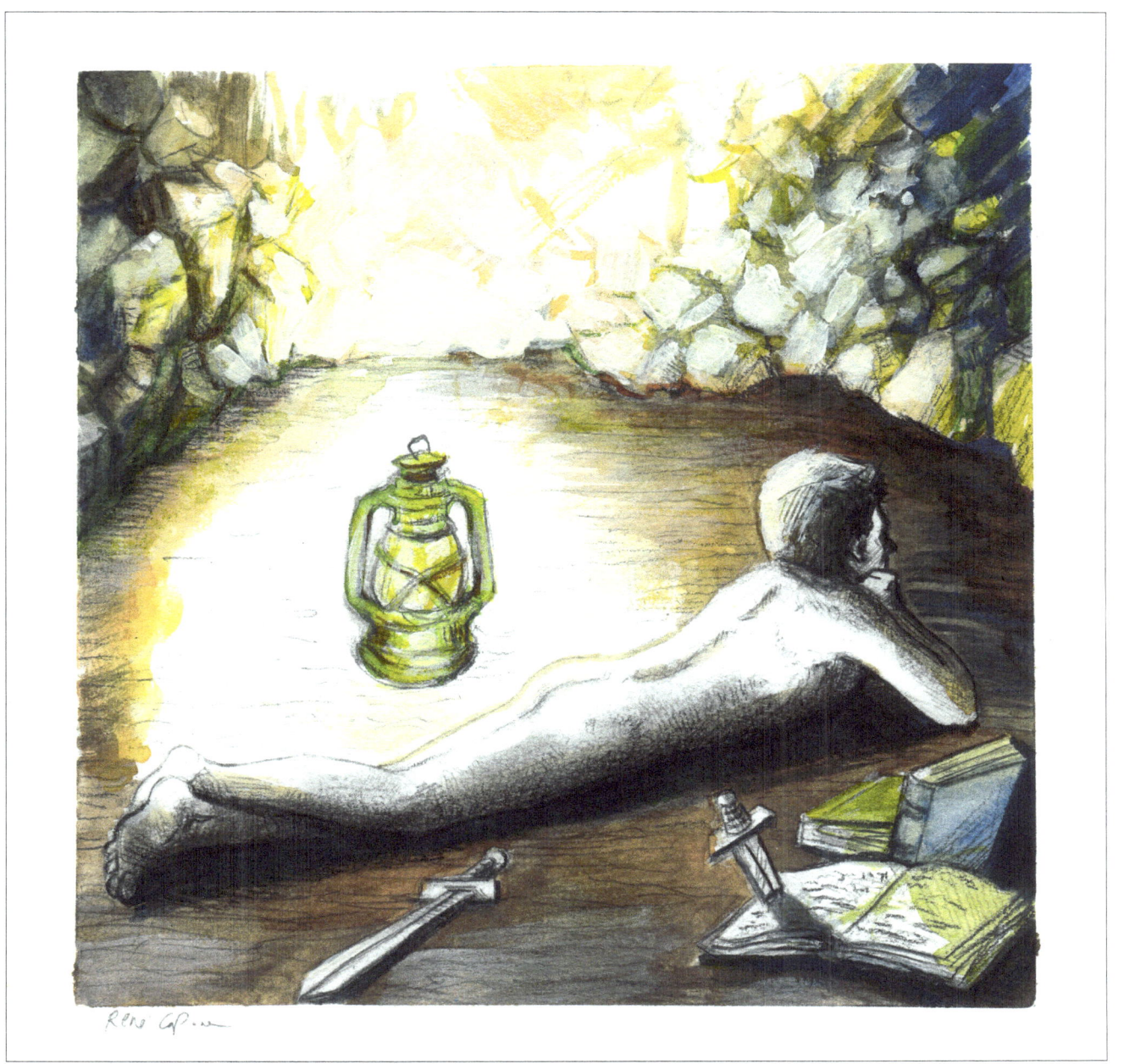

"Light My Way #2" watercolor & pencil, 8"x8", 2012

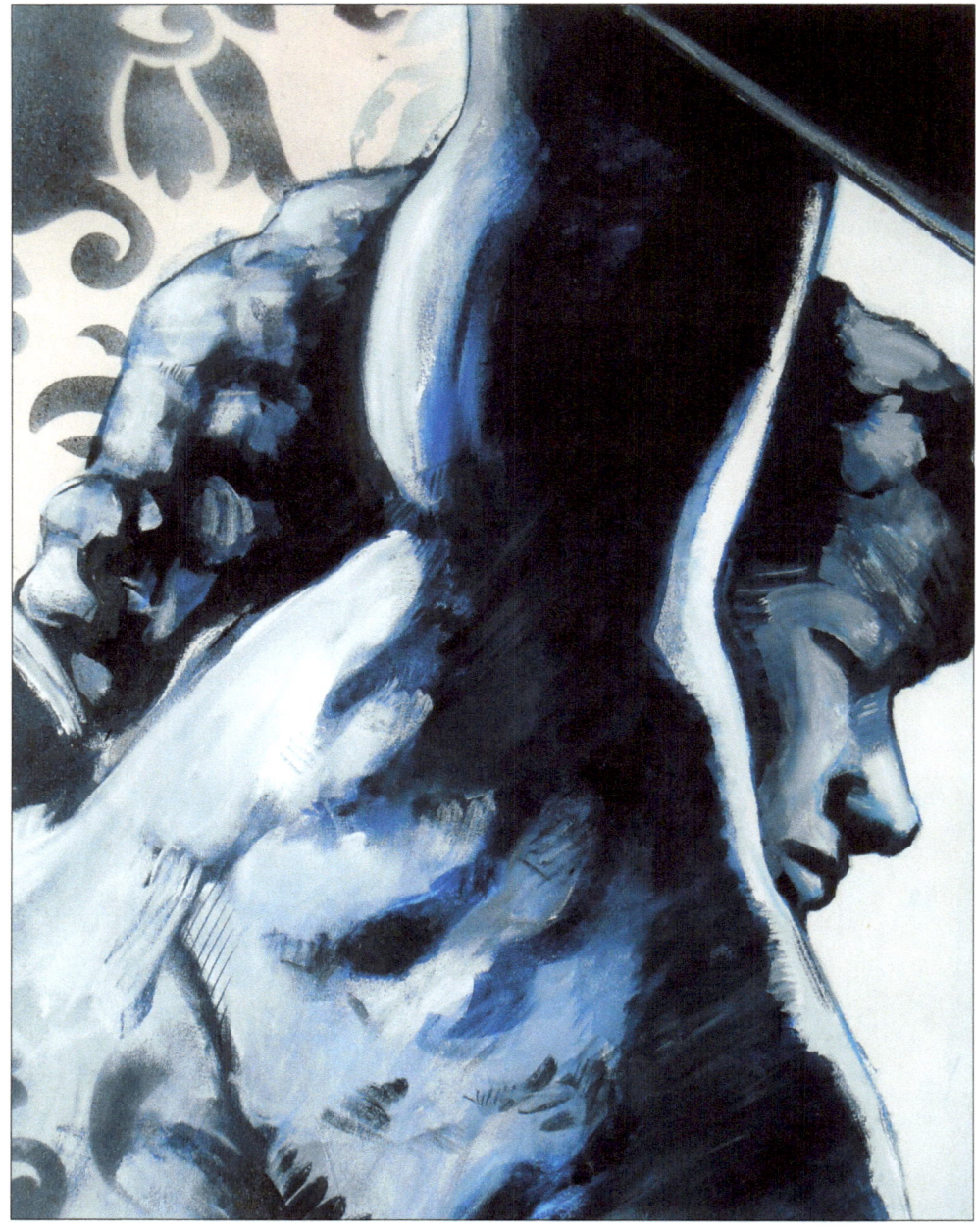

"Moving Iron #1" acrylic, 20"x24", 2012

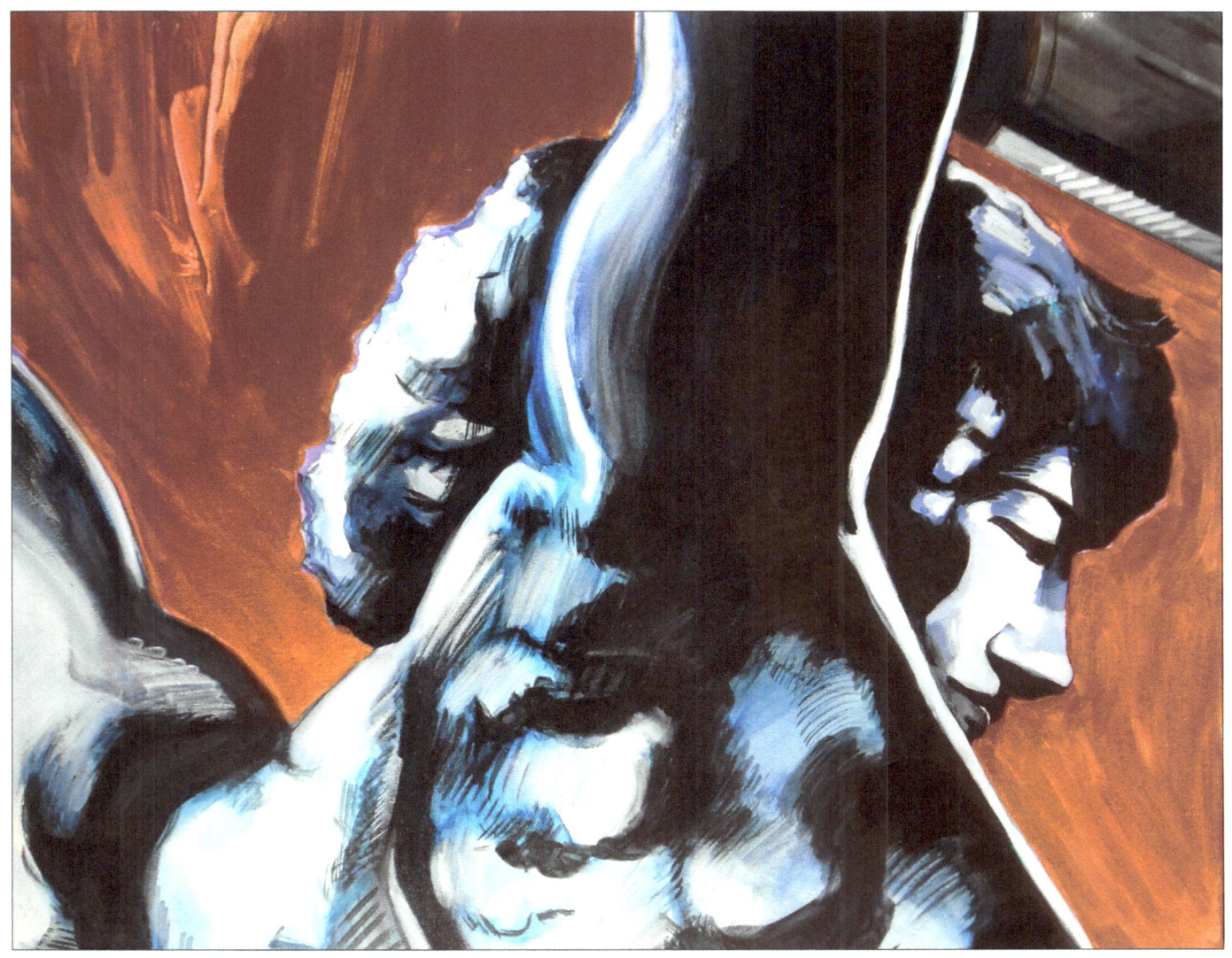

"Moving Iron #2" watercolor & ink, 36"x34", 2013

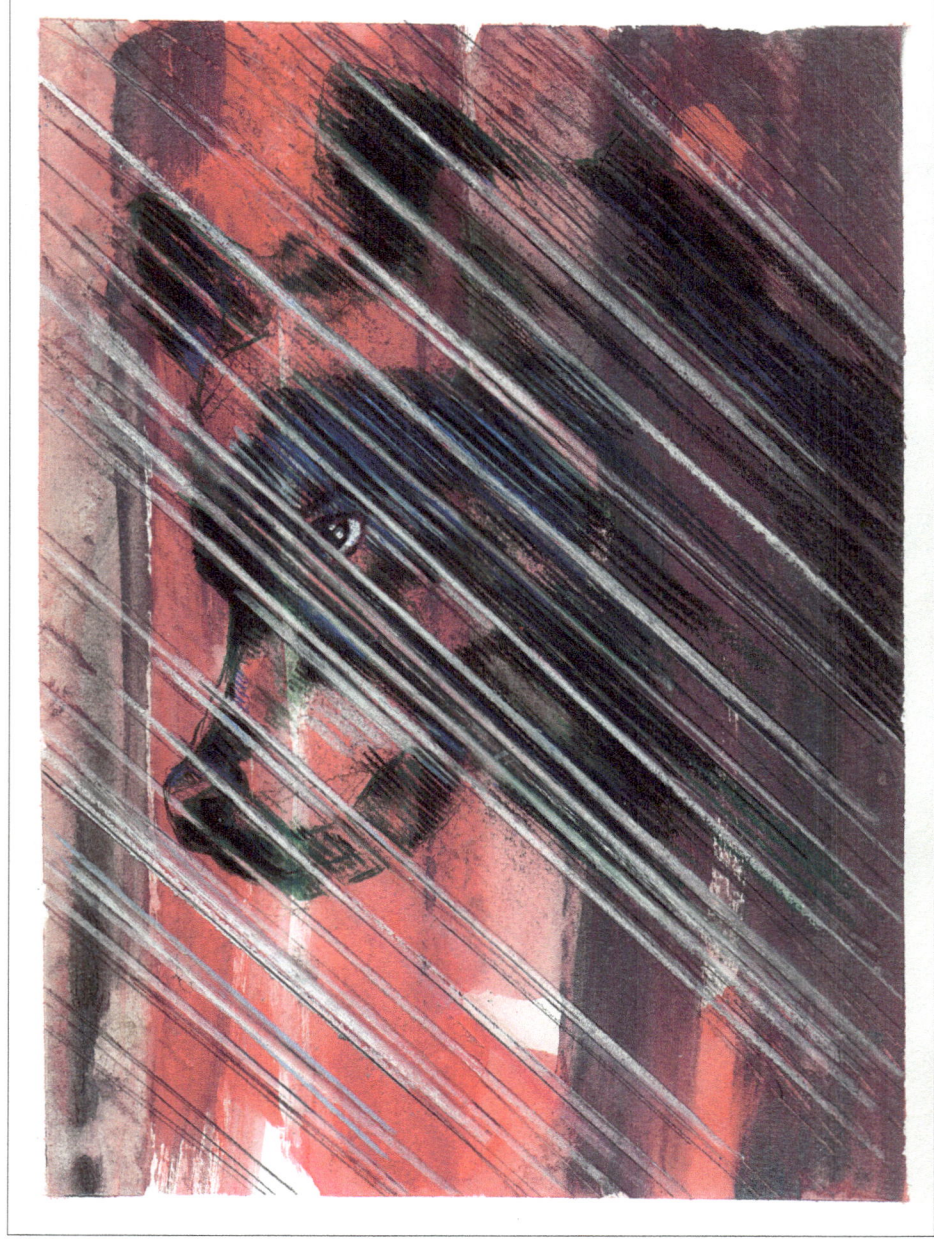

"The Wolf That Guards Your Dreams" watercolor & color pencil, 9"x12", 2013

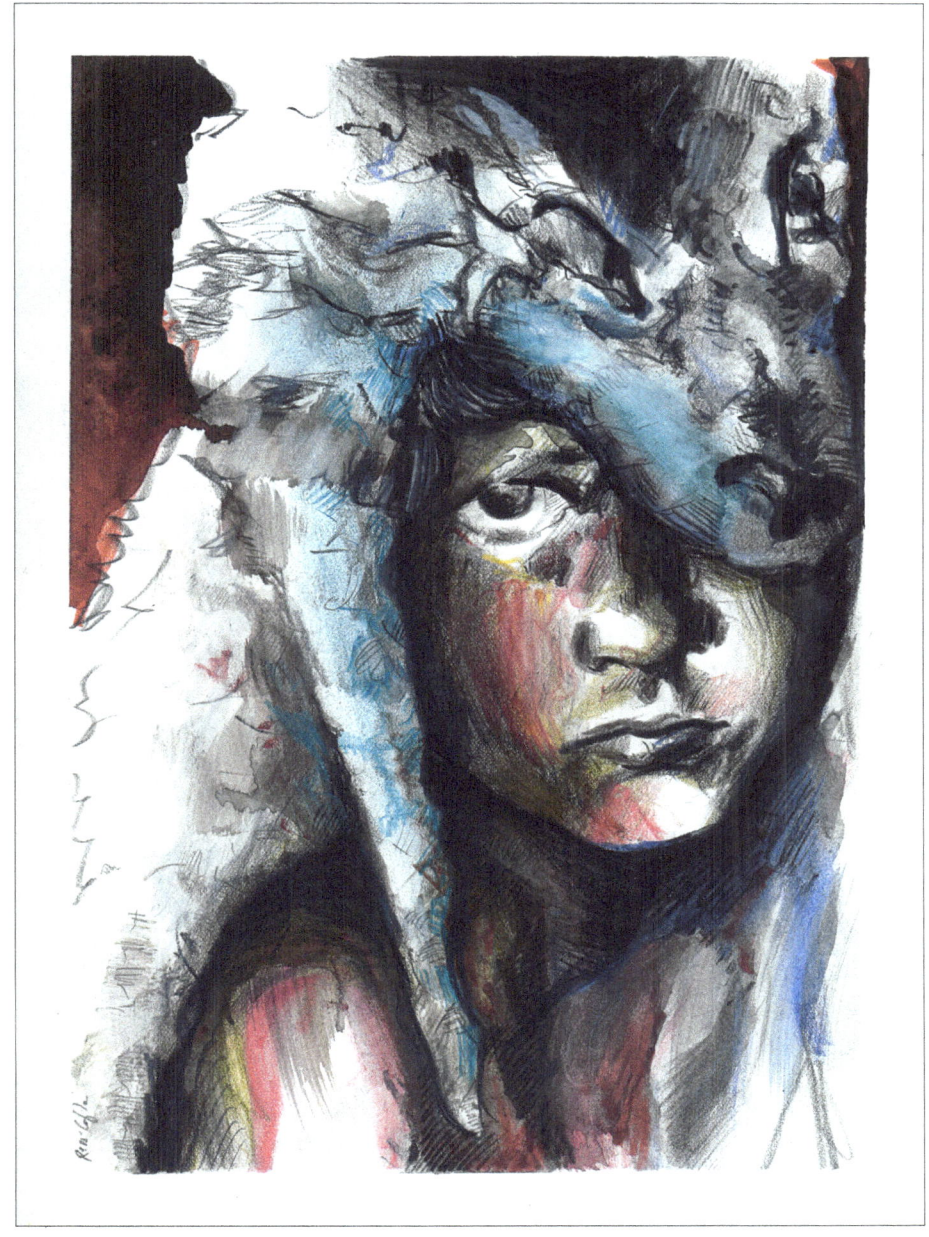

"No Child Left Behind" watercolor & color pencil, 9"x12", 2013

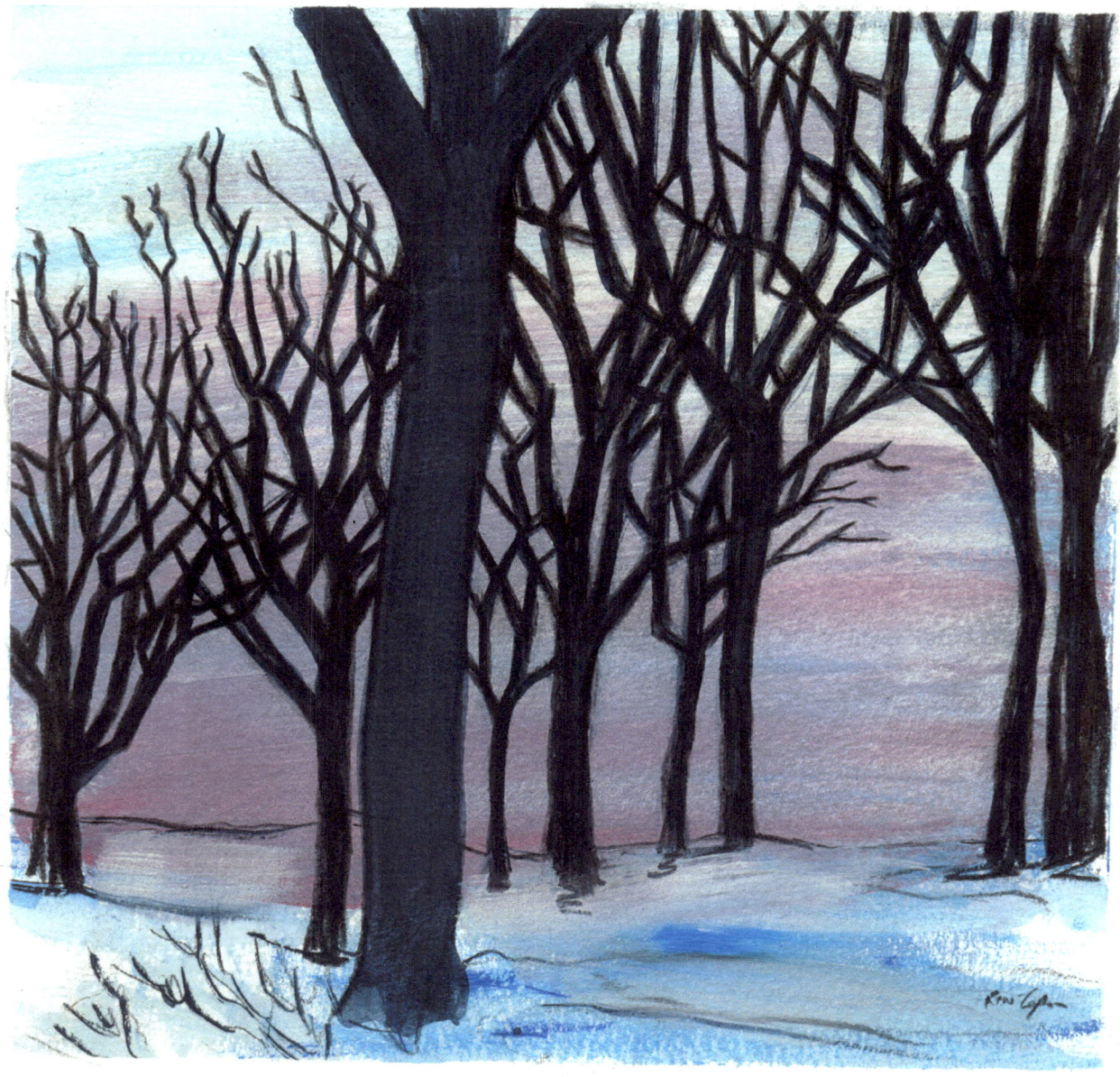

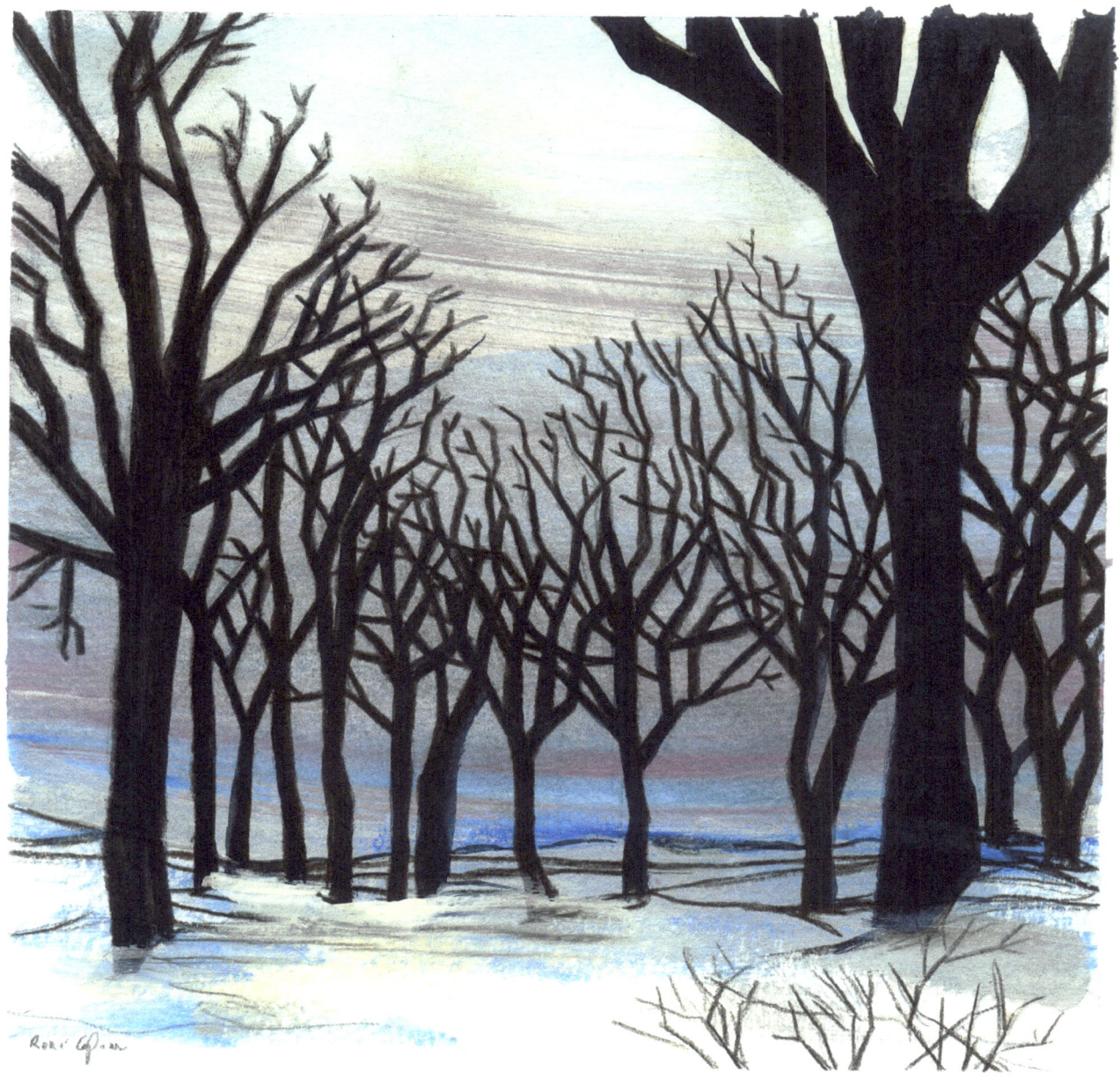

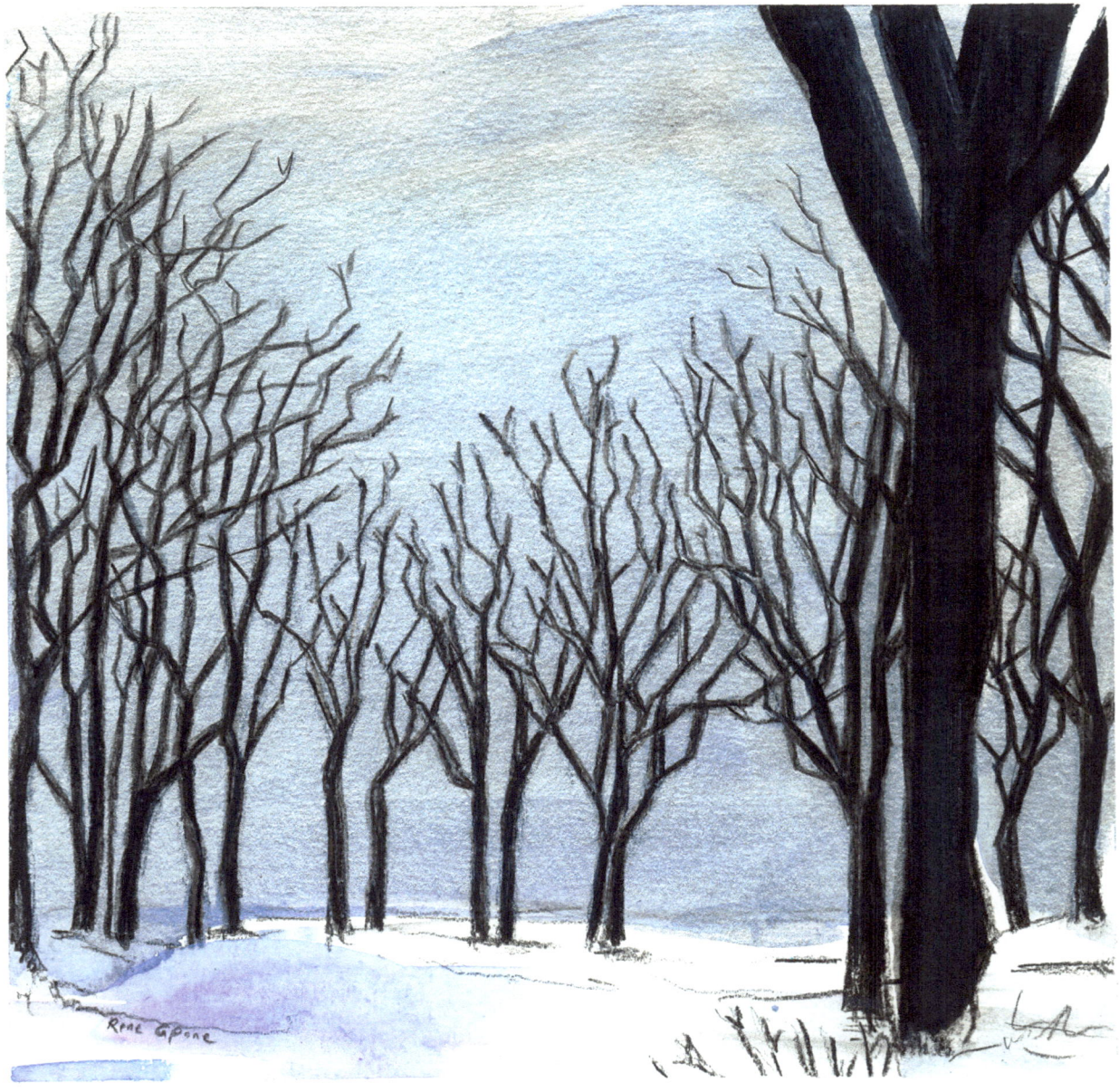

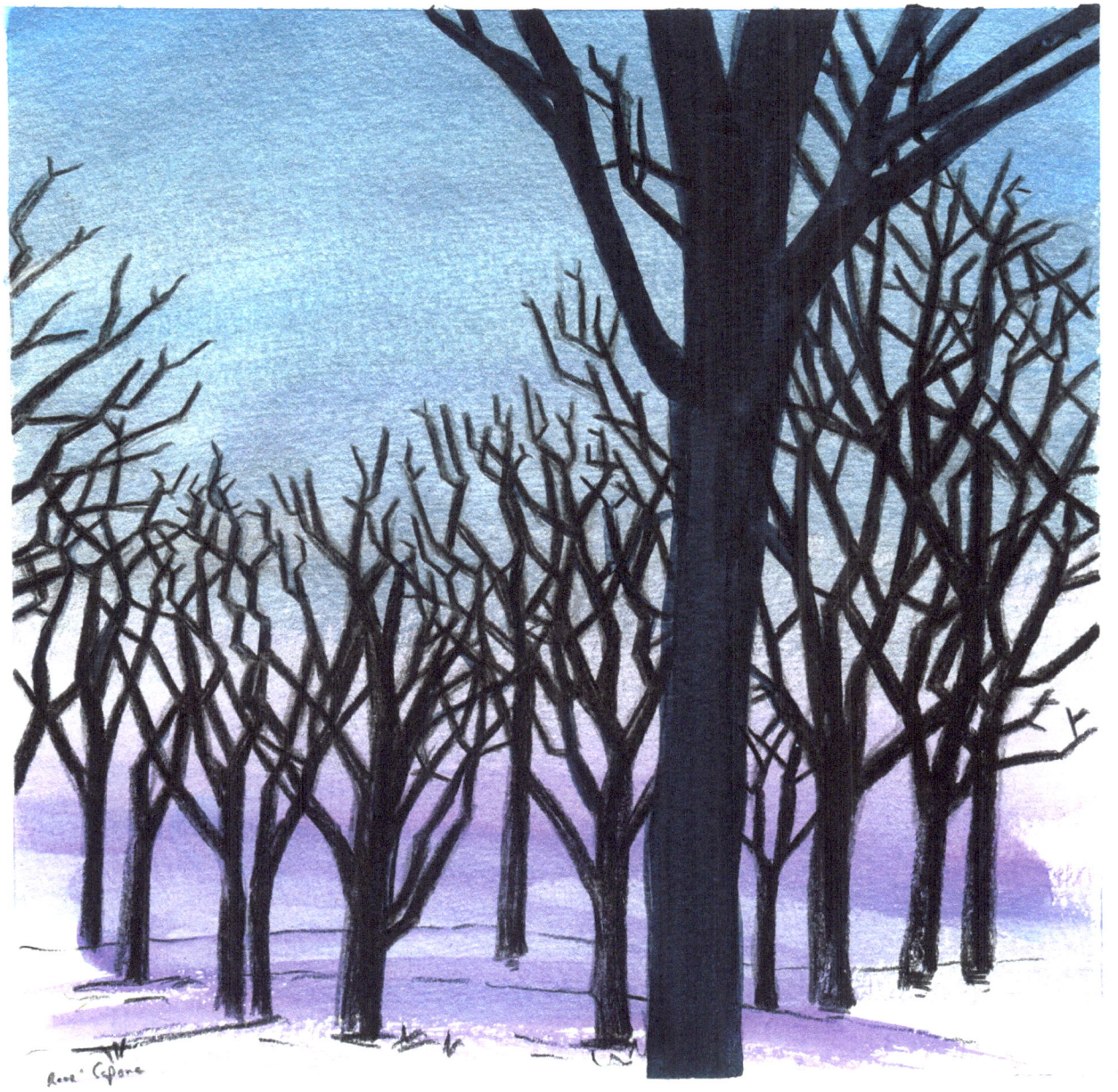

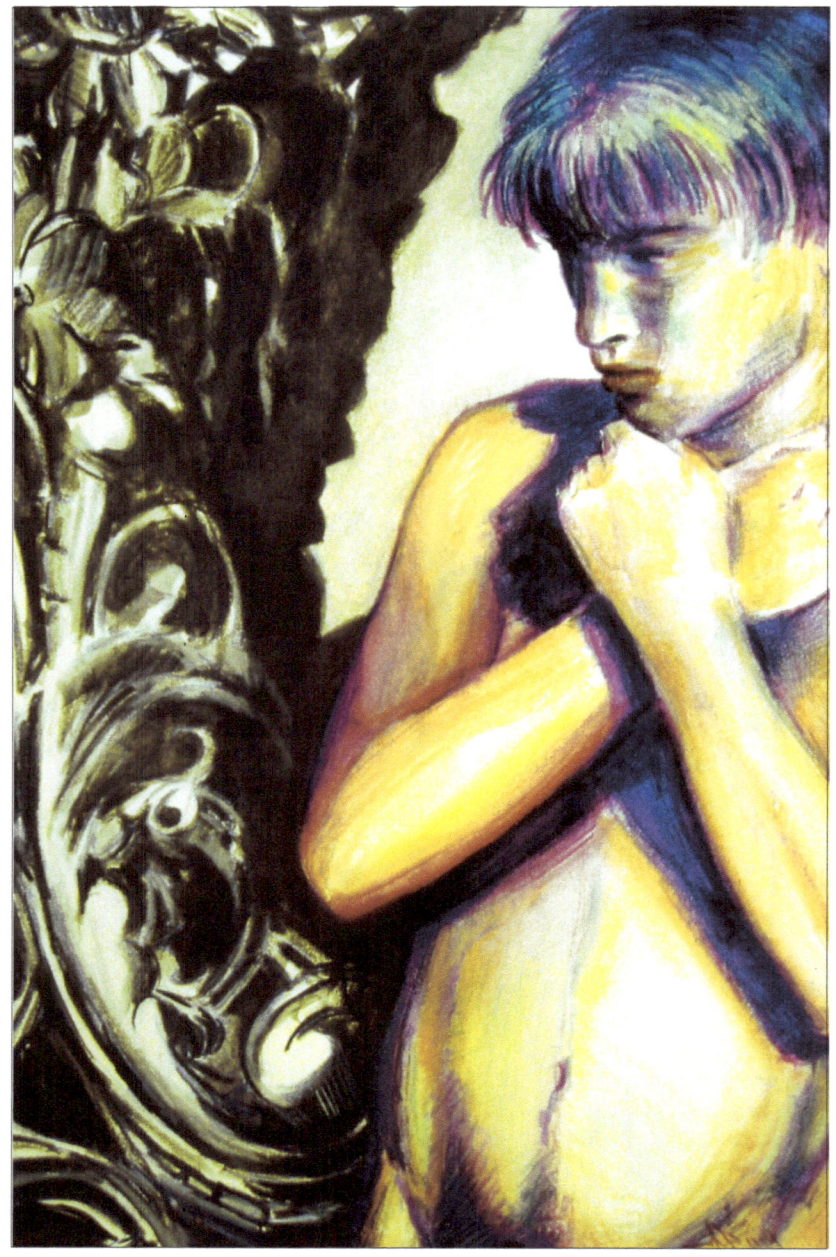

"Tremble #3" watercolor & color pencil, 6"x12", 2011

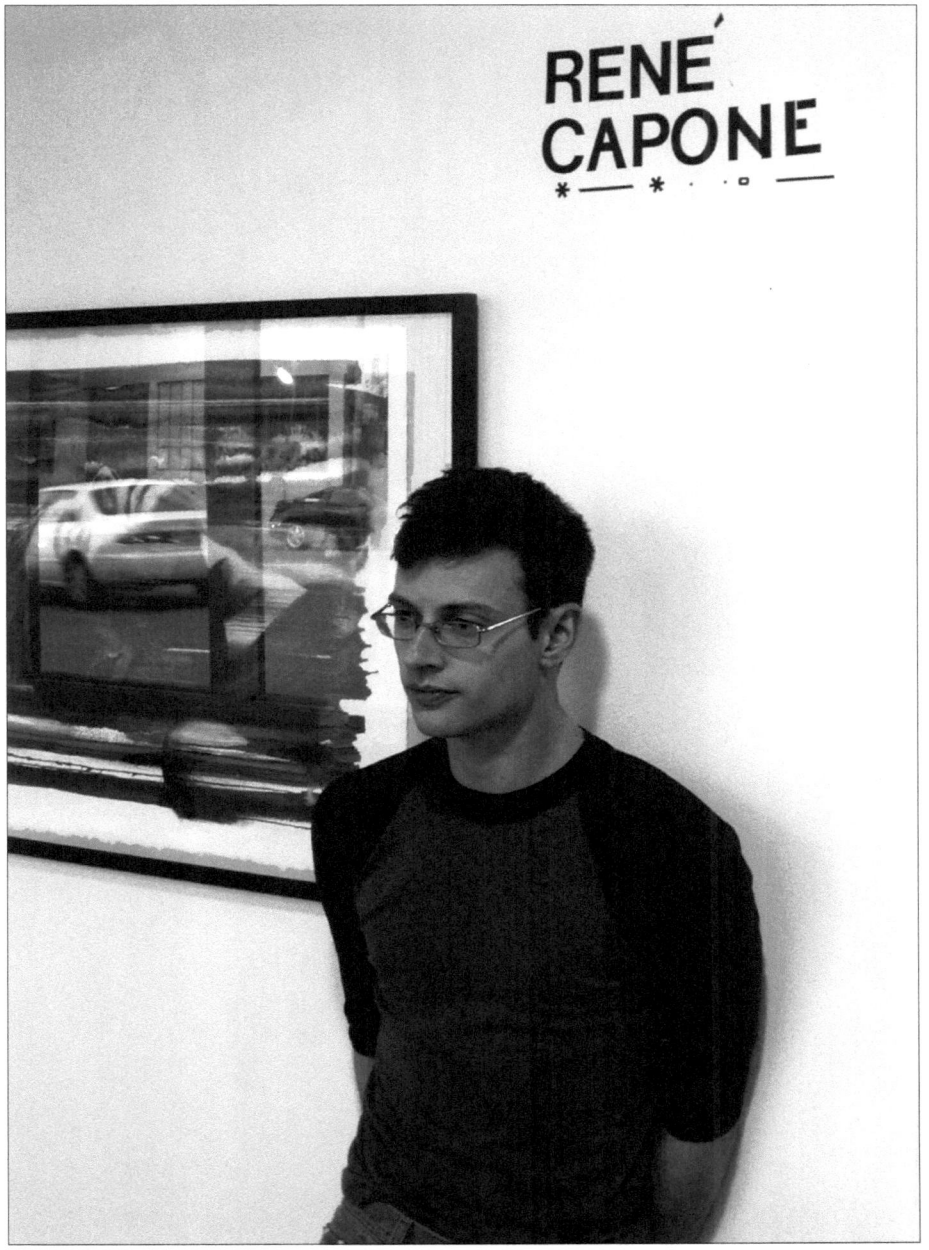

photo: Max Barlow

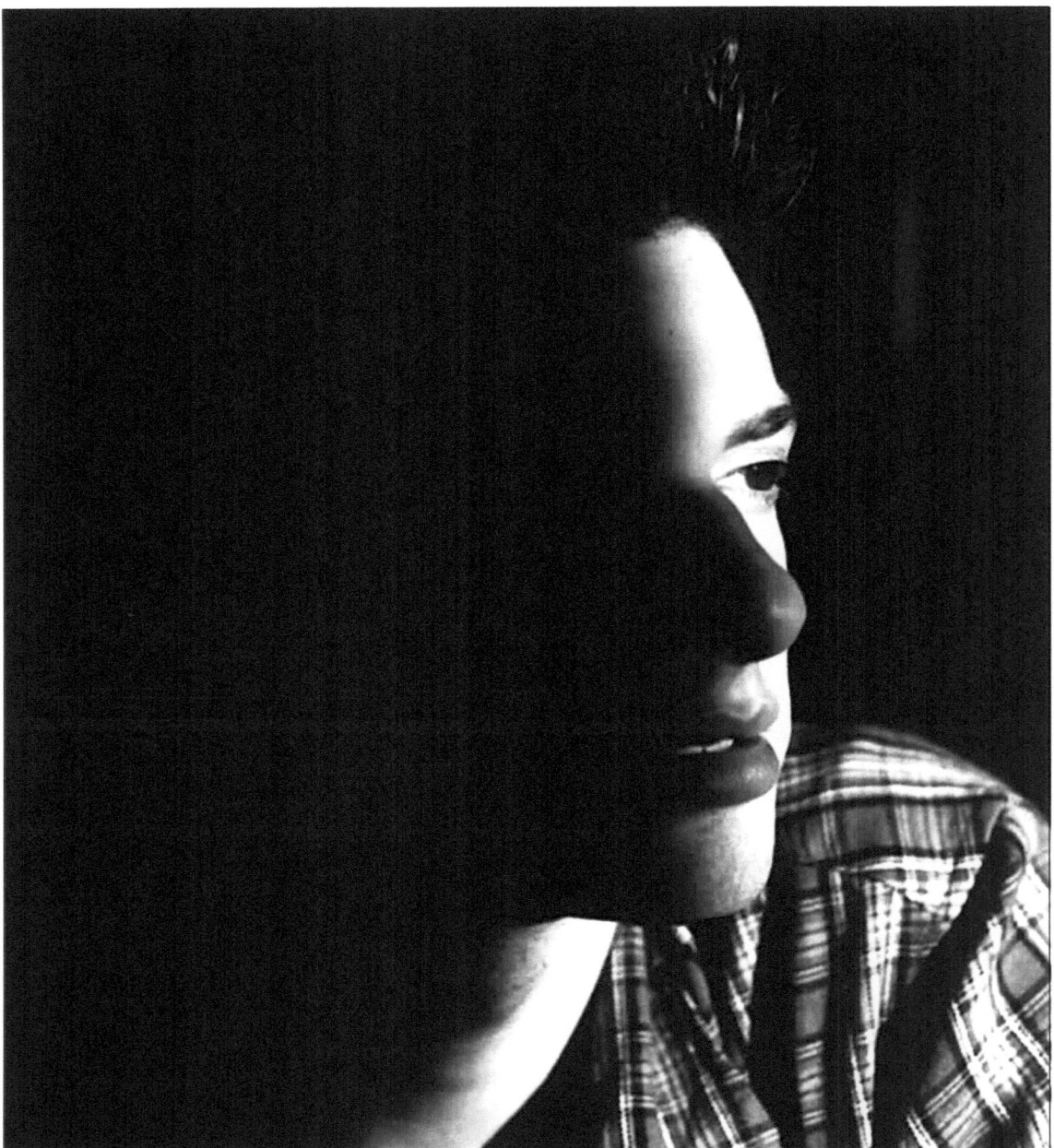

photo: Stephen Honicki

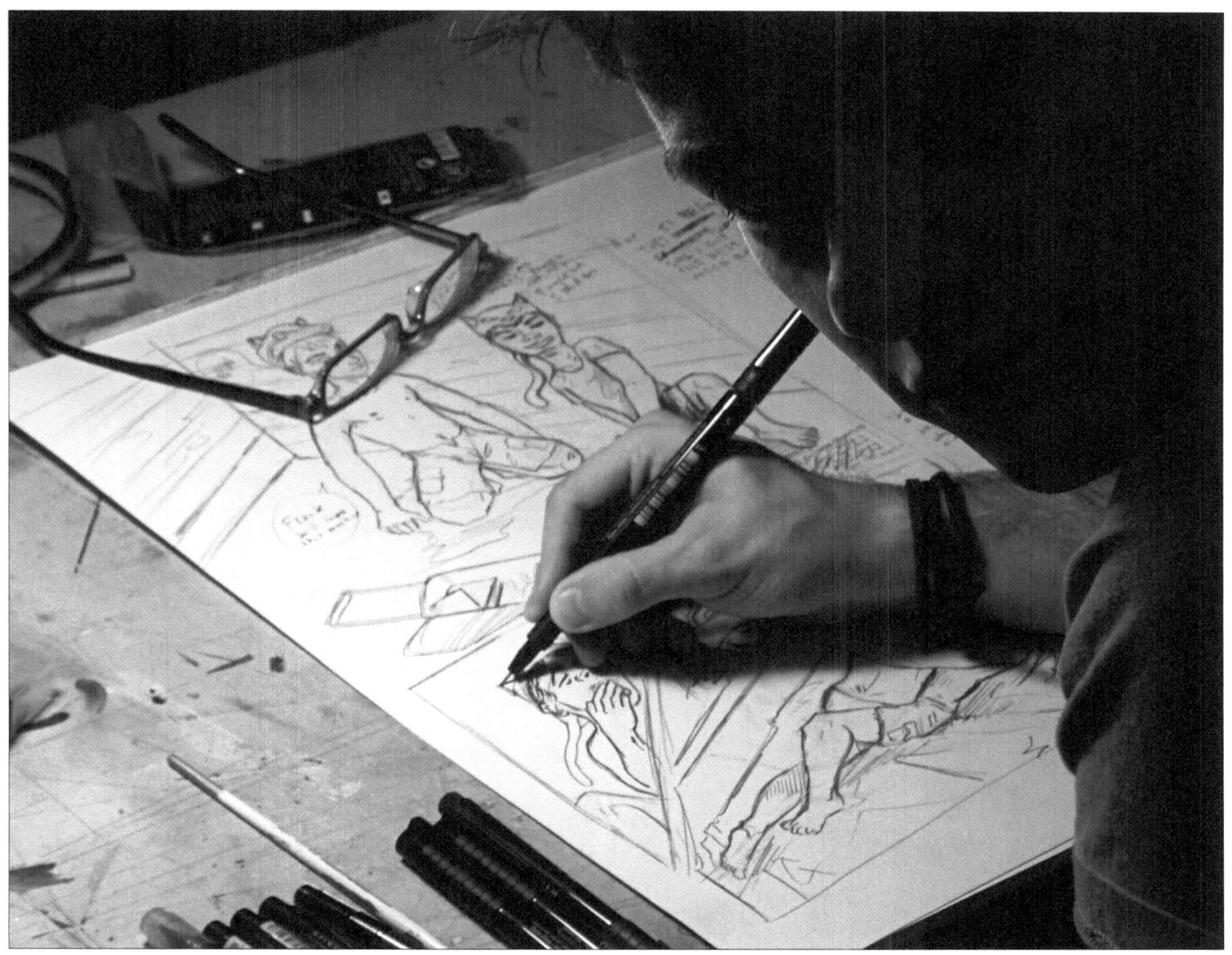

photo: Max Barlow

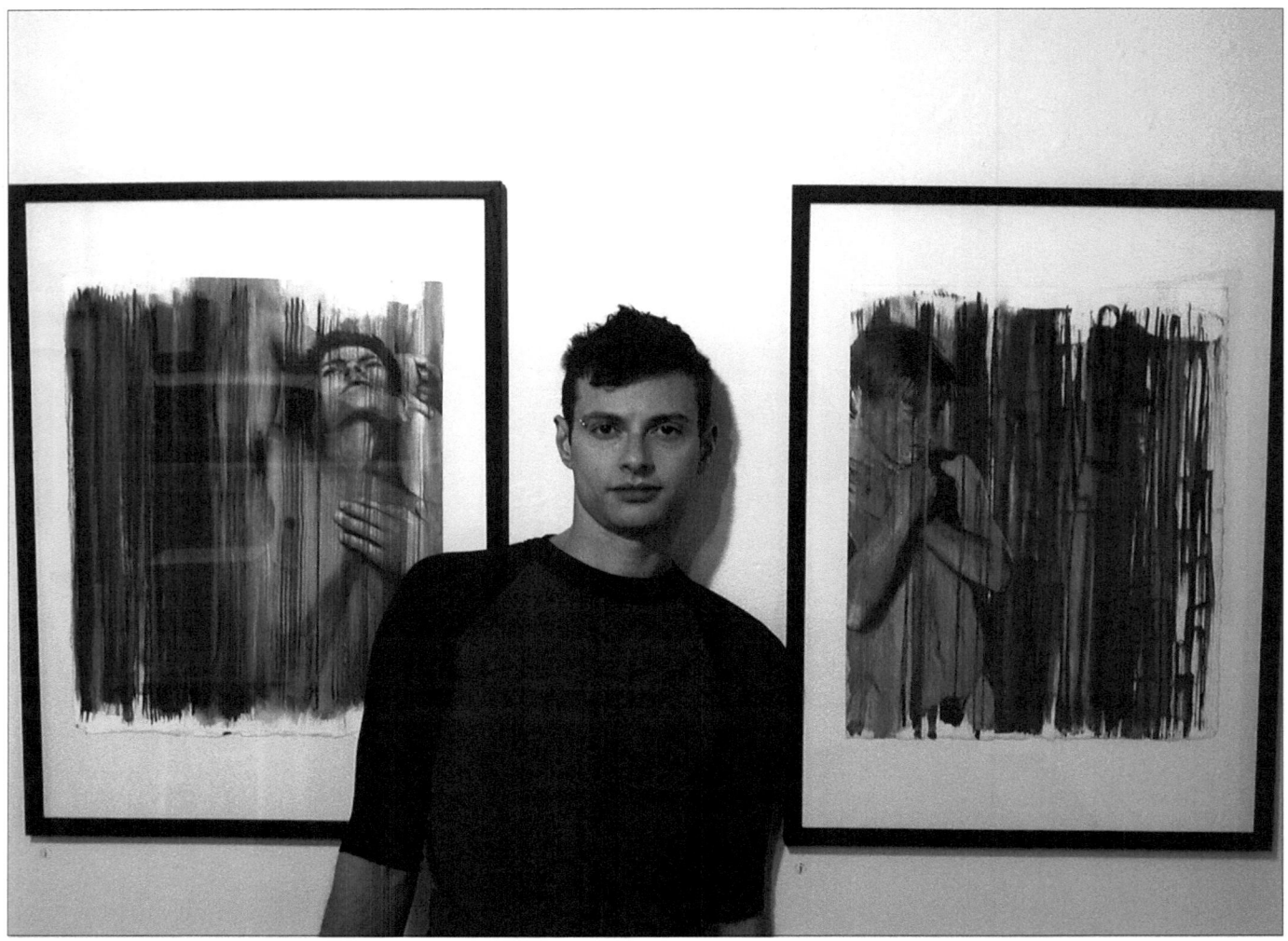

photo: Max Barlow

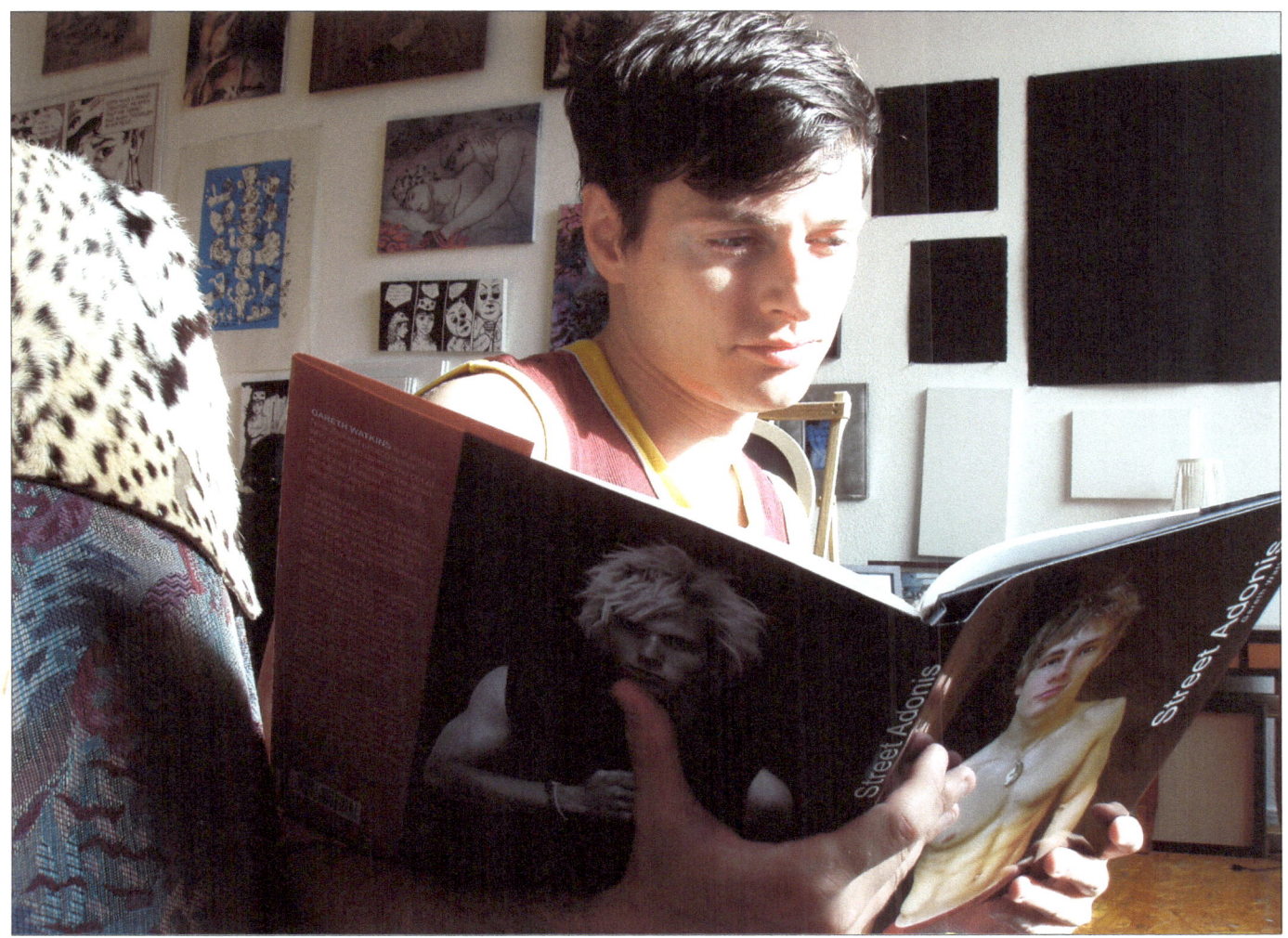

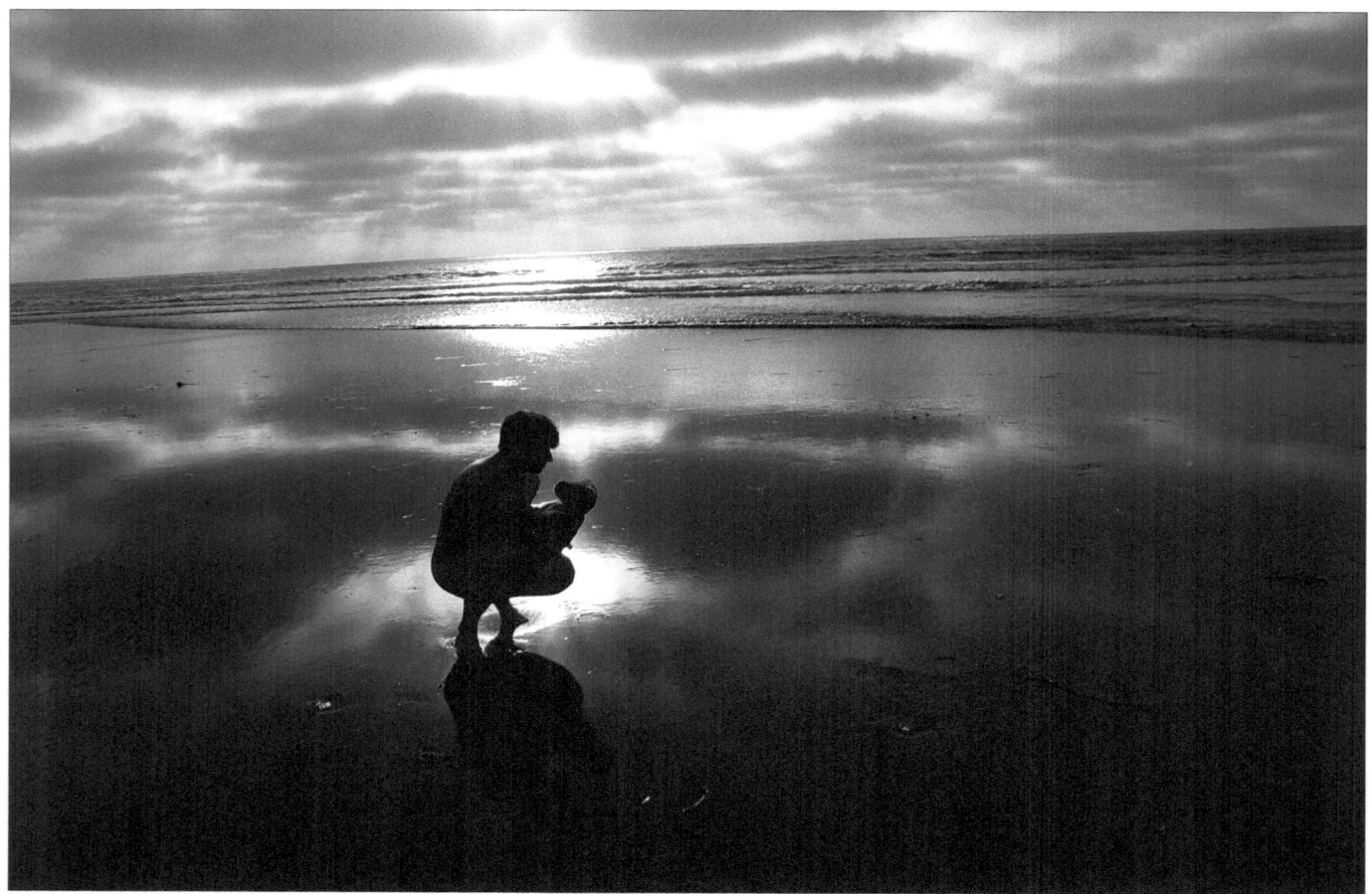

photo: Tom Blair

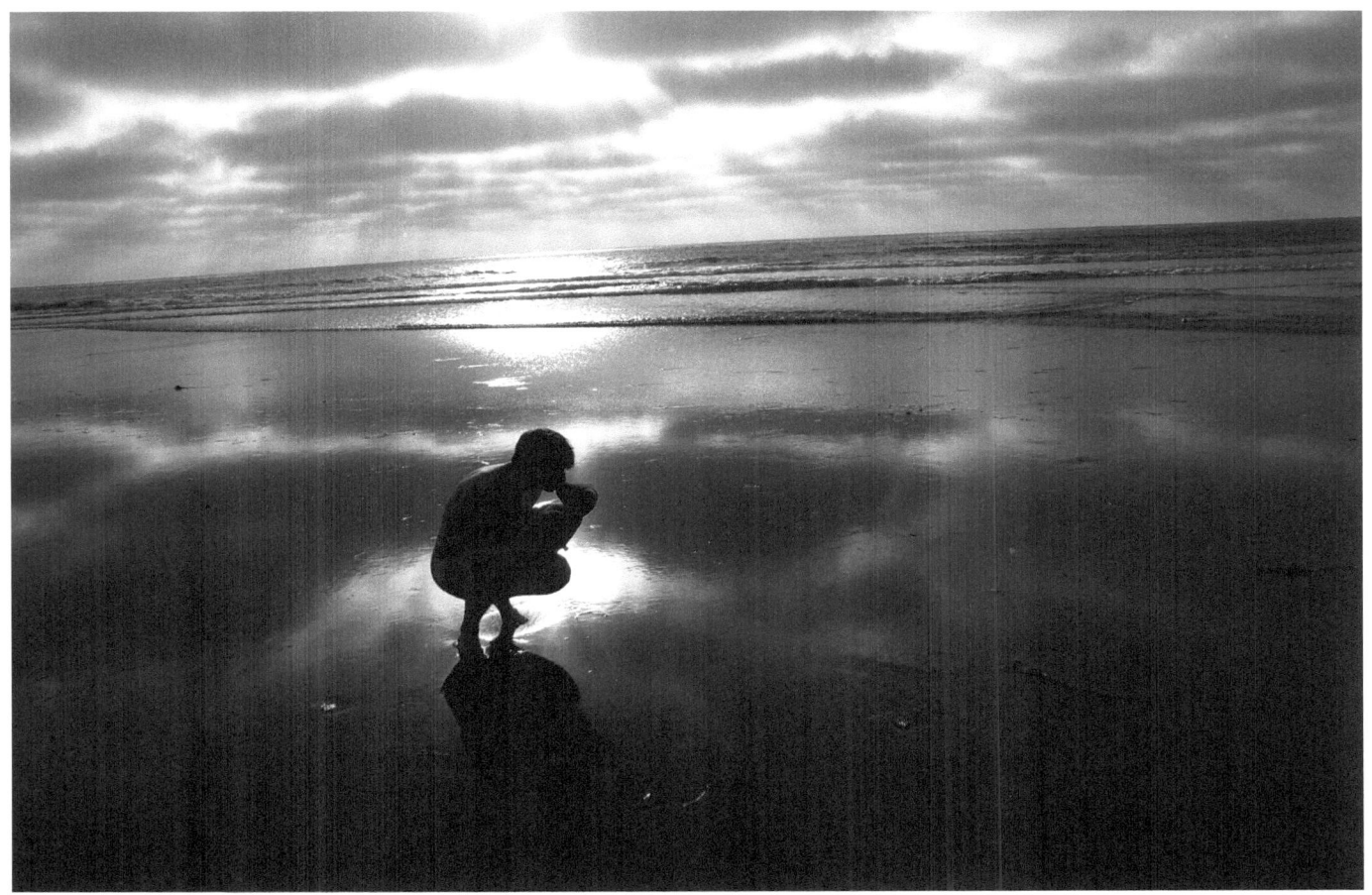

photo: Tom Blair

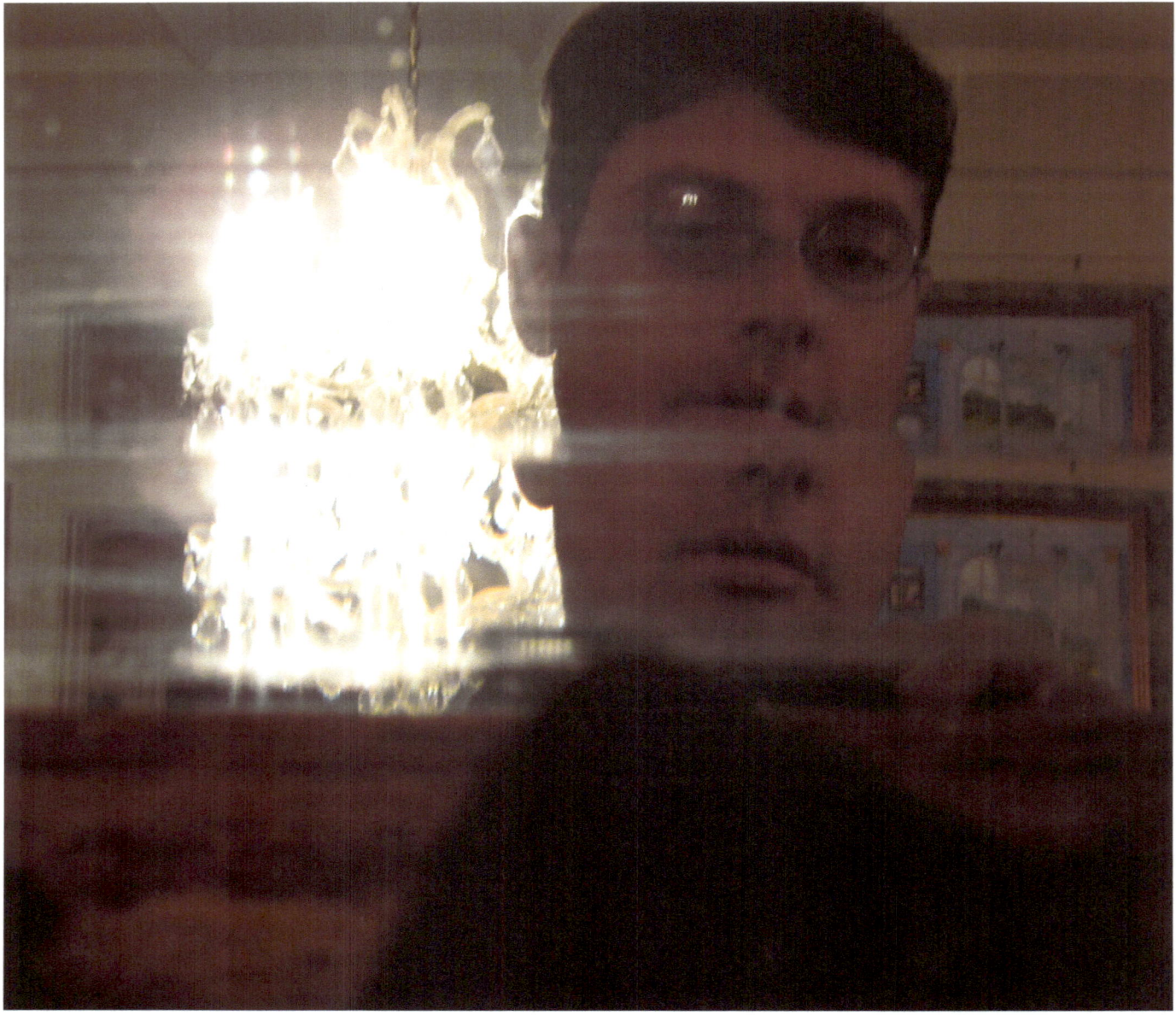

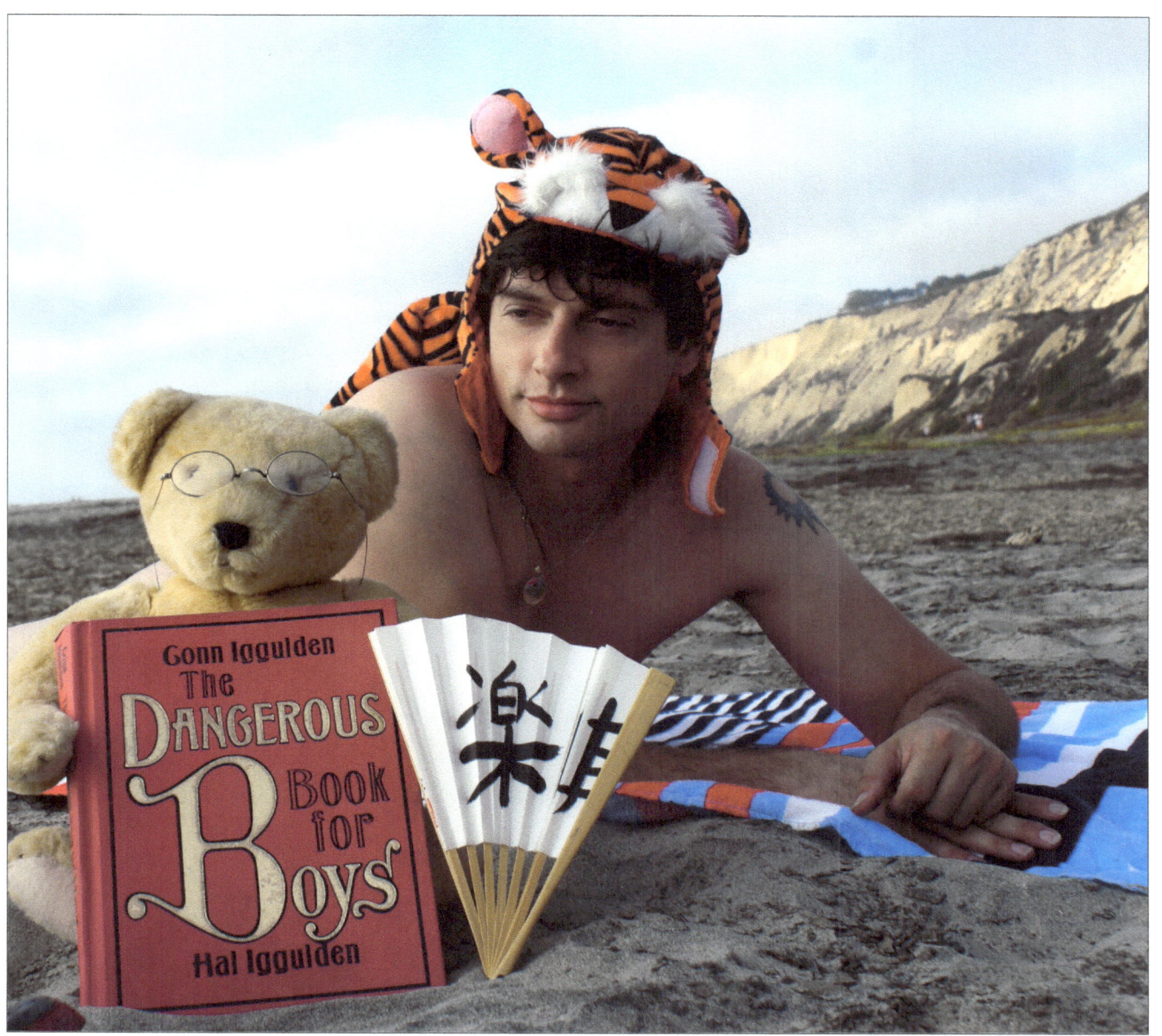

photo: Tom Blair

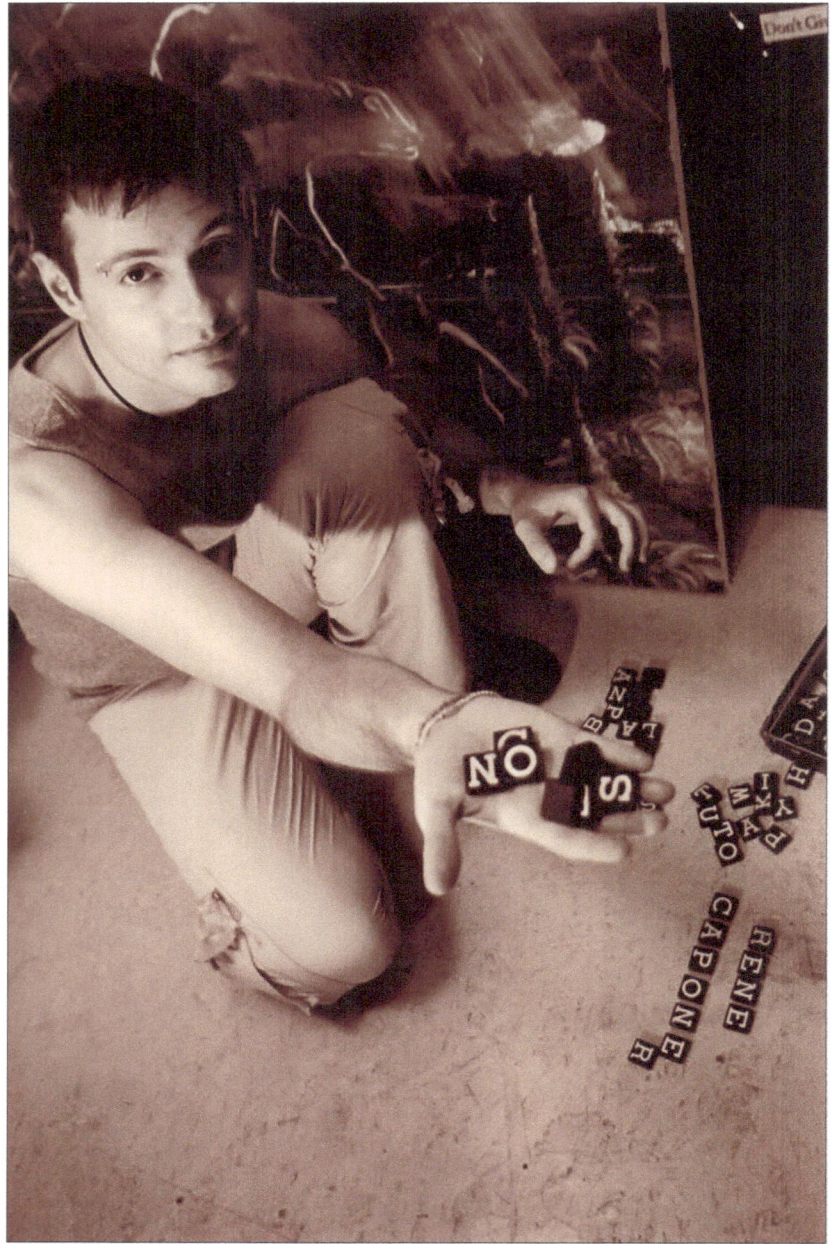

photo: Jarred Webster

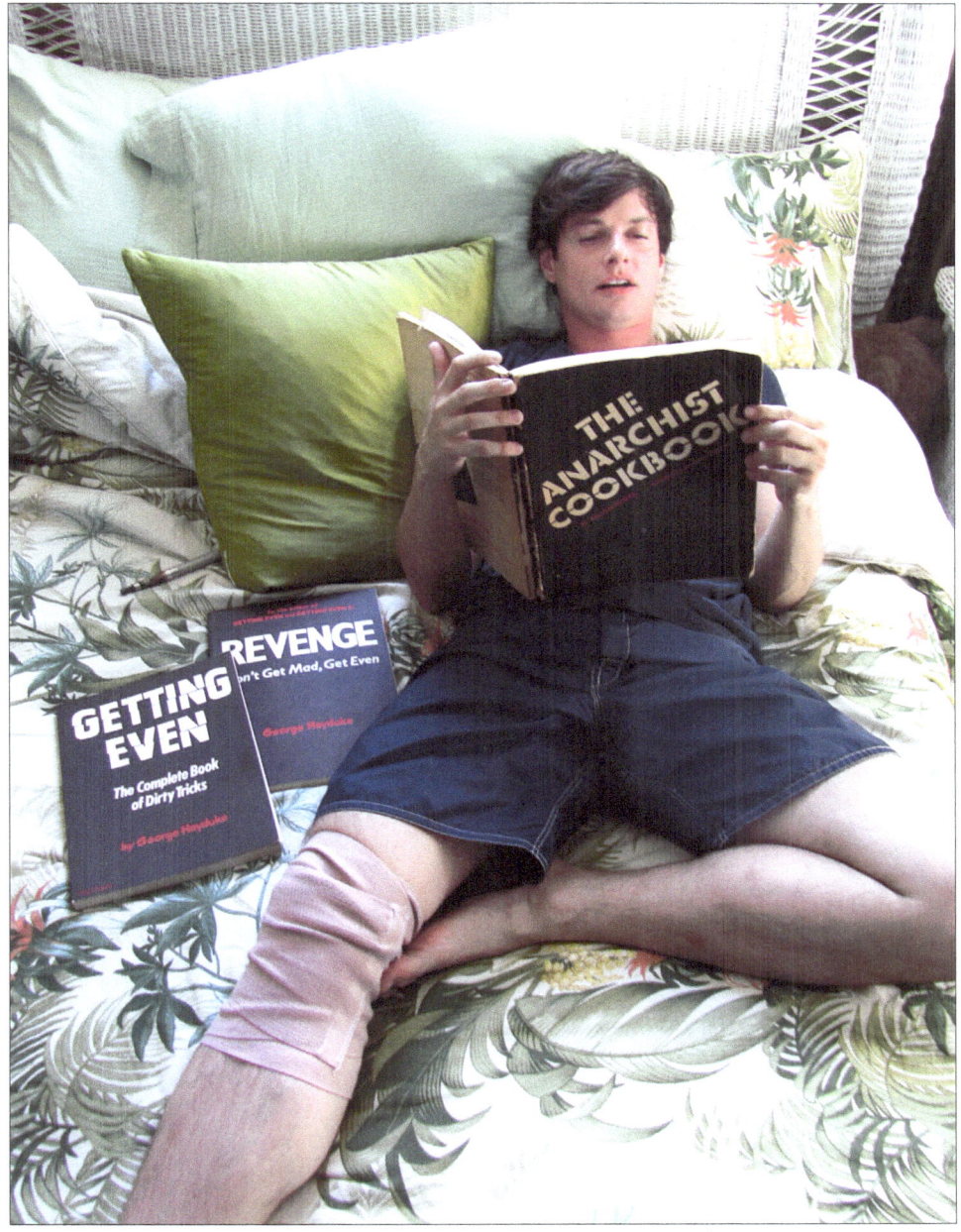

photo: Tyson Wrensch

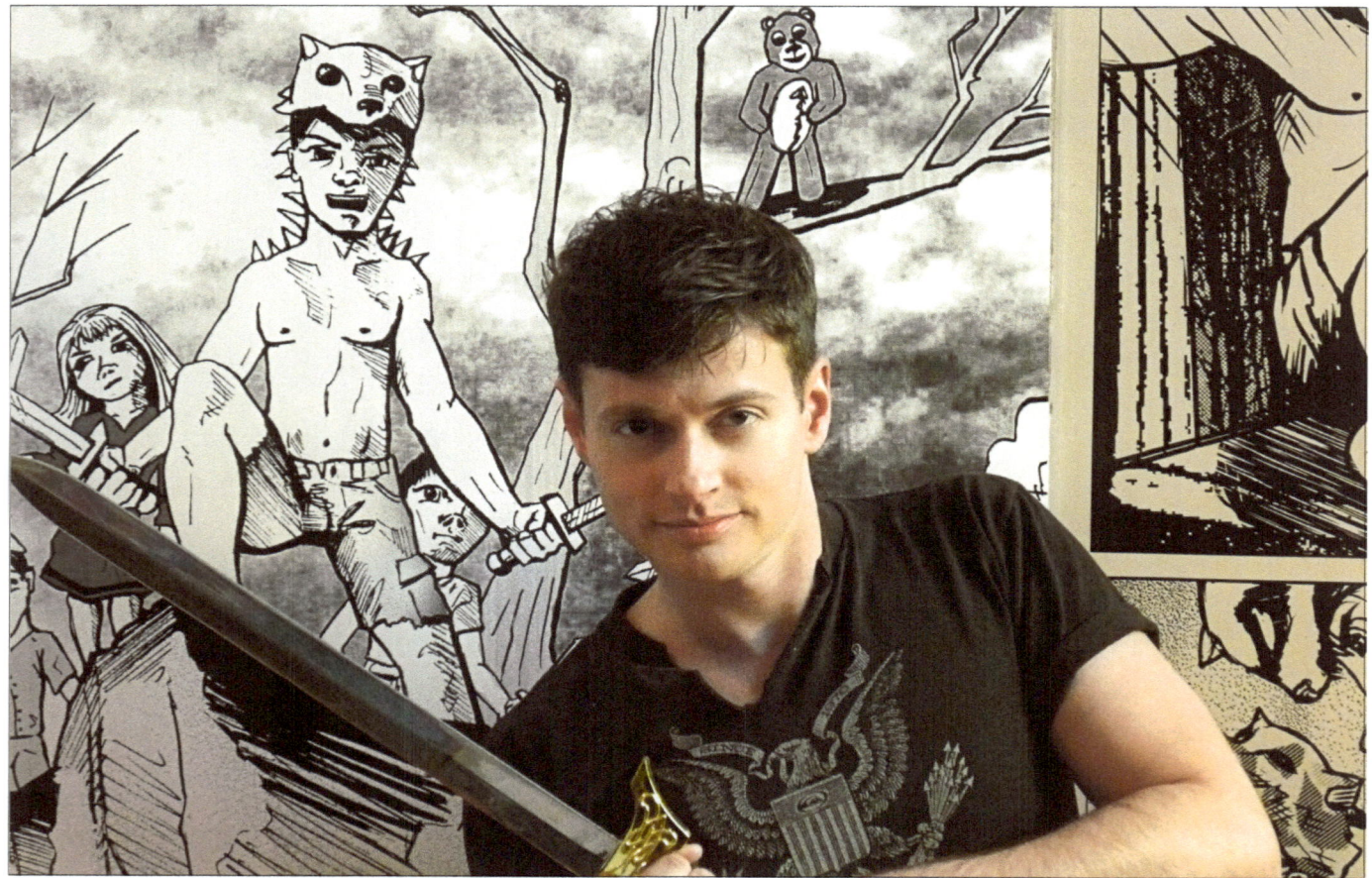

photo: Michael Johnstone

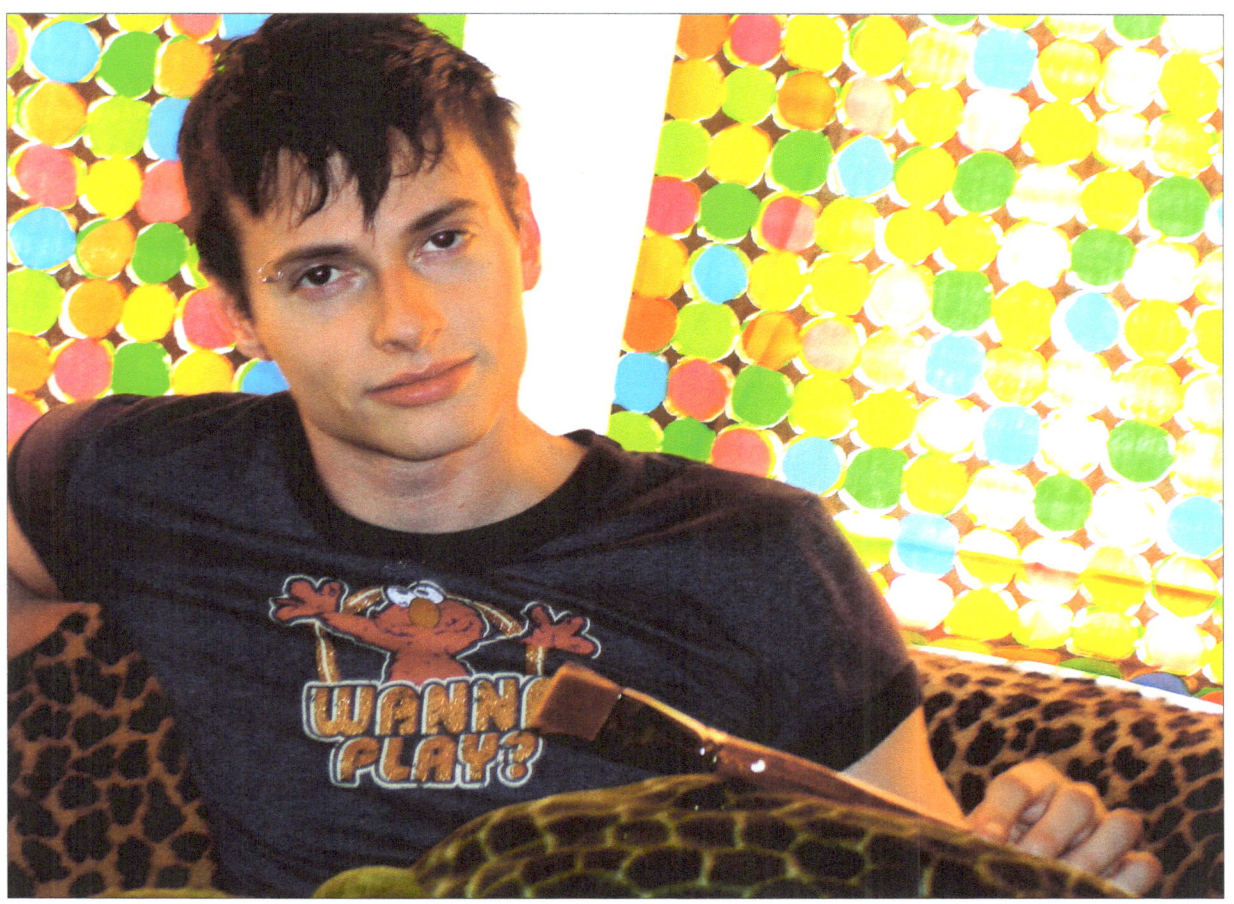

photo: Michael Johnstone

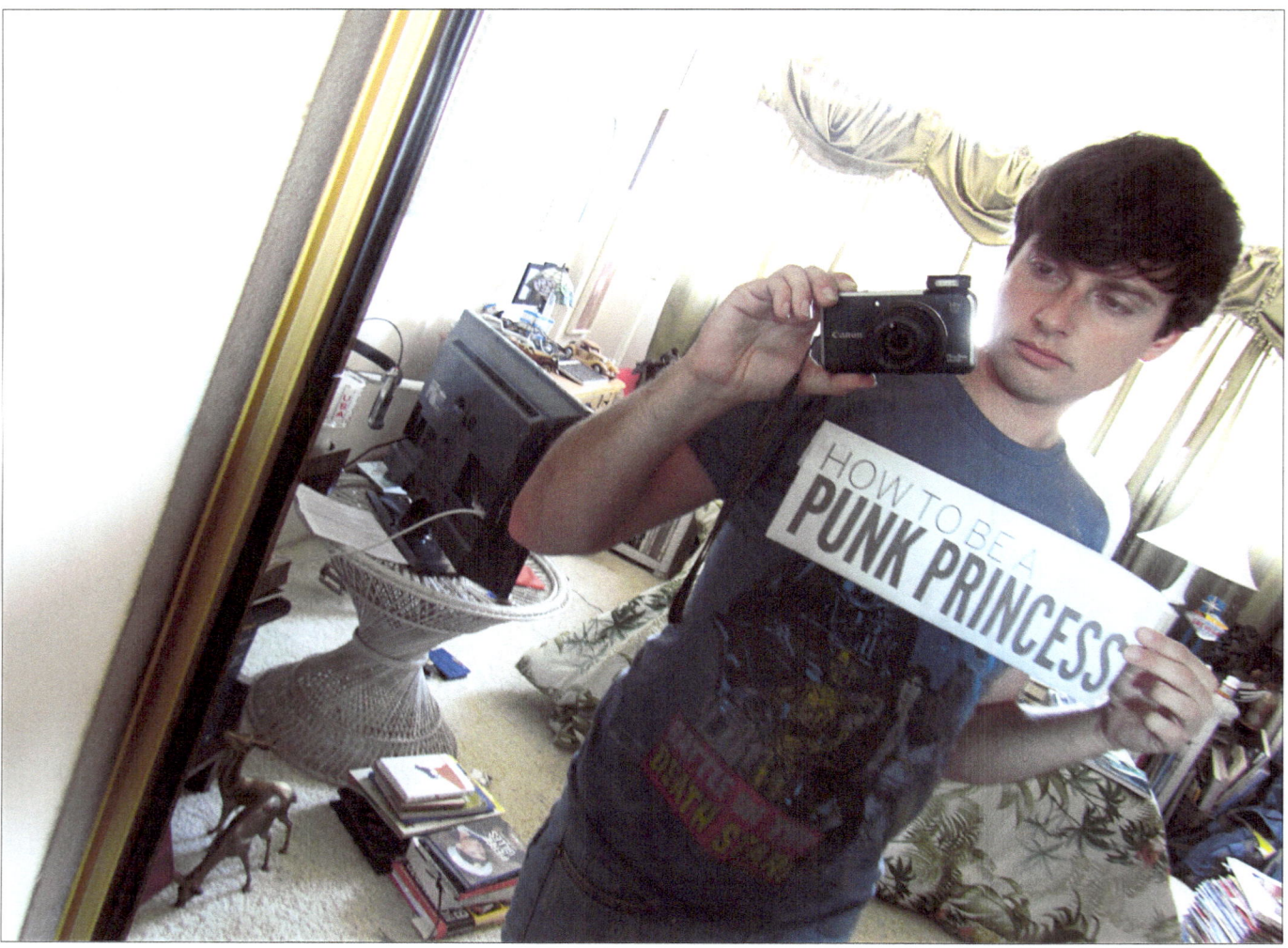

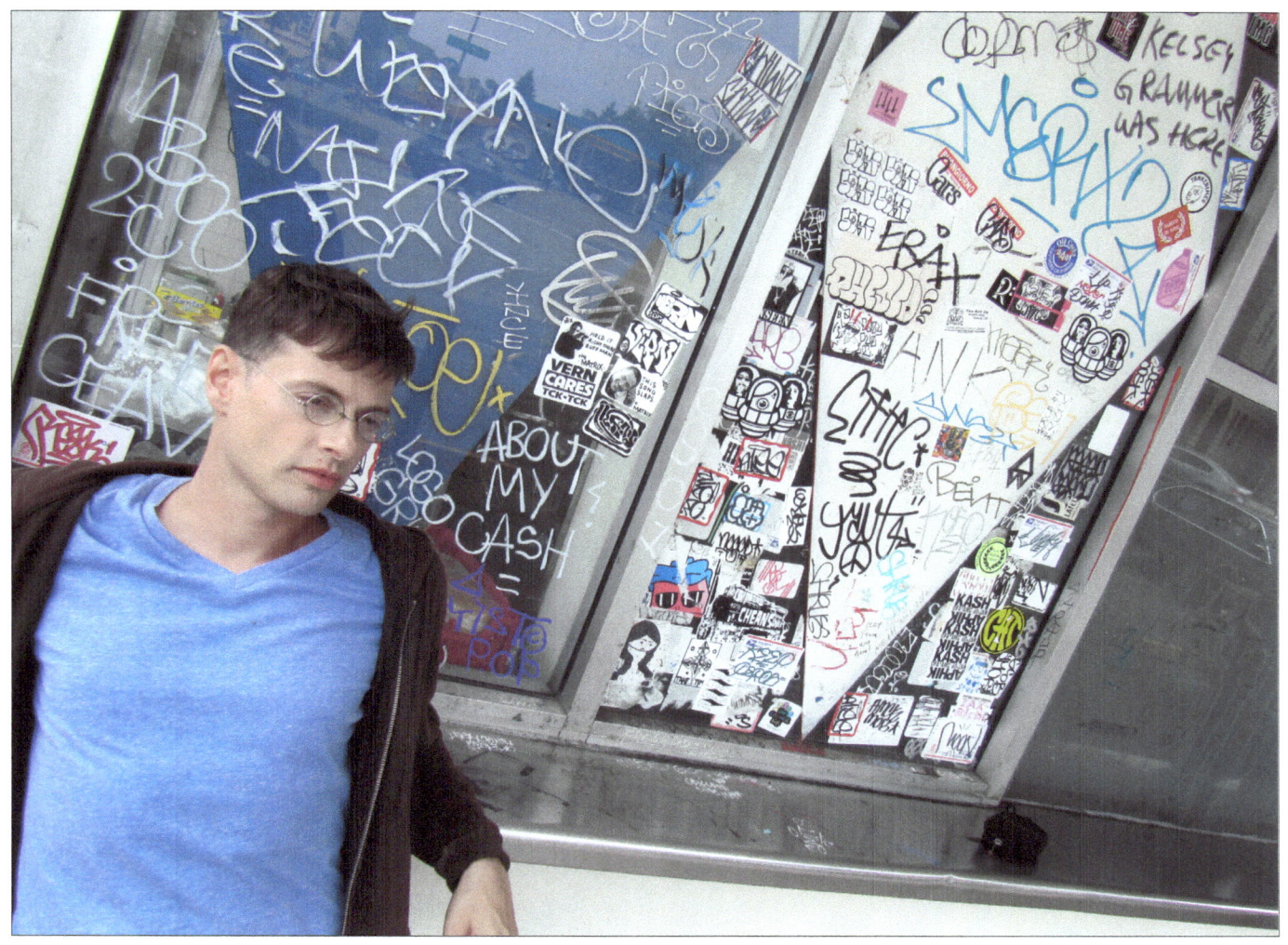

photo: Peter Palmer

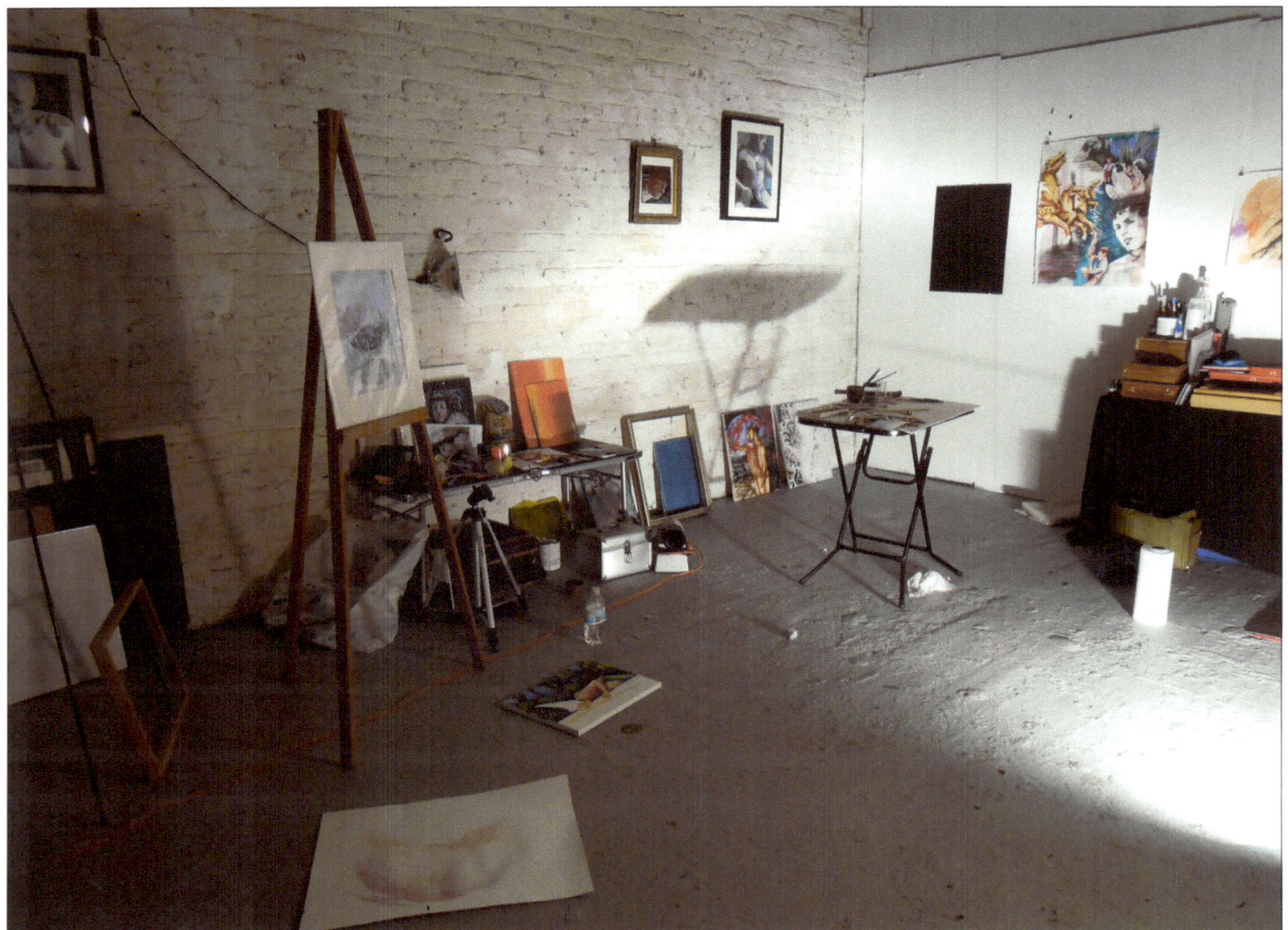

"Live Art" Studio & Gallery in San Francisco

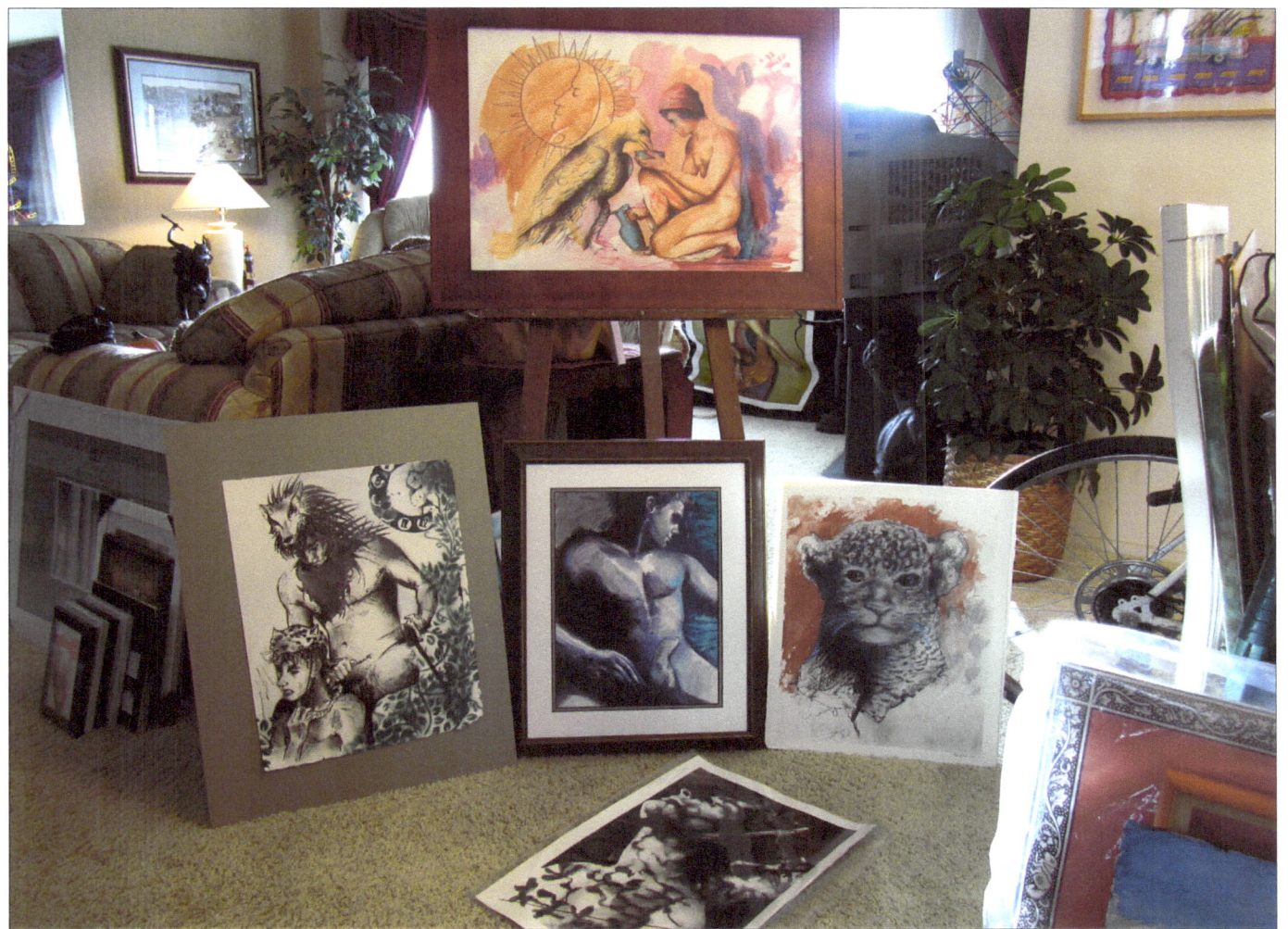

Art Studio: Newport Beach

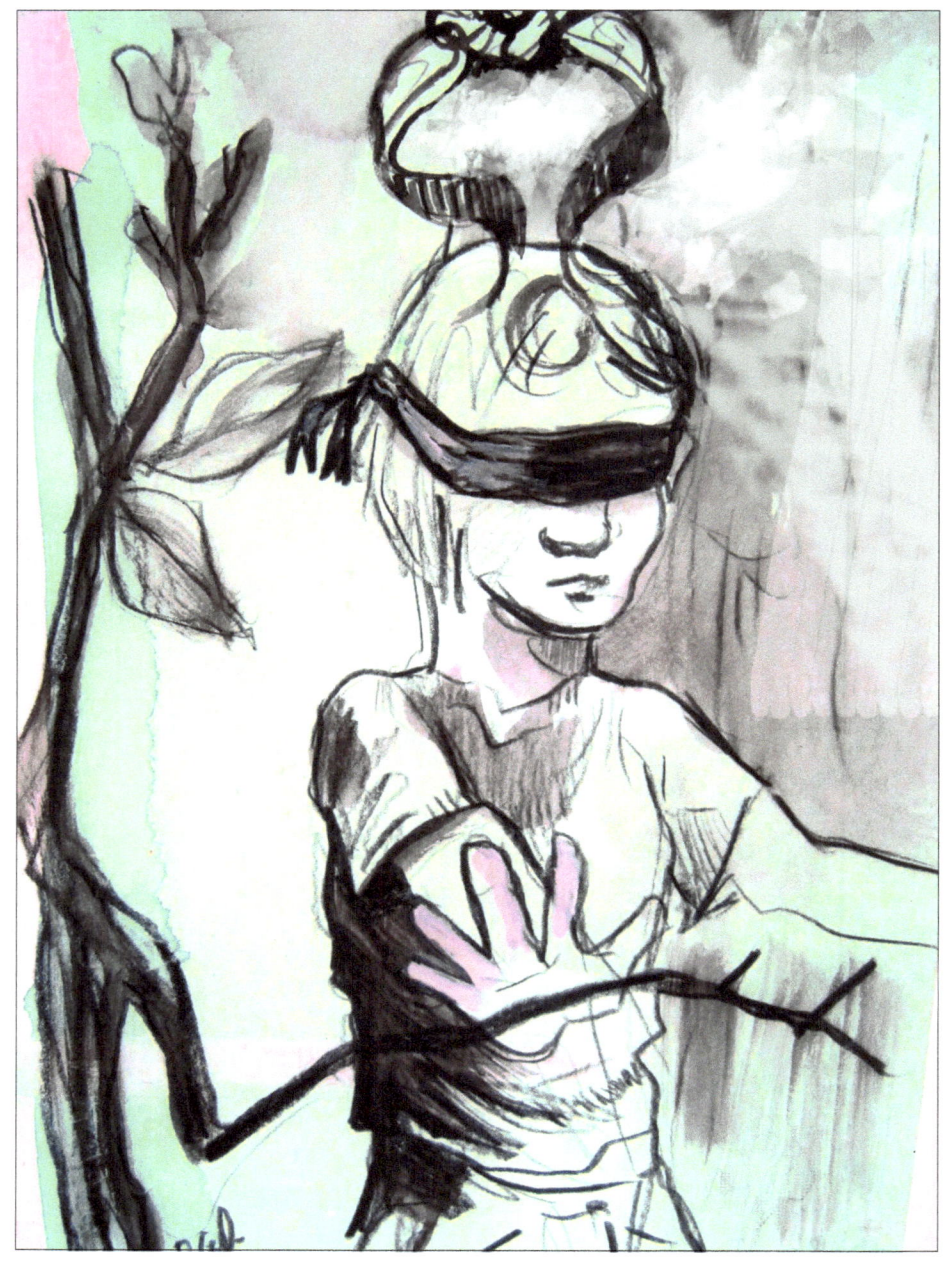

Real life (part 1)

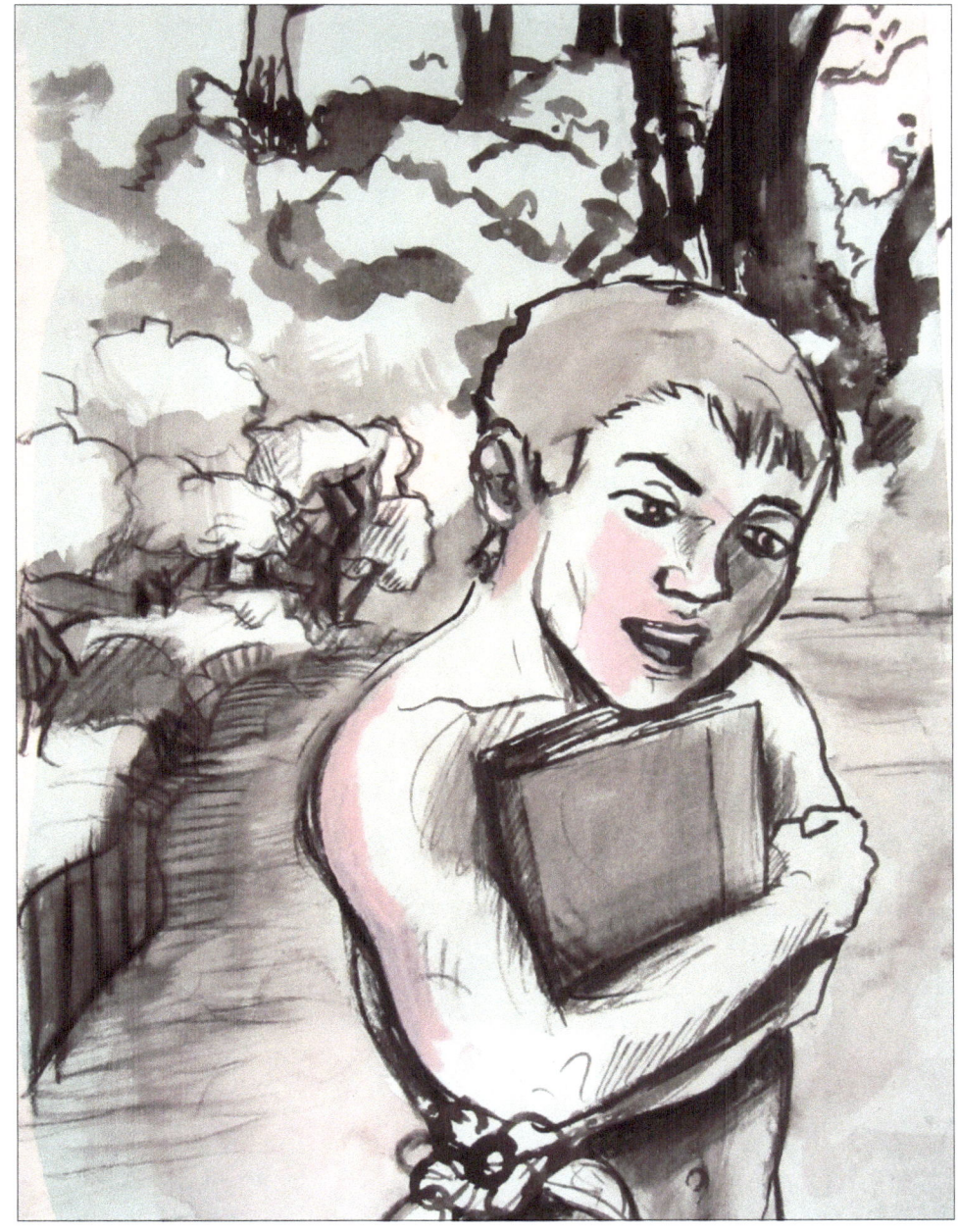

Real life (part 2)

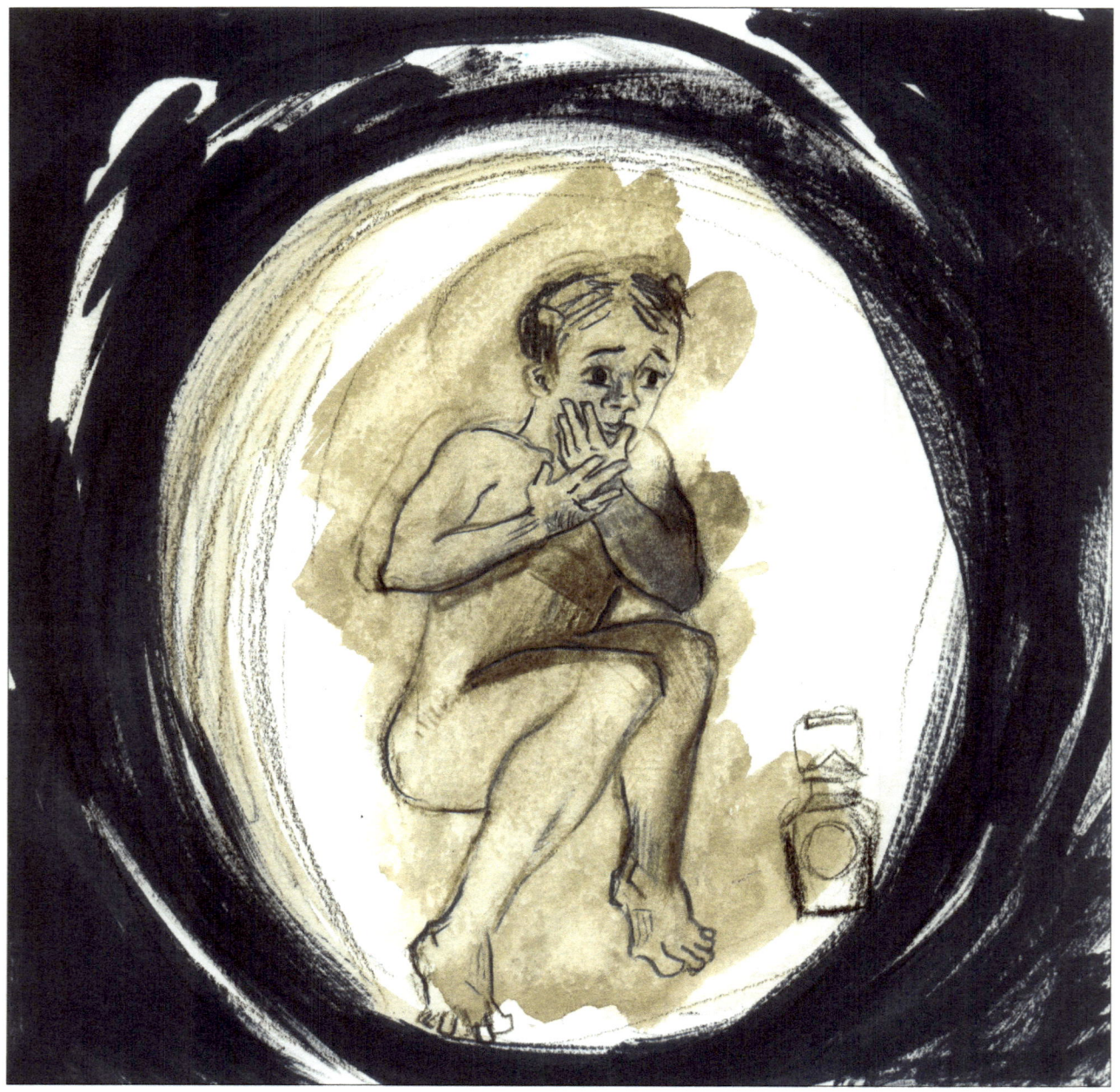

"Flashlight" watercolor, ink & pencil, 8"x8", 2012

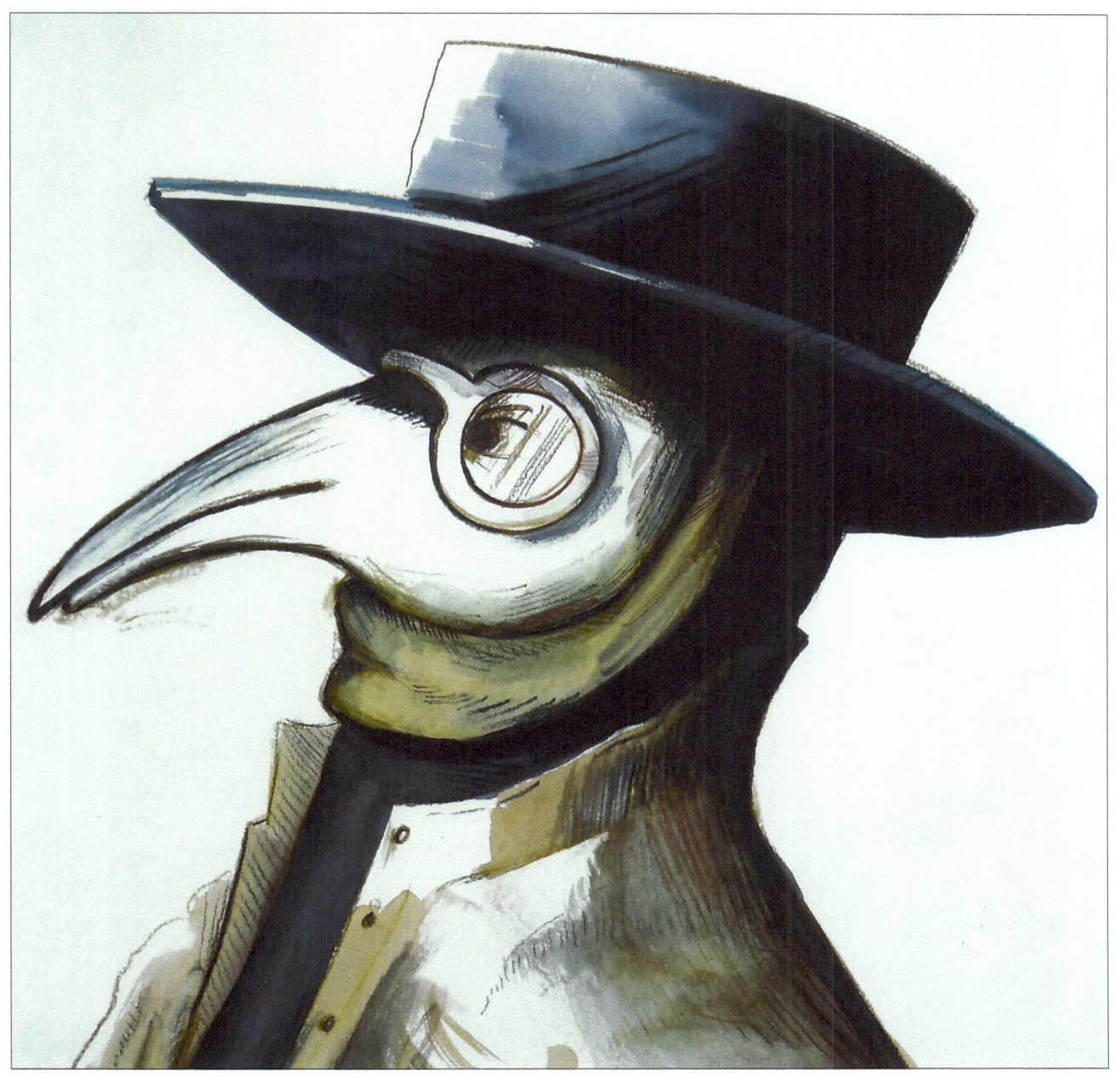

"Mr. Pennyworth" watercolor, ink & color pencil (detail) 9"x12", 2012

www.ingramcontent.com/pod-product-compliance
Lightning Source LLC
Chambersburg PA
CBHW050726180526
45159CB00003B/1139

9780615966076